Liturgy for the People

ESSAYS IN HONOR OF

Gerald Ellard, S.J.
1894–1963

Edited by WILLIAM J. LEONARD, S.J.

SECRETARY, THE LITURGICAL CONFERENCE

THE BRUCE PUBLISHING COMPANY
MILWAUKEE

NIHIL OBSTAT:

    James A. Donohue
    Diocesan Censor

IMPRIMATUR:

    ✠ Richard Cardinal Cushing
    Archbishop of Boston

    June 2, 1963

BX
1970
L414

Library of Congress Catalog Card Number: 63–21155

© 1963 The Bruce Publishing Company

MADE IN THE UNITED STATES OF AMERICA

112724

Foreword

FATHER GERALD ELLARD died on April 1, 1963, during the
Golden Jubilee year of his membership in the Society of Jesus.
The present volume, originally intended as a Golden Jubilee gift
and as a token of admiration and grateful affection by his col-
laborators through the years and by a number of his juniors
who have entered into his labors, has now become a memorial.
The theme of the volume, LITURGY FOR THE PEOPLE, was
chosen because Father Ellard elected long ago, in spite of his
scholarly training and tastes, to work in the field of popular
liturgy, and his influence has been most powerfully felt in that
area. Few men in America, at the time when he began his
work, were equipped as he was to interpret the liturgy to
modern Catholics and make it attractive to them. As he said in
the Foreword to *The Mass of the Future*, "In the Catholic Church
nothing can be said to have a future save in so far as it has a
past and is deeply rooted in tradition," and he had read widely
in that past, that tradition. By temperament and grace he was
sympathetic with men's aspirations and problems and keenly sensi-
tive to the winds of change blowing in his age. Lastly, he was
endowed with courage to present unfamiliar ideas and with patience to wait until they had been assimilated.

Father Ellard was born in 1894 at Commonwealth, Wiscon-
sin; his friends have seen in the town's name a happy omen
for one who was to do so much for the Christian community.
He was educated at Ironwood, Michigan, and at Regis High School
in Denver, and in 1912 he followed his brother, Father G. Augustine Ellard, into the Society of Jesus. His Jesuit education took
him to the novitiate at Los Gatos, California, and to Mount St.
Michael, the house of studies affiliated with Gonzaga University
in Spokane; in accordance with Jesuit custom, he then taught for
four years at Regis before beginning the study of theology at St.

Louis in 1923. After his ordination by Archbishop (later Cardinal) Glennon in 1926, he pursued further theological and ascetical studies in the United States and in Austria, finally proceeding as a doctoral candidate to the Ludwig-Maximilian University in Munich. He took the degree in 1931; his thesis dealt with ordination anointings in the Western Church before the year 1000, and was published as a monograph of the Medieval Academy of America in 1933.

1963 was the thirtieth year of his uninterrupted service to St. Mary's College in Kansas, the School of Divinity of St. Louis University. A full generation of Jesuit seminarians has passed through his classes on their way to the altar, their minds shaped by his teaching to sympathy with liturgical renewal. These men are now pastors, university presidents, missionaries, professors, journalists, retreat masters, sponsors and supervisors of a thousand projects for the glory of God, so it is not difficult to imagine the enormous scope of his influence.

Even before his ordination Father Ellard had written, in April of 1925, a letter to the editor of *America* calling for the "opening up of the liturgy" in this country by means of classroom instruction, articles, books, lectures, and sermons. The letter evoked similar letters on the same theme from other interested people, like the farsighted and vigorous pioneer, Monsignor William Busch of St. Paul; it put the author in touch with Monsignor Martin Hellriegel of St. Louis, whose writing, lecturing, and pastoral example have made him the venerated father of liturgical achievement in the United States; it brought him an invitation, a year later, to collaborate as associate editor of the new magazine, *Orate Fratres* (now *Worship*), which, with the learning and zeal of its two editors in chief, Fathers Virgil Michel and Godfrey Diekmann, remains the authoritative organ of the liturgical movement in America and the most substantial of the many contributions of the Collegeville Benedictines to the cause of corporate worship. In 1951 the magazine awarded to Father Ellard the "Blessed Pius X Medal" in grateful recognition of twenty-five years of generous collaboration — the only medal he has ever worn in public.

Meanwhile there began to flow from the little room at St. Mary's a constant stream of books, articles, reviews, pamphlets, letters to the editor, program materials, suggestions and encouragement for questioners and beginners, correspondence with colleagues in Europe, Africa, Asia. *Christian Life and Worship* became in 1933 and still remains a standard text in Catholic colleges all over America. Later works were carried beyond the seas by missionaries and wartime chaplains; *The Mass in Transition* appeared in Italian and French translations and earned approval from the Holy See itself. A leaflet version of the dialogue Mass, first published in 1938, is still being revised and republished after selling hundreds of thousands of copies.

However, Father Ellard had been no recluse. He taught summer courses at Boston College, Marquette University, the University of San Francisco, and at many other institutions. He lectured at "institutes," "liturgical days," and "liturgical weeks" in almost every state in the union. He conducted retreats for priests, religious, seminarians, lay people. From the time of its organization in 1940 he was a member of the Board of Directors of the Liturgical Conference, and for many years, as chairman of the program committee, he suggested the theme and the program of the annual national "Week." Perhaps his supreme achievement, so far as popular education was concerned, was the twelve years he spent on the faculty of the "Summer School of Catholic Action," a peripatetic institution that moves from city to city during the twelve weeks of summer. More than a hundred thousand persons attended the sessions during those years, to take part in the "six days you'll never forget" and to bring home with them the SSCA *Blue Book* which was conned by thousands of others. A staff member of the central office of the Sodality of Our Lady, which sponsors the Summer Schools, wrote (*Orate Fratres,* January, 1951): "I would cite Father Gerald Ellard's work as most important. He worked with the office here both through his writings and his classes in the Summer School of Catholic Action. It was his influence which initiated the dialogue Mass at these schools. The practice was carried back to many schools and colleges throughout the land, and to not a few parishes as well. Whatever success this type of Mass participation has had on a large scale can be attributed to him and to his work with us. In addition, he contributed informational and inspirational material for social worship to both school and parish programming services sent out to thousands of schools and parishes in the United States."

Father Ellard described his decision to champion the cause of the vernacular in the liturgy as a conversion, slow and painful but in the end utterly convinced. A fluent Latinist himself, he loved the sonorous rhythms of the language in which the Christians of the West have prayed for so long, but, just as he chose at the outset of his career to dedicate his time and energies to popular liturgy rather than to scholarly research, so now, putting his own preference aside, he began to work for what seemed to him an indispensable requisite for a living liturgy — a living language. The first version of the American Ritual was largely his work, done under extreme pressure because of the exigencies of the moment. Many articles, many chapters in his books witness to the zeal with which he studied the progress of the vernacular languages as instruments of worship and cleared the way for the use of English.

If service be the criterion by which we evaluate the good Christian, the good priest, then Father Ellard has deserved well of the Church in America. If the public worship of God now corresponds more nearly to the ideal held up by St. Pius X fifty years ago, if the vitality of modern Christian groups and individuals is derived more abundantly from its "primary and indispensable source," if the community is more vividly aware that its vocation summons it both to adore God and to serve men, then very much of the credit belongs to Father Ellard. Let this homage of his colleagues stand as their acknowledgment of his merits and their profound affection for him personally. *Requiescat in pace.*

WILLIAM J. LEONARD, S.J.

St. Mary's Hall, Boston College
July 27, 1962

CONTRIBUTORS TO THE VOLUME

Father John LaFarge, S.J., missionary pastor for many years in southern Maryland, associate editor and editor in chief of *America* for many more, has been identified with almost every good cause sponsored by the Church in the United States in this century.

Father Eugene H. Maly, professor of Holy Scripture at Mount St. Mary's Seminary in Cincinnati, Ohio, is currently president of the Catholic Biblical Association of America and editor of *The Bible Today.*

Father David M. Stanley, S.J., on leave of absence from the Jesuit House of Studies in Toronto, has been teaching for three years at the State University of Iowa. His contribution to the present volume was read originally at a symposium in November, 1962, at St. Mary's, Kansas, held in honor of Father Ellard's Golden Jubilee as a Jesuit.

Mother Kathryn Sullivan, R.S.C.J., professor of theology at Manhattanville College of the Sacred Heart, is the first woman elected to office in the Catholic Biblical Association of America. She has written and translated many volumes on Holy Scripture and ascetics.

Father Terrence R. O'Connor, S.J., is professor of patrology and liturgy at Alma College, the Jesuit house of studies in California.

Father Matthew J. O'Connell, S.J., is professor of theology at Woodstock College, Maryland, and has written many articles for scholarly journals.

Father Shawn Sheehan, whose graduate work in history was done at the Catholic University of America, was president of the Liturgical Conference from 1956 to 1959. A priest in parish work for ten years, he is now professor and dean at St. John's Seminary, Brighton, Massachusetts.

Father C. J. NcNaspy, S.J., now one of the editors of *America,* taught classics for many years to the young Jesuits at St. Charles College, Grand Coteau, Louisiana, and served as dean of the College of Music at Loyola University in New Orleans.

Mr. Theodore N. Marier, organist, choral director, composer, editor, teacher, and author, has made a distinguished contribution in Boston and elsewhere throughout the country to the cause of sacred music. In recent years he has organized and trained the nationally recruited choir which has sung at the annual Liturgical Weeks.

Father Clifford Howell, S.J., is the well-known English liturgist and musician who has lectured so often in the United States and Australia.

Father Rembert Weakland, O.S.B., is a musicologist and professor at St. Vincent's Archabbey in Pennsylvania.

Father Daniel Berrigan, S.J., professor of theology at LeMoyne College, Syracuse, New York, has published several volumes of theology and of poetry. He gave the keynote address at the Liturgical Week of 1962 in Seattle.

Father Josef Jungmann, S.J., is the distinguished professor and sometime rector of the Canisianum at Innsbruck, Austria. His *The Mass of the Roman Rite* remains the definitive history of the Mass liturgy of the West.

Monsignor Martin Hellriegel, pastor of Holy Cross Church in St. Louis, author, lecturer, retreat master, former president of the Liturgical Conference, has been a distinguished leader for forty years of the American liturgical movement.

Father Francis X. Weiser, S.J., of the Boston College faculty, has published more than twenty books on popular liturgy and has lectured and preached tirelessly in all parts of the United States since coming here from his native Austria thirty years ago.

Father H. A. Reinhold, now working in Pittsburgh, Pennsylvania, has been writing and lecturing on the liturgy for many years. His books on the pastoral reform of the Mass and on American parish life summarize the stimulating ideas he has been presenting in many periodicals.

Mrs. Mary Perkins Ryan, of Goffstown, New Hampshire, has written, translated, or edited many articles and books on the liturgy, on lay spirituality, and on Holy Scripture — the Psalms in particular.

Contents

LITURGY FOR THE PEOPLE

...1...

Progress and Rhythm in the Liturgical Movement

JOHN LA FARGE, S.J.

As FATHER GERALD ELLARD looks back at the time that has elapsed since his *Christian Life and Worship* first appeared in 1933,[1] and recalls the years of writing, teaching, and lecturing that preceded and followed that attractive and authoritative volume, he cannot avoid contrasting the present nationwide and worldwide acceptance of the restored liturgy with the bleak loneliness of that early period.

Fr. Ellard's experience as an apostle of the liturgy has been similar to that of other pioneers in the liturgical movement, here and abroad. A teacher will be fortified by the consciousness that he has a "good idea." Relying on the soundness of his proposition, he will bravely face a mountain of shortsighted opposition. The truth, after all, has its own vigor. A clear-sighted teacher learns to suffer a barrage of contradictions and complaints, safe in the consciousness that the truth will triumph in the end, if given a decent chance, and if proposed with due modesty and rational arguments. But Fr. Ellard's warfare against the incrusted misconceptions that had crept into our liturgical usage was nourished on stronger fare. Throughout the sequence of his writings he has made clear that he is moving with a mightier current: that of the Holy Spirit working in the Church.

It has taken much time and patience to familiarize people — clergy and laity alike — with the idea of any change or improve-

---

[1] Milwaukee: The Bruce Publishing Company.

1

ment in the conduct of the Church's sacred worship. Much patient exposition is required to distinguish between those elements in our worship that are permanent and unchanging, that belong to its very essence, and those which are mere accidents of a given culture or social structure at a given epoch. Hence a variety of misunderstandings and suspicions on the part of otherwise intelligent and progressive exponents of the meaning of our Christian practice.

Through all this period Fr. Ellard has witnessed a steady development and progress. Cautions and warnings which the movement has received at different stages of this progress, though annoying to eager spirits, in the long run have helped to strengthen and solidify it. With this progress, time has brought into much clearer focus the distinction between two interrelated, but still distinct factors in the evermore widespread revival, and has helped to assign its proper place to each of these elements.

One such tendency is centered in a cultural renewal, that is to say, a revival of knowledge and appreciation of those elements in the liturgy which reflect the achievements of Christian culture in the service of divine worship. This revival has brought to light and made available for our worship of today, especially for our public and communal worship, the rich and sublime treasures of earlier ages: in the field of architecture, craftsmanship, music, etc. An outstanding example is the revival in our period of the ritual music of the past: the chant with its modes, tones, and vast storehouse of consecrated melodies, as well as the more essential practice of congregational singing and response. In this category, too, one could include the restoration of the true face or aspect of the traditional ceremonies, many of which have become obscured by neglect or by theatrical practices. It means the restoration of genuine liturgical art in place of the degenerate and shoddy products that have gained prevalence, often by a spirit of misplaced commercial profit or by assimilation of current standards of taste or mistaste.

The other tendency that has developed is of a quite different character: the *pastoral* or *mission* aspect of the liturgy, the movement which received a rebirth and a lasting impetus through the initiative of St. Pius X and has been contained in one form or another by his successors, despite interference of two world wars. How this pastoral movement grew through the recent decades is told graphically by Fr. Ellard in his synopsis entitled "The First Fifty Years," Chapter 20 of his book, *The Mass in Transition*.[2] This chapter, says the author, "seeks to provide specific tokens of . . . papal initiatives, and typical instances of local reaction in various countries from 1906 to 1956, under Popes St. Pius X, Benedict XV, Pius XI, and Pius XII." The last seven years — to the date of this writing — could of course supply a proportionately still greater number and variety of instances.

This pastoral concept of the liturgy is none other than the activating of the Church's mission to the world: in our times, to the modern world, which has undergone and continues to experience such rapid and bewildering transformations. The liturgical aspects of this "mission" are as yet far from being solved. One gains an idea of the number and intricacy of the problems involved by exploring the immense variety of proposals — practical and impractical alike — that have been proposed for the consideration of the Fathers at the ecumenical council, Vatican II. We could face the problems of the mission to the future with greater ease if we had been more faithful to the problems of the Church's mission in the more recent past. Yet, once more, we rely upon the wisdom of the Holy Spirit to guide us in our quest.

In all this development of the liturgy's pastoral character we notice one ever increasingly predominant note. This is its insistence upon the *communal* nature of our worship. What this means was succinctly and cogently stated by Fr. Ellard in his "Retrospect," at the close of his *Christian Life and Worship*:

> *Lifted Up in Christ.* A deep sense of how much human nature is ennobled by being elevated to the divine life in and through Christ should be one of the most abiding and transcendent lessons of this study. Another most important conviction, which should be built into one's everyday consciousness as a result of this course, is a

---

2 Milwaukee: The Bruce Publishing Co., 1956.

sense of fellowship, of corporate being, so to speak, with Christ and His Members. Christian *worship* is social and corporate, that of the members with the Head, "No man goeth to the Father save through Me"; Christian *work* is likewise corporate, that of the members with the Head. "Without Me ye can do nothing." When these truths are pondered, and their vital consequences little by little drawn out in the diversities of life, they should produce a twofold modification of one's appreciation of Christianity. Toward Christ a new bond is formed in the deepened knowledge of His mediatorial character, and in the realization of a sharing in His life and eternal priesthood. Respecting the neighbor, there is a far loftier estimate of social obligations toward actual or potential fellow members of the Mystical Body. Contact with religion in its holiest rites, sacrifice, and sacraments has its enduring gains from the unifying concepts of Christ-life and Christ-work. In fine, in the light of the new knowledge, a synthesis results in which the close-knit solidarity of all things under the scepter of Christ is perceived as never before.

From the first page onward our never-failing Scriptural guide has been the Apostle of the Gentiles, from whose inspired writings have been drawn all our proofs. He now furnishes us with the apt phrases set out above, in which we can sum up and, as it were, outline the leading ideas of the whole book.[3]

In the earlier stages of the liturgical movement, the emphasis lay upon the revival of our knowledge and appreciation of the visible, tangible, audible heritage from the past, and its adaptation to the peculiar needs — as well as the unique opportunities — of the present. In its later phases, the movement has widened into a continually greater penetration of the inner nature and meaning of our communal life in Christ. The liturgical movement in our day has brought us to a deeper understanding of our inward fellowship with those who are externally associated with us in the act of worship. Such practices as the joint singing of the choral parts of the Mass, the emphasis upon its catechetical character, and the dialogue Mass all bring to life that communal idea, that worshiping fellowship which made the direct appeal of the Church's mission to the pagan world in its earliest epoch, and had its deep roots in the communal worship of the Old Law.

Hardly a day passes that some new proof is not offered of the

---

[3] *Christian Life and Worship* (1956 ed.), pp. 397–398.

steady growth of understanding for the importance of this communal spirit. Indeed, just as this paragraph is being written, I am interrupted by the news that Philadelphia's Archbishop John J. Krol, in a letter to the clergy, religious, and laity of the archdiocese, calls for a "conscientious observance" of the Instruction of Pius XII on sacred music and the liturgy, and lays down a series of 26 directives to be initiated immediately in all places of worship in the archdiocese, illustrating the principle of the participation of the faithful in divine worship. The ultimate goal, Archbishop Krol emphasizes, "is that indicated by the Supreme Pontiffs, namely, full active participation at all low and sung Masses."

Future historians will wonder how it was that the communal nature of our worship should have become obscured in our recent times, and will speculate upon the causes — such as the social structure of the Middle Ages or the cruel persecutions, bloody or unbloody, of Catholics in later times, which drove Catholic worship underground, as it were. In the days of Maryland's Protestant ascendancy, for instance, it was difficult for the communal aspects of Catholic worship to take anything but a most modest and undemonstrative form.

Today, however, as the outward manifestations of the communal spirit become more and more evident in our public worship, there is the equally urgent need that we keep clearly in sight the inmost nature of our Catholic, Christian communal bond: that we see it always in its true nature, and do not let it become confused with one or the other of those emotional substitutes which can so easily lead us astray.

Hence Fr. Ellard hails as immensely significant the exposition of the inmost nature of the Christian community contained in the great encyclical *Mystici Corporis* ("The Mystical Body," June 29, 1943) of Pope Pius XII, and its particular application to the Church's worship in the companion document, *Mediator Dei* ("The Divine Mediator," November 20, 1947).

Let me explain this point a little further, in view of the actual confrontation that our Catholic faith is obliged to make at the present time.

Our Catholic communal idea, taught at the very dawn of Christianity, is of limitless breadth and depth. In its broadest aspect, it takes in the entire range of the Church: the Church's mission to the entire human race. For there is no human being, alive or dead, who is not to some degree involved in the mystery or the worldwide community of the redemption: either as actual, living members of that community or as potential members. This includes furthermore the fellowship, through the Communion of Saints, of the faithful departed.

In its depth, its inmost intimacy and sublimity, this concept is focused in the community that shares in the daily sacrifice of praise, adoration, thanksgiving, and petition of the Mass; the *communicantes* par excellence.

Today this Catholic community is confronted by two conflicting forces, each of which is profoundly hostile to the other, each in its own way.

One of these is the radical denial of the communal spirit through an exaggerated individualism, our heritage from the individualistic doctrines of the eighteenth century. Such individualism is sharply distinguished from the stress upon the individual human person which the Mystical Body of Christ exalts and perfects, since it lays its principal emphasis upon the self-centered individual either alone or as associated with others of the same radical persuasion.

The other is the perverted communitarian idea of atheistic Communism, in which the operation of communal living in the material order is made the motive and goal of the community. Hence today our Christian fellowship needs to be clarified with a sanity and an intensity as never before.

From the point of view of the merely natural man, the worship of the liturgy might seem out of step with the progressive spirit of the age. Each year, the first Sunday of Advent begins the same cycle of prayer and praise, of lessons and psalms and hymns, of feasts and fasts. The order is unchanged, save where the Sacred

Congregation of Rites inserts some element of passing variety — welcome or unwelcome for its novelty, according as the worshiper's temperament may be, but usually with the idea of bringing contemporary worship more in line with the Church's modern pastoral mission.

To the pagan mind, this ever recurring yearly cycle might seem the same as in pagan worship. One can even draw a certain resemblance between the rosary of the Buddhists and that of the Christians. Yet any such analogy profoundly misses the liturgy's true spirit. True, there is repetition, even a degree of immobility. Yet the liturgy's inherent rhythm is the rhythm of a march, not that of a fixed and revolving wheel: it is always a movement toward a goal.

This onward note or characteristic of our worship impresses itself with the progress of the years. As you yourself advance toward the moment that finds its issue in the transcendence of eternity, you become ever more conscious of the onward movement of the cycles themselves. Each year, as the Advent cycle begins, you are conscious that the entire march of Christian worship moves ever forward. Even though the new calendar may repeat the cycle of the preceding year, it is moving toward an ultimate consummation.

In these days, I think we are particularly conscious of such forward movement, and more inclined to make it a measuring rod for all valid human action. Modern, contemporary man is time-conscious as never before; so much so, that any movement that ignores this factor is doomed to failure. In one form or another, it supplies the dynamic element in all popular, overmastering ideologies. Not merely that they move, but that they are understood — rightly or wrongly — to be progressing toward a higher goal.

The classic example, of course, is the ideology of Communism, which manages to harmonize all its inner contradictions and variations by forcing them all to march under the banner of the "new dawn," the alleged and never attained ultimate consummation of dialectic materialism. And, as Professor Michael Polanyi has skillfully pointed out, it accomplishes its purpose by clothing this destructive forward march with the high dignity of a moral purpose. Yet other popular ideologies, however violently they may be supposed to disagree, derive much of their appeal, their inner force, from the same source. The ideological conservative steals much of his thunder not from the actual attractions of a bygone age, but from the magic that change and revolution are supposed to bring to a foot-dragging age.

The well-nigh universal popular appeal of a movement toward a brighter future is a natural result of the incredibly heightened and accelerated material and scientific progress of our age. Yet at the same time our Christian worship orients even our natural world progress toward a goal which lies hidden in the mystery of man's future; it guides our inner spiritual progress toward a goal revealed by our faith, grasped by our hope, and consummated in perfect charity; this is none other than the eternal kingdom of God: the goal of all redeemed mankind.

The more deeply, then, we enter into the spirit of our worship, into its eschatology, the nearer we come to an understanding of what the movement of our contemporary times really means. The forward movement of our liturgy is the key to our understanding the inner movement of our age. Hence, as I happen to see it, the imperative importance of entering into this inner, eschatological movement of the liturgy, if we wish to combat at its roots the various types of false progressivism in our times, and to see humanity's progress moving on a serene and even keel.

The more intimately we are attuned to the inner rhythm of the liturgy's glorious cycle of praise and sacrifice, of recurrence and remembrance and repetition, the more we shall liberate ourselves from the enslaving bonds of a false concept of human progress, the better we shall understand the words spoken by the sacred prophets centuries before even the birth of the Redeemer, who hailed the march of the poor and the tread of the humble as they walked toward the ultimate liberation from the tyranny of time itself. At each morning's Lauds we hail the new dawn, but at each morning's Divine Sacrifice of the Mass the baptized community, toiling in Peter's bark, greets Him who stands on the shore and *is* the dawn, who has conquered the limitations of space and time, of mortality and sin: we are just so many stadia nearer to the Life that is the goal of all Christian life and worship.

Israel — God's Liturgical People

EUGENE H. MALY

For the Hebrews reality had more than one dimension. It embraced not only the secular world about them, but extended into, and was ultimately controlled by, the world of the divine. Similarly history for them was no bare concatenation of events with no meaning beyond the stark data of natural reality. It was a providential disposition of affairs whose meaning, invested with a divine purpose, had an eternal value. It was not confined by the once-for-allness of a single historical act. Such a theological investiture of the natural often requires, for us of a Western and secularized mentality, a deliberate act of reflection; for the Hebrews it was the normal expression of a living faith.

Biblical historical writing presupposes such a mentality. It rests on the conviction that the saving acts of God, once accomplished in history, are more than the object of historical research; they are the ever present expression of God's continuing redemption of His people. "The Lord, our God, made a covenant with us at Horeb; not with our fathers did he make this covenant, but with us, all of us who are alive here this day" (Dt 5:2–3). "But it is not with you alone that I am making this covenant . . . it is just as much with those who are not here among us today as it is with us who are now here present before the Lord, our God" (Dt 29:13–14).

Because of this almost innate manner of approaching historical reality the biblical historians never display that "statistics" mentality which marks the competent historian of the modern world. An event of the past, sparked by the divine purpose, has its meaning for the people of today. Hence it must be reread in the light of today; it must be dressed anew in the trappings of a contemporary world while it retains its eternal and never changing significance as salvation history. Thus did Israel's rich heritage never become a record of desiccated data of the past; it was always a living reality in the hands of those who recorded it.

Israel was graced with a number of inspired historians. Each wrote in accord with his own religious emphases and to meet the needs of the people of his own day. For the Deuteronomist it was the covenant sealed by God with His people that was the guiding criterion of Israel's fortunes in her national life, and that covenant must become, for a people living in exile, the basis of a new life with God. For the Chronicler, writing after the return from exile, and at a time when Zorobabel represented the continuation of the Davidic line in his own person and the restoration of the cult in his building activities, history takes on a messianic character that would provide a needed stimulus to the discouraged remnant. Years later the author of the Book of Wisdom, faced with the apostasy of many of his coreligionists to the allurements of Hellenic culture, could rewrite the story of the Exodus in terms of a new liberation to be achieved beyond the grave in a life of union with God. The chosen people of old are the types of the faithful just ones of his day who must retain, if they are to be worthy of the perfect redemption, the divine realities that Israel's salvation history alone exhibited.

It is with still another of Israel's historians that we are concerned here. We call him the "priestly" author. The title could be misleading since the priestly history was a composite effort developed gradually over the years and then incorporated into the much larger work that we know as the Pentateuch.[1] But it was

---

[1] It is the common consensus of all modern biblical scholars that the Pentateuch contains four principal "traditions," each of which had developed independently before being incorporated in the canonical Pentateuch. They are given the names of Yahwist, Elohist, Deuteronomist, and Priestly. The last named, the object of our study, comprises about one fifth of the Book of Genesis, about a half of Exodus, all of Leviticus, and about two thirds of Numbers. Those who are interested in a detailed indication of the texts attributed to the four traditions may consult P. Ellis, C.SS.R., *The Men and Message of the Old Testament* (Collegeville, Minn.: The Liturgical Press, 1963), pp. 57–72.

under one overriding conviction that this mass of material was brought together and given a definitive shape. It is this conviction and the manner of its presentation that is the object of our study.

The priestly historian, like his biblical counterparts, was writing from no ivory tower of pure research. He was caught up in the moil of history along with his contemporaries and wrote in answer to the problems of his day. The exile of 587 B.C. had completely disrupted the harmony of Israel's political, social, and, above all, her religious life. A twofold danger was present. She could be contaminated by the practices of pagan Babylon, and she could forget the imposing liturgy of her religious past. Either would constitute, in the eyes of the priestly historian, the grossest perversion of the worship due to Yahweh. He was the "holy one of Israel," and holy must His people be — completely divorced from all the marks of a man-made morality or of a man-made cult.

It was, therefore, no legalistic preoccupation that motivated the cataloguing of all those moral prescriptions that make up so much of the priestly code. Underlying them is the profound conviction of Israel's separateness, of her union with the transcendent God. But morality was, in a sense, only the negative aspect of that union; it *characterized* her unworldliness and her Godlikeness, but it did not constitute it. For the priestly author this was achieved in a positive way through the divine liturgy. If the people of God had, through that abandonment of the covenant that had brought on the exile, lost their right to be considered God's own community, they could only regain that right by experiencing anew the saving acts of God. This new creation was accomplished in the liturgy.

The priestly code has left numerous traces of such a guiding conviction. It is true that the many and minute instructions on the types of sacrifices, on the ceremony of ordination, and on the cultic calendar all betray a concern for a proper worship. But in themselves these reveal little of the author's theology of worship. They could be, and frequently have been, interpreted as the expression of an extreme rubricism. It is only when they are seen in the whole context of the author's story that they take on their intended significance. For, unlike her neighbors, Israel had no book of rubrics, just as she had no code of laws or collection of ethical maxims, that was not conceived and presented as an integral part of her salvation history. This was as true for the priestly author as it was for his Yahwistic, Elohistic, and Deuteronomistic predecessors. His theology of worship, therefore, will be revealed, not in some supposed fascination for rubrical detail, but in his theology of history.

Like the Yahwist he has traced history from the very beginning of man's earthly pilgrimage. The first chapter of Genesis[2] is the most brilliant of all the priestly writings; it also gives us the first insight into his liturgical thinking. The passage has been described as "a heavenly liturgy. With a severe and solemn rhythm the same expressions occur again and again throughout the whole chapter like a litany. . . ."[3] Dominating the scene is the picture of the supreme, unapproachable deity who brings into being, by the mere expression of His will, the various regions of the universe and then their inhabitants. For the creation of man, the climactic act of the six-day work-week, a consultation of the Lord with His royal court determines that man shall be unlike the rest of creatures. He will be made in the image and likeness of God Himself.

This description of man's creation was a necessary stroke of the inspired author's hand. Like the Yahwist historian[4] he was convinced that man had not come from God's hand in a fallen state. But unlike the Yahwist he has expressed that conviction in a truly sublime fashion. Moreover, by putting the whole of creation within the framework of a liturgical hymn, he has, it would seem, given voice to a further conviction that the divine likeness found in man is effected by a liturgical act in which the transcendent God raises man to His own august heights. Through the liturgy, he is saying to his contemporaries, man regains the image and likeness of the God who created him.

This is somewhat confirmed inasmuch as, in the priestly author's

---

[2] The priestly story of creation is contained in Gn 1:1–2:4a.

[3] C. Westermann, Der Schöpfungsbericht vom Anfang der Bibel, Stuttgart, 1960, p. 10.

[4] Cf. Gn 2:25.

view, it is the liturgical worship of God, not only the creation of man, that is the final end of the creative act. This is hinted at, first of all, by the fact that the universe takes on the aspects of a cosmic temple whose appointments, as in the Jerusalem temple, are all severely regulated. It is understandable, then, that the heavenly lights should be designated as serving primarily to determine the sacred calendar (Gn 1:14). But also there could be no six days of creation unless they were followed by the seventh day of rest, the day which the Creator has blessed and made holy above all other days. On this day man must recognize the enthroned Lord of hosts who, having completed His work, awaits in the attitude of majestic repose the liturgical response of His creature. "God seeks the communion of him who was created in his image, but not in the sense that this creature is to place himself as a second god at his side, but only in the sense that God remains Lord and that all must worship him alone."[5]

The priestly history from the first man to the Exodus has been only sketchily preserved for us in Genesis. But what is there permits us to analyze his theology of this long period. Basic to it are the many genealogies that serve to emphasize what has been called the process of gradual elimination. The descendants of Adam are given down to Noe on whom the interest then centers to the exclusion of all the others (Gn 5). Again, all the descendants of Noe are listed until the figure of Abraham appears (Gn 10:1–7, 22–23, 31–32; 11:10–27, 31–32). With Abraham, as with Noe, history takes a significant turn and the others are eliminated from the scene. The obvious purpose of these lists is to show the continuity of history between God's primeval act of creation and the creation of His people, Israel. But there is, at the same time, a process of separation, of "making holy." Israel is the people chosen from among all other nations to be holy (i.e., "separated" from all that is profane) as the Lord her God is holy. The author has insinuated, by his method of tracing man's descent, that this sanctification had been inaugurated from the

[5] W. Zimmerli, 1. Mose 1–11; Die Urgeschichte. 1. Teil – 1. Mose 1–4, Zurich, 1943, p. 112.

very beginning. Israel as God's holy people was the final goal of a protracted divine program.

What is more, we can see that a liturgical framework has been superimposed on this story of mankind's halting steps toward the fulfillment of God's plan. We shall see shortly that the priestly historian has presented the whole story of the Exodus from Egypt and the wandering in the desert as a grand liturgical procession. There are indications that he has similarly conceived the principal stages of mankind's historical pilgrimage from Adam to Israel. The Exodus from Egypt was the Paschal liberation on which all other liberations were modeled. But in the priestly document the Exodus occurred on a Wednesday.[6] It is no accident that our author has also placed on a Wednesday the first ebbing of the floodwaters (Gn 8:3), on another Wednesday the liberation of the mountains (8:5), on still another the appearance of the land (8:13), and finally on a Wednesday the complete drying of the land that permitted Noe to descend from the Ark (8:14). All of these "liberation" events, by being endowed with a cultic significance, are made to share, as the *prooemia* of a divine pedagogy, in the Paschal liberation *par excellence*.

Friday, too, has been accorded a special importance in the priestly theology. It is the day of "arrivals."[7] It was on this day, according to their reckoning, that the people of God arrived at the land of promise (Jos 4:19), and that Ezra reached the land of Palestine after the exile in Babylon (Ezr 7:9). It is understandable, then, that the arrival of the Ark at the mountains of Ararat (Gn 8:4), and, above all, that the arrival of the Creator at the climax of His work, the fashioning of man, should fall on a Friday (Gn 1:26–31).

Similar liturgical overtones can be seen in the manner in which the sacred writer has conceived the division of world history. It is a fourfold division based on the covenants made by God with man. Each period is marked by the inauguration of a permanent

---

[6] Cf. Ex 12:31–51 and Nm 33:3. Cf. T. Maertens, *C'est fête en l'honneur de Jahvé*, Bruges, 1961, p. 165.
[7] Cf. Maertens, *op. cit.*, p. 167 f.

institution, and in each can be noted the gradual development of man's ritual worship of God. For the first period, from Adam to Noe, there is no express mention of a covenant, but one can be readily supposed from the words of God to His creatures (Gn 1:28–30). The institution of the Sabbath (Gn 2:3) marks this period, during which man calls upon God by the merely descriptive title of *Elohim*. Like the animals man is a vegetarian (Gn 1:29 f.).

The second period is inaugurated by a covenant with Noe, and its outward sign is the rainbow (Gn 9:8–17). God is still known simply as *Elohim*, but some progress in the development of a ritual might be seen in the fact that man is now permitted to eat flesh as long as it has been drained of blood (Gn 9:3–5). There is no distinction yet between "clean" and "unclean" animals, a necessary requirement for sacrificial worship, but the groundwork has been laid for such a distinction. The third covenant, marking the beginning of the third period, is made with Abraham. Here God reveals Himself more intimately as *El Shaddai* (Gn 17:1), and the sign of the covenant is ritual circumcision (Gn 17:10–14). The final period is, of course, inaugurated at the time of the Exodus and the covenant of Sinai. Now alone is God known and worshiped by His proper name of *Yahweh*; now alone is the fully developed sacrificial worship revealed. It is evident, therefore, that the priestly author has presented the story of man as the story of his religious and cultic relationship to his God.

It is at the point of fulfillment of the divine plan, however, that the liturgical framework of the whole emerges in all its clarity. Here, in the reconstruction of the story of the Exodus and the wandering, is the midrashic art of the historian employed to its fullest to bring out the cultic bond that tied Israel to her God. It is well known that the Deuteronomist, Israel's historian of the *covenanted* people, has defined that people as the *Qahal Yahweh*, the assembly convoked by Yahweh to seal the covenant at Sinai. The intimate association of the term with the notion of the covenant is indicated by the Deuteronomist's use of the word for the first time in his description of the covenant's enactment

(Dt 5:22). We can say that he has conceived a new creation here and fittingly applies to that creation a new term that defines its nature.[8]

With no less profound convictions has the priestly historian conceived and presented the creation of God's *liturgical* people. The term he uses most frequently to define that creation is *'edah Yisra'el*, the "congregation of Israel." The author sees the divine act of creation in the liturgical setting of a Paschal liberation and redemption. To indicate the nature of this creation he, too, like the Deuteronomist, adopts a new expression for the first time in his description of that liturgical act which both symbolized and re-presented to the successive generations of Israel their definitive redemption, the Paschal meal (Ex 12:3).[9] The cultic emphasis of the priestly historian is even more in evidence inasmuch as he names both Moses *and* Aaron, the high priest, as the responsible authorities for the carrying out of the liturgical meal (Ex 12:1), while the Deuteronomist, in his re-presentation of the covenant sealing, names only Moses as the mediator between God and people (Dt 5:22 ff.). This is in line with the former's general tendency to emphasize the role of the priests (and of Aaron in particular) in the whole history of the Exodus and wandering.[10]

If this "congregation of Israel" is by nature a liturgical people of God, we should expect this to be brought out in the further history of that people. We are not disappointed. First of all it can

---

[8] The Septuagint translation of the word, *ekklēsia*, has been taken over by the New Testament writers to denote the assembly of God's new people.

[9] Before the carrying out of the Passover ritual the Hebrew people are referred to simply as "the Israelites" (cf. Ex 1:7; 2:23 ff.; 6:5; etc.), or as "my (God's) people" (Ex 6:7). It is interesting that the Septuagint translation of the Hebrew *'edah Yisra'el*, i.e., *synagogē*, was not adopted by the New Testament writers as was the Deuteronomist's term. Undoubtedly this was because of the overtones that the Greek word had for the young Christian Church in connection with the Jewish "synagogue" at the time of Jesus. The only occurrence of the term in a Christian sense is in Jas 2:2; the strong Jewish character of this epistle is sufficient explanation for its use there. The Qumran sectaries referred to their "brotherhood" as the *'edah Yahweh*, and the priestly influence in that community and in its writings would explain their preservation and adoption of the term.

[10] Cf., for example, the role that Aaron plays in the mission to Pharao: Ex 7:1-13, 19-20a, 21b-22; 8:1-3, 12-15; 9:8-12; 11:9-10. These are all from the priestly tradition. The same emphasis can be noted in the events connected with the wandering in the desert.

be noted that the term *'edah Yisra'el* is used a little over a hundred times in the priestly document; it is almost invariably used in a cultic context, or where such a context can be inferred. Even more striking is that many of the major events of the Exodus and wandering of this community are given a liturgical coloring either by being directly related to the later feasts that commemorated them (cf. Ex 23:15; Nm 9:1 ff.), or by the fact that they are said to have taken place on a day which was of some importance in later Israel's cultic calendar. Among the latter events can be mentioned the setting out from Rameses in the land of Egypt (cf. Nm 33:3), the erection of the tabernacle (Ex 40:2, 17), and the setting out from the desert of Sinai (Nm 10:11). All of these events take place on a Wednesday, which, as we have seen, was an important day in the calendar of the postexilic period. Similarly the community arrives at the desert of Sinai (Ex 16:1), the directions are given for the convocation of the people for the census (Nm 1:1, 18), and Aaron dies on Mount Hor (Nm 33:38) — all on a Friday, another day that was of special significance in the later period. Israel, therefore, is depicted by the priestly historian as a liturgical community whose movements are directed according to a well-defined cultic calendar.

The manner in which these events are described betray the same concern of the author. We have no picture of a pell-mell flight of released slaves. Rather, the whole scene evoked by the priestly writer is one of order and solemnity, precisely what might be expected of a liturgical group marching in procession. The Lord is at their head (Ex 12:42) as they leave the land of Egypt "company by company" (Ex 12:51). The procession moves along by stages (Ex 13:20; 17:1; 19:1-2), with Moses and Aaron acting as the masters of ceremony (cf. Nm 33:1), and the glorious presence of the Lord, indicated by the cloud covering the tabernacle, determining their stopping and their setting out (Ex 40:34-38; and especially Nm 9:15-23). During the procession each is to keep his proper place (Nm 2:17). And the order of encampment is strictly regulated, with the Levites given the privileged place around the tabernacle (Nm 1:50), and the other tribes assigned their place "at some distance from it" (Nm 2:2). Because of their special cultic role, Moses and Aaron are to camp in front of the tabernacle (Nm 3:38).

Despite its solemnity it is a glorious procession marking a victory over the forces of evil. The Israelites "march away in triumph" (Ex 14:8), and even the waters of the Red Sea are presented as forming a rigid guard of honor as God's people pass through (Ex 14:22, 29). As befits the glorious solemnity of the liturgical event, silver trumpets are blown by the priests to assemble the community and to dismiss them, all in accord with a well-thought-out ritual (Nm 10:1–10). The note of glory is particularly evidenced in the descriptions of the Lord's presence. Doubtless the priestly author was influenced here, as elsewhere, by the awe and reverence associated with the liturgical worship at Jerusalem's temple and so majestically re-created in the priestly Isaia's inaugural vision (Is 6). A similar picture is evoked in the descriptions of Moses' talk with the Lord on Mount Sinai (Ex 24:16–18; 34:29–35), and of the divine presence in the tabernacle (Ex 40:34–38; Nm 9:15–23).

It is within the framework of this liturgical procession marking the salvation of Israel that all the ritual prescriptions of the priestly code are set. The framework is intended to confer on these prescriptions a dynamic character; they become part of Israel's salvation history and thereby lose any rubricist spirit they might otherwise have. Moreover, the cult is seen as attended to by a hierarchized priesthood directly organized by God (Nm 1:50; 3:6 ff.). To stress the continuation of this sole legitimate priesthood of Aaron through his son Eleazar, from whom the priests of the postexilic period traced their descent (cf. Ezr 7:1–5), the author gives a highly stylized account of the death of Aaron and of the transference of his sacerdotal office to his son. In the presence of the whole community, which acts as official witness to the sacred event, the priestly garments of Aaron are placed upon Eleazar (Nm 20:22–29). Thus are the people of the author's day assured of the divinely instituted orders of their own priests, while the people themselves represent the continuation of the liturgical community of old.

It is this latter note, it would seem, that our historian has especially tried to strike throughout his work. Men, created in the beginning to worship God, had been divinely prepared over a long period of time and by successive divine self-revelations to carry out this supreme mission. The fulfillment of the divine plan came when the Hebrews, slaves in a foreign land, had been liberated by the powerful hand of God. In that liberation they became a liturgical people of God marching processionally through the desert, hierarchically grouped behind their Lord, and solemnizing their deliverance from every crisis by an appropriate cultic celebration. Before the author's eyes are his own contemporaries, exiled in the land of Babylon, but now called once again to be God's liturgical people and to solemnize their deliverance by the cultic worship of the Lord at the temple of Jerusalem. On this twofold level of history has the writer conceived his work and presented his message. The salvation history of old can live again; God only awaits the liturgical response of His liberated creature.

...3...

The Fonts of Preaching[1]

DAVID MICHAEL STANLEY, S.J.

THE renascence of interest in the liturgy and the Bible, comparatively recent phenomena in North American Catholicism, might well be expected to affect our attitude towards preaching. Accordingly, we venture here to suggest the value for a revitalized preaching of certain principles emerging, on the one hand, from our new insights into the meaning of public worship and, on the other, from the new directions in scriptural studies.

Three rather broad topics must be qualified at the outset. By liturgy is to be understood the eucharistic liturgy, the Mass. Scripture is taken to mean the selections from the Bible employed in the Roman Mass formulae. Preaching is here restricted to the homily pronounced during Mass. To restate our purpose: we wish to recall, by reflection upon those qualities of Scripture which make it apt for liturgical use, the aim and scope of the sermon considered as an integral part of the liturgy.

Three questions present themselves for consideration: 1) what basic characteristics does the liturgy possess in common with the Bible? 2) what facets of the scriptural Word make it readily adaptable for public worship? 3) how should this affinity existing between liturgy and holy writ be made operative in our preaching? We shall address ourselves in turn to each of these questions.

[1] Reprinted from *Worship*, 37:3 (February, 1963), with the kind permission of Father Godfrey Diekmann, O.S.B.

21

I. WORSHIP AND WORD: COMMON GROUND

At the Assisi Conference Cardinal Bea pointed out a feature of Christian public worship which he considered distinctive: the manner in which the Mass combines instruction with sacrifice.[2] The validity of this observation is attested by the Acts of the Apostles. Luke gives us a picture of an early Christian liturgy conducted by Paul at Troas where the Eucharist is preceded by teaching (Acts 25:7-12). It is significant also that in one of the summaries describing the daily life of the Jerusalem community we find "the teaching of the apostles" juxtaposed with "the breaking of the bread" (Acts 2:42). We may then conclude that from the earliest years of her existence, the Church has included the liturgy of the Word as an integral part of her public worship in the eucharistic action. Can we discover any reason for this practice?

In the first place, as my colleague, R. A. F. MacKenzie, S.J., has pointed out, the Church's attitude to the Bible is similar to her view of the Eucharist. Speaking of the Church's reverence for the Scriptures, Father MacKenzie remarks:

> She acknowledges them for what they are; she did not make them what they are, namely, the word of God. They are gifts bestowed upon the Church by her divine Spouse. She has both the privilege and the responsibility of preserving them, and of exploiting them for the salvation of men. . . . In this respect (as in others) an illuminating comparison can be drawn between the Scriptures and the Eucharist: the Word of Life and the Bread of Life. . . . The Eucharist is not something that the Church herself instituted; it too is a gift from her Spouse. . . . It too is a means and manifestation of Christ's presence among His members. Thus both Scripture and Eucharist are part of the Church's divinely bestowed equipment for carrying on the Saviour's work of redemption.[3]

In the second place, the proclamation of the Word of God has

---

[2] A. Bea, S.J., "The Pastoral Value of the Word of God in the Sacred Liturgy," *The Assisi Papers* (Collegeville: The Liturgical Press, 1957), p. 76.

[3] R.A.F. MacKenzie, S.J. *Introduction to the New Testament*, N.T.R.G. 1 (Collegeville: The Liturgical Press, 1960), p. 40.

ever been regarded in the Judaeo-Christian tradition as possessing the same fundamental effect as that of the Eucharist. Each, in its own way, produces the efficacious unification of God's people.

In the Old Testament, the Hebrews were created into Israel, the chosen people of Yahweh, by Moses' reading of the covenant. And in subsequent eras of history — particularly at critical moments like the religious reform under King Josia or the re-establishment of the exiles in Judaea by the work of Ezra — it was through the recital of God's Word that the people were re-formed, re-constituted, and re-united.

Thirdly, in the Christian dispensation it is clear that the Eucharist, like the Bible, can only be understood in relation to the Church. If Church and sacraments are necessarily correlative, the same is equally true of Church and Scriptures. (I might add that from the inspired record of the apostolic age, the same may be said of preaching.)

The New Testament's essential relationship with the Church is immediately evident when it is recalled that these books are simply the Church's witness to Christ, that they are considered as a record of her testimony normative for the Christian life. The Old Testament too can only be properly comprehended in the context of the Church. Unless read in function of Christ, the inspired writings of Israel have no discernible unity. In fact, since in Israel or in Judaism there was no infallible institution that could unerringly list the canonical books of Scripture, the Old Testament canon cannot be said to have come into existence except with and through the Church.

In the fourth place — this may come as a surprise to some — the Eucharist and the Scriptures possess a common quality. Each is proclamation. The Bible proclaims God's self-revelation to man. The Eucharist proclaims "the death of the Lord until he comes" (1 Cor 11:26).

Jesus instituted the Eucharist as the sacrifice of the new covenant (Mt 26:28; Mk 14:24; Lk 22:20; 1 Cor 11:25). The scriptural accounts reveal, moreover, that Jesus enjoined the repetition of this eucharistic action as a memorial — *anamnesis* (Lk 22:19; 1 Cor 11:24–25). In virtue of this command, remembering acquires significance as a religious activity of a sacramental nature. The Roman liturgy recalls this fact each day: "*Unde et memores . . . Christi . . . passionis . . . resurrectionis et gloriosae ascensionis. . . .* — Accordingly, remembering . . . Christ's passion . . . His resurrection and glorious ascension . . ."

In the intention of our Lord, the eucharistic liturgy was orientated basically towards making contemporary the twin event by which He wrought man's redemption: His death and exaltation. Paul certainly understood this, as we see from his commentary upon Jesus' command of iteration: "As often as you eat this bread and drink from this cup, you proclaim the death of the Lord until He comes" (1 Cor 11:26). Note that by "the Lord," the Apostle understands the risen Christ. This "proclaiming" as *anamnesis* (remembering) falls within the scope of the eucharistic liturgy. And it is obviously the aim of Scripture as testimony to Christ.

Fifthly and finally, the Eucharist-action makes present the risen Christ, our heavenly intercessor, "the Lamb that has been slain." He offers Himself together with the Church, while the Church offers Him, together with herself, to the heavenly Father.

But the risen Christ, as Stephen long ago observed, is also the key to our Christian understanding of the Bible. It is only when the risen Christ, through the activity of the Spirit whom He sends, is present in the reading of the Scriptures that they become for us what they were intended by God to be — His divine self-revelation.

It is then ultimately this twofold presence of the exalted Christ — in the Eucharist and in the Scriptures — which adequately explains their intimate relationship and the Church's use of them both in her public worship. If the Eucharist is Christ's sacramental body, the Scriptures are His sacramental voice, through which He addresses the Father and allows the Church to address Himself and the Father "*propter nos et propter nostram salutem* — for ourselves, for our salvation."

II. THE WORD: OLD YET EVER NEW

Now let us turn to the Bible. There are two aspects which an adequate comprehension of the Scriptures must take into account. On the one hand, they present themselves to our modern, Western mentality as something distinctly alien. If we are to grasp their message, we must follow the advice of Pius XII: "It is absolutely necessary for the interpreter to go back in spirit to those remote centuries of the East, and make proper use of the aids afforded by history, archaeology, ethnology and other sciences, in order to discover what literary forms the writers of that early age . . . employed."[4]

On the other hand, we can discern in the Bible a tendency towards what may be called up-dating. The Old Testament writers no less than those of the New Testament display a preoccupation with making God's Word contemporary for every generation. This aspect of Scripture may require some further amplification; for it is a facet of the Bible which is a consequence of its character as salvation-history.

The Biblical narrative is distinguished from modern historiography principally in two ways. First, by its manner of interpreting the facts it recounts. The historian of today finds the rationale of happenings in the interplay between human personality and historical phenomena; the writer of biblical history sees in the events he records God's self-revelation. The insights provided by scientific historical method are the fruit of human reason; the insights of the hagiographer are the fruit of supernatural faith.

The second notable distinction between these two kinds of history lies in their respective aims. Scientific history addresses itself merely to man's intellect, its ultimate purpose being information about the remembered past — as past. Salvation-history seeks to involve the whole man. As Paul remarks to Timothy, Scripture is orientated to man's *formation* in justice (2 Tim 3:16–17). In Paul's view, the vicissitudes of Israel's wandering in the

---

[4] *Divino Afflante Spiritu* — "On Biblical Studies and Opportune Means of Promoting Them" (London: Catholic Truth Society, 1944), par. 39.

desert "happened to them with symbolic significance and were recorded for our formation" (1 Cor 10:11).

Salvation-history seeks to re-present the past, that is, to make it present inasmuch as the *magnalia Dei* (God's wondrous deeds) are believed to be operative, through the Word of Scripture, in the experience of contemporary man. It is this ability of the Bible to involve the man of today in the sacred events of the past which makes it the best medium for creating the atmosphere of faith in which the Mystery of Faith, the Eucharist, is re-enacted.

Actually this contemporizing capacity of sacred Scripture flows from the historical character of revelation. God revealed Himself in a sequence of past events; but by His intention to have the past committed to writing He continues to reveal Himself to us in the present. "These things have been written," says the author of the Fourth Gospel, "that you may grow in your belief that Jesus is the Messias, the Son of God" (John 20:31).

According to Acts (1:22), the apostolic testimony consists both of a witnessing to Christ based upon personal experience of Jesus' public ministry (eyewitness testimony), and also of an attestation of Christ's resurrection (the testimony of Christian faith). It is this second aspect which makes the apostolic message contemporary.

It may not be out of place here to exemplify briefly this updating tendency of the Bible, the quality which has led the Church to enshrine the eucharistic action in the liturgy of the Word. I would observe in passing that the eucharistic liturgy should be considered not as juxtaposed to, but rather as incorporated in the liturgy of the Word.

The book of Deuteronomy, while it recounts the making of God's covenant with Israel through Moses' mediation, reached the form in which we have it only in the seventh or sixth century. In the intention of the exilic or post-exilic author, the book is directed to his own contemporaries: "Hear, O Israel, the statutes and ordinances which I am delivering in your hearing *today*. . . . The Lord our God made a covenant *with us at Horeb*. It was not with our forefathers that the Lord made this covenant, but *with ourselves,* who are *all here alive today*" (Dt 5:1-3).

The covenant is regarded not merely as an event of the past, but as a continuing event by which the living God addresses Himself to each succeeding generation of Israel. Accordingly it was necessary for the people of God to renew this pact with Yahweh at stated intervals.

The majority of Old Testament scholars would concur with the view of Walther Eichrodt that the varying biblical versions of the Sinai-event come from cultic recitals of it: "Form-critical examination of the Sinai pericope (Ex 19–24), of the narrative of the Joshua covenant (Josh 24), and of the Book of Deuteronomy has revealed as the underlying pattern of all three the scheme of a festival of covenant renewal."[5] According to Eichrodt, "the purpose was to renew the source and basis of the life of the federation of the twelve tribes by means of a regular cultic representation of its origin. . . "[6]

We have an instance of this up-dating in the New Testament in the sermons Matthew has composed of the logia of Jesus, and which he, i.e., their author, addresses to his Christian reader. The Matthean version of Jesus' command to practice Christian baptism (an injunction Jesus undoubtedly gave) provides another instance of up-dating. Matthew has put into our Lord's mouth the liturgical formula employed in the Church of his own day ("in the name of the Father, . . ."), since he regards this command as a continuing injunction which is addressed to every minister of the sacrament "until the end of the world."

If Pierre Benoit be correct in assuming that the words of institution of the Eucharist reported by Mark were actually taken over from the liturgy of the Roman church of his day (Mk 14:22–24), such a literary borrowing is surely evidence of the Church's awareness that in each celebration of the Eucharist she was hearing Christ utter these words to her anew. It will have escaped no one's notice that this scriptural up-dating attained sacramental efficacy — the actual realization of what it represented — in the celebration of the Eucharist.

---

[5] Walther Eichrodt, *Theology of the Old Testament* Vol. I, trans. J. A. Baker, (Philadelphia: Westminster Press, 1961), p. 123. [6] *Ibid.*

III. PREACHING A CONTEMPORIZED WORD

To come to the final section of this paper — the aim of our preaching is to make God's Word contemporary. The preacher must speak to the man of today. He must, however, be conscious that he is merely the voice by which Christ speaks to contemporary man.

The preacher's preliminary task then is to re-mythologize — to explain the Christian message (and this of course includes the Old as well as the New Testament) in function of the culture of the present day. This presupposes that he has himself gone back in spirit to the ancient East, understood what the sacred writers meant to say, and expressed their insight into the Christian Mystery in contemporary language.

But the principal objective of the preacher should be to permit the Good News to be heard today. The preacher cannot afford to settle for the fringe benefits of moralistic application. The structures of the so-called practical application to modern life should not fetter the Word of God. The preacher must respect the reaction of Christian faith on the part of his hearers. He must be aware, as the prophets foretold (Is 54:13; Jer 31:33–34) and Jesus Himself insisted, that "they shall all be taught of God" (John 6:45). He cannot afford to forget Paul's trenchant remark — which might be understood as a criticism of preaching — "the letter kills; it is the Spirit who gives life" (2 Cor 3:6).

In virtue of the faculties for preaching given him by the bishop, the preacher stands before the faithful as the successor of the apostolic preachers, armed with a two-edged sword which is the proclaimed Word of God. Through their Christian faith his audience possesses the Spirit who will lead them, as Jesus promised, "into the full range of truth" (John 16:13). The words of the preacher, uttered as successor of the apostles, evoke in his hearers that inner Word, the Gospel in the fullest sense (as Paul was so well aware), spoken by the Spirit in the depths of their hearts.

... 4 ...

"Blessed be the God and Father of
Our Lord Jesus Christ"
Εὐλογητὸς ὁ Θεός (Eph 1:3–14)

KATHRYN SULLIVAN, R.S.C.J.

THE importance of hymns in the liturgical life of the early Church is clearly stated several times in the New Testament. Of the first Christians it is said, "Breaking bread at home, they took their food with gladness and simplicity of heart, praising God in song"[1] (Acts 2:46–47). In the captivity epistles, two passages make specific allusion to the primitive practice of hymn-singing. The directive given to the Colossians reads: "Let Christ's message with all its wealth of meaning abide in you; with fullness of wisdom teach and admonish one another, and from the bottom of your hearts gratefully sing psalms, hymns and spiritual songs to God" (1:16). In a parallel text the Ephesians were advised: "Recite among yourselves psalms and hymns and inspired canticles, singing and giving praise to the Lord with all your heart" (5:19).

Were these hymns charismatic improvisations or patterned forms of praise? Inspired, ecstatic utterances[2] undoubtedly were often the sign of the Spirit's presence at the agapē[3] and the expression

---

[1] "Praising God in song." Thus should the Greek αἰνοῦντες τὸν Θεὸν be translated. The word αἰνοῦντες was used, says Zorell, "in Sacred Scripture of religious hymns and public acts of thanksgiving." Cf. H. Schlier, Theologisches Wörterbuch zum neuen Testament, I, 176.

[2] Cf. P. Benoit, Les Epitres de la Captivité, super Col 3:16.

[3] Heinrich Schlier, Der Brief an die Epheser (Düsseldorf: Patmos-Verlag, 1958): "The situation (Eph 5:18) of the faithful to whom he writes resembles that of the assemblies referred to in 1 Cor 11:12 ff. It is also possible that these assemblies were later called Agapēs."

29

of the joy of the assembled Christians, but from the context it seems clear that the cultic hymn-singing recommended by the Apostles to his correspondents is not to be identified with such spontaneous outbursts but rather with the "liturgical song of the community."[4]

"Community hymns" containing early Christian credal concepts[5] were held in honor until they were superseded by psalm-singing as a corrective to gnostic abuses.[6] The liturgical origin of many of the lyric fragments found in the New Testament is now generally recognized,[7] and it is our purpose here to examine one of the most beautiful of the Pauline hymns of praise (Eph 1:3–14).

Paul's epistles, it is generally admitted, are structured according to contemporary patterns. He follows the literary form then currently used in private letters: greeting, thanksgiving, prayer, main topic(s), and epilogue, making such modifications as his desires or the needs of his readers may suggest. Commentators sometimes fail to point out — and, even when they do, they do not always explain — the deviation from his customary procedure in Ephesians.

---

[4] "One does not regard as a glossolalia (a spontaneous, inspired, charismatic utterance) the cultic hymns of the people." *Ibid.* Cf. *Theologisches Wörterbuch,* I, 164.

[5] D. M. Stanley, "Carmenque Christo Quasi Deo Dicere . . . ," *Catholic Biblical Quarterly,* 20 (2, 1958), analyzes several New Testament hymns and shows that they constitute an important part of the most ancient testimony to the Church's belief in the divinity of Jesus, e.g., Phil 2:5–11; Ap 5:9–10, 12, 13; 1 Pt 1:3–5; Eph 5:14; 1 Tm 3:16; Col 1:13–20; Jn 1:1–18. H. Leclercq, hymns he cites are Rom 11:36; Eph 3:21, 5:14; 1 Tm 1:17, 3:16, 6:15; 2928, cautiously admits that the Pauline lyric fragments may be "formulas taken from apostolic eschatology," but he does not believe that this claim can be proved. He cites 66 hymns belonging to the early and medieval Church. The Pauline hymns he cites are Rom 11:36; Eph 3:21, 5:14; 1 Tm 1:17, 3:16, 6:15; 2 Tm 2:11–13. His list is obviously incomplete.

[6] Balthasar Fischer, "Le Christ dans les psaumes," *La Maison Dieu,* 27, 1951, p. 88: "According to Rudolf Knopf's well known thesis, the psalter appears in fact never to have played a role other than that of a book of liturgical *readings* in the framework of the reading of the prophecies. It does not seem to have become a book of liturgical chant until the young Church, turning aside from hymns radically compromised by gnostic abuses, returned to the Bible."

[7] Lucien Cerfaux, *Le Christ dans la Théologie de St. Paul,* Editions du Cerf, Paris, 1954, p. 306. "Epistolary thanksgiving formulas are expanded in the captivity epistles and given a liturgical style. It seems probable that they preserve echoes of eucharistic thanksgivings. The most beautiful is found at the beginning of the epistle to the Ephesians, 1:3–14."

Here the introductory greeting, the *praescriptio,* a literary form containing the names of the sender and the recipient (1:1–2), is followed by a "praise-giving" or eulogy (1:3–14), the key phrase being "Blessed be the God" (εὐλογητὸς ὁ Θεὸς) (1:3); a thanks giving and prayer formula (1:15–2; 22); and a solemn invocation and doxology (3:1–21).[8]

Much has been written about the initial "praise-giving" verses which are marked by Semitic inclusiveness rather than Greek synthesis.[9] "Baffling," "obscure," "complex" or their synonyms, are often used to describe these twelve long verses which form a single sentence in the Greek text. All comment on the density of thought and the profundity of doctrine contained in this passage which is "a kaleidoscope of dazzling lights and shifting colors." Because certain seminal phrases ring out like a refrain, attempts have been made to use them as keys to unlock the meaning of the passage and reveal its pattern. The significant words "In Christ" or their equivalent are repeated at least ten times: *in Christ* (ἐν Χριστῷ) (verses 3, 10, 12), *in him* (ἐν αὐτῷ) (verses 4, 11), *in his beloved Son* (ἐν τῷ ἠγαπημένῳ) (verse 6), *in whom* (ἐν ᾧ) (verses 7, 11, 13a, 13b), and *unto him* (εἰς αὐτόν) (verse 5). Three times mention is made of the divine will — "conformably to the good pleasure of his will" (κατὰ τὴν εὐδοχίαν τοῦ Θελήματος αὐτοῦ) (verses 5, 11; cf. verse 9), and three times of the praise of the divine glory — "to the praise of his glory" (εἰς ἔπαινον δόξης) (verses 6, 12, 14). Three particles are considered by some authors to have special signifi-

---

8 "The terms of the mystery are expressed in an unusual style, which is solemn, priestly, 'liturgical.' . . . The involved style of the captivity epistles with its redundancies, its accumulated synonymous expressions, its succession of relatives and participles, probably reflects liturgical practice." *Ibid.* pp. 305–306. Alfred Wikenhauser, *New Testament Introduction,* Herder and Herder, New York, 1958, pp. 348–349.

9 J. Coutts, "Ephesians 1, 3–14 and 1 Peter 1, 3–12," *New Testament Studies,* 1957, pp. 115–127. Three older studies still have value. T. Innitzer, "Der Hymnus in Epheserbriefe, 1, 3–14," *Zeitschrift für katholische Theologie,* 1904, pp. 612–621. H. Coppieters, "La doxologie de la lettre aux Ephesiens," *Revue Biblique,* 1909, pp. 74–88. E. Driessen, "De auxilio Dei et salute hominis apud S. Paulum," *Verbum Domini,* 1940, pp. 225–233.

cance; and other repetitions, e.g., "redemption" (ἀπολύτρωσιν) (verses 7, 14), have also been noted.

Rejecting the explanation of mere casual repetition, commentators assume that these phrases control the division of the subject matter, yet no single theme or uniform pattern emerges. A sampling of some of the titles given to this passage indicates the variety of the themes that have been proposed. The major titles advanced by scholars include the following:

"Praise to God for the blessings of salvation" (Abbott).
"A description [of the divine plan of salvation] according to the divine purpose" (Benoit).
"A hymn of praise to the all-embracing efficacy of God's grace" (Meinertz).
"An act of thanksgiving for the graces which God has prepared for us and granted us in Jesus Christ" (Medebielle).
"The mystery of incorporation in Christ" (Prat).
"A description of the mystery of God's will for Jew and Gentile" (Robinson).
"The worshipful praising of God's blessing" (Schlier).
"A hymn of praise to God for the greatness of the spiritual blessings which all the faithful are receiving through Jesus Christ" (Steinmueller).
"The mystery of the recapitulation of all things in Christ" (Vosté).
"A hymn of praise to God for the redemption and consummation of all things in Christ" (Westcott).

Not only do different authors select different themes as the dominating motifs of this passage, they likewise vary markedly in their analyses of the structure of the passage as a whole. Two examples, one derived from an earlier author and one from a more recent writer, serve to illustrate this diversity. In 1904 Bover[10] analyzed the contents of this passage under the following headings:

[10] J. M. Bover, "Doxologiae Epistulae ad Ephesios logica partitio," *Biblica,* 1921, p. 460.

A a) blessing and election (verses 3–4)

   b) filiation and predestination (verses 5–6)

B a) redemption through Christ (verses 7–8)

   b) recapitulation in Christ (verses 9–10)

C a) the heritage of the Jews (verses 11–12)

   b) the heritage of the Gentiles (verses 13–14)

In 1957 Coutts proposed a division of the subject matter which may be summarized as follows:[11]

  I. An opening blessing to God the Father.

    1. who has blessed us in Christ Jesus,

    2. in whom we have been chosen,

    3. and foreordained to be His adopted sons.

  II. He has bestowed grace on us in the beloved,

    1. through whose blood we have been redeemed,

    2. in whom all things are to be summed up,

    3. in whom we have been chosen as God's portion.

  III. In him we have been sealed by the Holy Spirit.

Since the division of these verses according to grammatical structure does not seem to lead to any conclusive result, it is well to return to the *Sitz im Leben* of this hymn and to inquire if any literary form can be found that corresponds to its context. The opening word "Blessed" (εὐλογητός), is always used by New Testament writers in a religious sense and sometimes in a liturgical setting.[12] In the *Didachē* several prayers begin with phrases closely

---

[11] J. Coutts, "Eph. 1:3–14 and 1 Peter 1:3–12," *New Testament Studies,* 1957, p. 117. The author holds that both passages contain "a homily based on a form of prayer, and to some extent reproducing its words," p. 113.

[12] It has often been observed that the first ten words in 2 Cor 1:3, Eph 1:3, and 1 Pt 1:3 are identical. In 1 Pt the phrase introduces a eulogy for the gift of new birth and the pledge of an eternal inheritance; in 2 Cor it introduces a hymn of praise to God "the Father of Mercy and Consolation." Cf. the phrase in the Qumran hymn 10:14. For further references consult the article "εὐλογέω, εὐλογία" (Beyer) *Theologisches Wörterbuch* 2, 751–763. Elsewhere in the NT εὐλογητός occurs five times and is always used of God (Mk 14:61; Lk 1:68; Rom 1:25; 9:5; 2 Cor 11:31). In the Lukan passage it introduces the *Benedictus,* where it repeats a phrase from the LXX, Ps 40:14, 71:18; 105:48; the Hebrew word corresponding to εὐλογητός is *berakhah.* For a particularly valuable study see M. E. Boismard, *Quatre hymnes baptimales dans la Première Epître de Pierre* (Paris: Cerf, 1961).

resembling the opening words of this passage. It is possible that Paul is following the pattern of a "thanksgiving," a *eucharistia*, a liturgical prayer currently popular and based on the Jewish blessing or *berakhah*.[13]

Two forms of this prayer type have been identified, and the simpler is a spontaneous outburst of praise containing two literary elements: the blessing proper and the motive or motives for the blessing (usually a "wonderful work of God"). The later, more complex form contains three elements: a short, stereotyped invitation to praise God; the remembrance of some manifestation of divine power, wisdom, and love given to the people as a whole or to an individual; a second benediction, richer, deeper, more heartfelt than the first because of the experience of God's goodness just recalled. Perhaps some of the obscurities of Eph 1:3–14 may be clarified if we attempt to view the passage as an instance of the simpler (two-element) form of this prayer type.

A. *The Blessing* (1:3)

The opening words of the passage should be considered as an exhortation to "bless God" ($\epsilon\dot{\upsilon}\lambda o\gamma\eta\tau\dot{o}s\ \dot{o}\ \Theta\epsilon\dot{o}s$), on which all subsequent concepts will depend and to which all will refer.

> Thus one sees . . . how fundamental and decisive is that blessing with which God has blessed us. He who is the power of the Spirit in the Father's blessing of us in Christ opens up for us the lordship of Christ as *the* dimension of our being. We are therefore — God be praised! — blessed even to the roots of our existence, to the very depths of our personal being. Transcendent even in the midst of the pitfalls of worldly might, we are concealed in Christ Jesus as those blessed by partaking in His condition.[14]

Why should God be blessed? Because He has blessed us with

---

[13] J. P. Audet, "Εὐχαριστία in the First Century," *Studia Evangelica* (Berlin: Akademie-Verlag, 1959), pp. 648–649. Father Audet speaks of "the really wonderful 'evangelical' εὐχαριστία of Eph 1,3 – 3,21," p. 649. Without questioning the validity of this statement, the position adopted here is slightly different: the *berakhah* elements of 1:3–14 are isolated for examination.

[14] Cf. H. Schlier, *Der Brief an die Epheser* (Düsseldorf: Patmos-Verlag, 1958), p. 39.

every best blessing. Paul then hastens to adduce six specific *mirabilia Dei* for which we should give praise.

B. *THE MIRABILIA DEI*

1. *God's love for man and man's response* (1:4)

Rising at once to the thought of the eternal plan according to which those who are united with Christ through grace while on earth are privileged to share in the beatific vision *in patria,* Paul marvels at the dimensions of the divine gifts inspired by love and inspiring love. The words "out of love" (ἐν ἀγάπῃ) may be taken both with the words that precede and the words that follow: it is God's love for us that explains the divine election and the call to sanctity, and it is our answering love that alone can be called the perfect response.[15]

2. *Divine adoption* (1:5-6)

Conformed to the image of His Son, all men are invited to grow in likeness to their divine Model who is the perfect image of the invisible God, with all that this conformity involves: "adoptive sonship through partaking in the sonship of God's only begotten Son, a call to share his glory, to rise like him, so that he may appear as the first-born of countless brothers, clothed with the privileges of the eldest, marching at the head of the Church triumphant."[16]

3. *The Precious Blood* (1:7)

In the Pauline context of reconciliation, Christ's death on the cross, the shedding of His blood, is the expression of God's fathomless love for man. In recounting this third wonderful work of the Lord, the Apostle sees a reason for blessing God who has made possible the purification of our sins through the outpoured blood of His Son. Reconciliation is here closely linked with propitiation. As Père Dupont says: "Christ's death appears here as eminently realizing what judaism demanded of legal sacrifices 'for sin.' . . .

---

[15] Cf. C. Spicq, *Agapè* (Paris: Gabalda, 1959), II, 210.
[16] J. Huby, *Saint Paul: Epître aux Romains* (Paris: Beauchesne, 1940), p. 310.

We rise to the sacral plane. Reconciliation is brought about by an act of worship."[17]

4. The Mystery of Christ in the Churches (1:8-10)

In the captivity epistles the message of Christian salvation is called the "mystery" because God's magnificently wise and loving plan infinitely transcends human reasoning. In the beginning God created all things; in the fullness of time He restored the unity shattered by sin, reestablishing, first through the incarnation and redemption and later through the *parousia*, all things in Christ so that a perfect hymn of praise can rise from creatures through Christ to the Father.[18]

5. The privileges accorded by God to Israel (1:11-12)

God wished to fashion for Himself a people to whom He could give graces of predilection, from whom He could receive limitless and loving obedience. This is the history of salvation. Abraham, Moses and Josue, the Judges, the Kings and the Prophets all played their role in preparing for the Messia and His message of salvation. In recalling this *mirabile Dei*, Paul dwells on the gratuitousness of the divine goodness and the obligation of those so singularly blessed to praise the divine glory.[19]

6. The privileges accorded by God to the Gentiles (1:12-14)

Turning from his own people to the Gentiles, he reminds them that they, too, have now received the full revelation. No longer through hints and symbols but plainly and unmistakably the universal gospel of salvation has been proclaimed. The long-promised Holy Spirit, the pledge and installment, is now given to all those who believe. For the third and last time, Paul repeats the triumphant refrain and invites all men to take part in the purpose for

---

[17] J. Dupont, *La Reconciliation dans la Théologie de Saint Paul* (Bruges: Desclée de Brouwer, 1953), p. 42.

[18] L. Cerfaux, *Le Mystère du Christ* (Paris: Editions du Cerf, 1954), pp. 318-322.

[19] J. Giblet, "The People of God," *The God of Israel, the God of Christians* (New York: Desclée, 1962), pp. 34-84.

which the world was made — the exaltation of the glory of God. *In laudem gloriae.*[20]

So the hymn comes to an end. Six of God's gifts to men have been recalled as so many reasons for praising Him. Like the prologue to the Gospel of St. John, this passage is a great gateway leading to the heart of this epistle: the wisely ordained plan of salvation centering in the Person of Jesus. More than that, this hymn of praise is an introduction to an important concept of biblical theology, containing as it does the definitive summation of Pauline soteriology.[21] For this grace of redemption the perfect response is: "Blessed be the God" — Εὐλογητὸς ὁ Θεός.[22]

---

[20] M. Meinertz, *Die Gefängenschaftsbriefs* (Bonn: Hanstein, 1931), pp. 65–67.

[21] D. Stanley, *Christ's Resurrection in Pauline Soteriology* (Rome: Pontificio Instituto Biblico, 1961), pp. 216–220. Coutts, *op. cit.*, lists six blessings. Cf. *Bible Jerusalem*, Col 1:3–14.

[22] Unfortunately before the preparation of this essay I did not have the advantage of seeing the scholarly study of S. Lyonnet, "La Benediction de Eph 1, 3–14 et son arrière-plan Judaique," *A la Rencontre de Dieu, Memorial Albert Gelin*, pp. 341–352 (Paris, 1961). A comparison of Eph 1, 3–14 with the Ahabah prayer adds further support to some of the conclusions reached here.

...5...

The Ignatian Exercises and the Liturgical Kerygma

TERRENCE R. O'CONNOR, S.J.

IN THOSE sections of the encyclical *Mediator Dei* which vindicate the legitimacy and need of various forms of subjective or personal piety, Pope Pius XII teaches that the proper use of such piety, including the Ignatian *Exercises,* requires an orientation toward objective piety, the official liturgy of the Church (*M.D.* 28–33, 180).[1] One of the most basic aspects of this orientation can be faithfully paraphrased, I believe, as follows: As the various prayers and rites with which the Church has embellished the central sacramental system serve as proximate preparation disposing the faithful for more fruitful reception of grace *ex opere operato,* so subjective piety should serve as a remote preparation for the same end (*M.D.* 22–27, 35–36, 101, 152–153). This is best accomplished when subjective piety draws constant nourishment from the liturgy (*M.D.* 33–37, 81, 184). There is a mutual interaction involved here. Its need becomes more apparent when the encyclical describes the liturgy as "the most efficacious means for achieving sanctity" (*M.D.* 26). For the *Spiritual Exercises,* as an instrument for achieving sanctity, are committed by their very purpose to a serious use of this "most efficacious means."[2]

---

[1] Abbreviations: *M.D.* – Encyclical *Mediator Dei,* trans. G. Ellard, S.J. (*On the Sacred Liturgy,* New York: America Press, 1948); *S.E.* – *The Spiritual Exercises of St. Ignatius,* trans. L. J. Puhl, S.J. (Westminster, Md.: Newman Press, 1951). References to both of these are according to section.

[2] Concerning the liturgy as a form of prayer: "Unquestionably, liturgical prayer, being the public supplication of the illustrious Spouse of Jesus Christ, is superior in excellence to private prayers" (*M.D.* 37).

Since, however, the Institute of the Society of set purpose departed from that emphasis on the liturgical life characteristic of the older monastic orders, the individual Jesuit, however prompt his spirit of obedience, is apt to feel that in implementing liturgical directives he is somehow moving onto an alien preserve. He may fear that his implementation may verge toward a soulless activism. For though the technique of "learning by doing" has real place in the liturgy, a more activated liturgy is not brought about simply by more liturgical activity.

The following remarks are an attempt to bridge this psychological gap by moving from the more known to the less known, from the most central, characteristic ideas of the Ignatian *Exercises* to the most central, characteristic ideas of the liturgy. Two postulates, which cannot be elaborated at length here, will render these terms more specific:

Postulate I: The most central, characteristic ideas of the Ignatian Exercises are those of the meditations on the Kingdom and the Two Standards.[3]

Postulate II: The most central, characteristic ideas of the liturgy are those of the traditional initiation rite. In the developed form of this rite (late third to early sixth centuries) the period of catechumenate (six to eight weeks) came to a climax with a continuous ceremony including baptism, confirmation, and first Mass and Communion.[4] The ancient catechumenate is no more, but the doctrinal emphases of the early catecheses remain in the liturgy down to the present day in the rites of baptism and confirmation, in the Mass, in the Lenten cycle and particularly in the Easter vigil. The Lenten liturgy derives from the early catechumenate instruction, and the teaching unfolded in the Easter vigil is intended as a pedagogic recapitulation of that instruction.

In these sources we have the core of the liturgical preaching or *kerygma*. Its importance can hardly be overstressed. Here the Church is not simply defining particular doctrines, nor confuting

---

[3] Cf. H. Rahner, S.J., *The Spirituality of St. Ignatius Loyola*, trans. F. J. Smith, S.J. (Westminster, Md.: Newman Press, 1953), pp. 34–40.

[4] Cf. G. Bareille, "Catechumenat," *DTC*, II, 2, 1968–1987.

specific heresies, nor applying a remedy for some passing contingency. Here she stands back, as it were, and asks herself: "What are the perennially important truths, values, and attitudes which should motivate and inspire the faithful for leading the Christian life?" Her answer presents to the whole man a whole view of the faith, timeless and ever timely, mysterious yet neither abstruse nor esoteric. Here the Church, *Mater et Magistra,* is most preeminently traditional, authentic, and kerygmatic.[5]

I. THE KINGDOM

A. *The Analogy of the Soldier-King*

The opinion is sometimes expressed that the *Kingdom* meditation is no longer pertinent because kingdoms are practically a thing of the past. Adaptation may be called for, but it should be tempered by the fact that both the kingdom idea and the warfare analogy of Ignatius are prominent in Scripture and even more prominent in the liturgical *kerygma.*

The classical Old Testament type of baptism is the crossing of the Red Sea, a military event which probably helped influence the "holy warfare" symbolism of baptism. In the religious instructions of St. John Chrysostom we read: "They had the great-souled Moses as leader and general (*stratēgon*); we have another Moses, God Himself, as both leader and commander (*stratēgounta*)."[6] This represents the characteristic development of the analogy: Moses, the leader chosen of God, serves to highlight the even greater attributes of Christ. It is precisely the same kind of *a*

[5] "From the time of her apostolic origins, Holy Mother Church has given singular emphasis to the yearly commemoration of the central mysteries of Jesus Christ" (Sacred Congregation of Rites, November 16, 1955; *AAS,* 47 [1955], 838). Because of the substantial stability of these rites, "one can find in them the traditional teaching of the Church Herself, free from the accidental differences of historical circumstances and various cultures" (J. Lecuyer, C.S.Sp., "Aspects missionaires de l'initiation chrétienne selon les Pères de l'Église," *Nouvelle revue de science missionaire,* 15 [1959] p. 1). See also L. Bouyer, Orat., *The Paschal Mystery,* trans. Sr. M. Benoit (Chicago: Henry Regnery Co., 1950).

[6] A. Wenger, ed., *Jean Chrysostome, Huit catéchèses baptismales inédites* (Paris: Editions du Cerf, 1957), Catech. III, 25, 166.

fortiori development as that of the *Kingdom* meditation, where the "human king" is introduced to emphasize "how much more worthy of consideration is Christ our Lord" (*S.E.* 95).

The emphasis in the initiation rite on the idea of a military campaign can be sufficiently indicated here by a brief summary.[7] Enrollment in the catechumenate was seen as an enlistment (*conscriptio, syntagē*) in response to the call of the Great King. Until the time of baptism, the catechumens are recruits (*neoi stratiōtai*) in basic training. Assembly on the night of baptism is the final roll call mustering them for the definitive "joining up" (*sýntaxis*) in the royal ranks. Fully trained and ready to enter the campaign, they are stripped and anointed as for combat in the arena. Profession of faith by recitation of the Creed is compared to the military oath (*sacramentum, synthēkē*) made to the commanding general, and the indelible character of baptism is seen as the tattoo the soldier bore on his arm to signify his allegiance.[8]

B. *The Basic Duality: Suffering as the Condition of Victory*

The kinship between the initiation rite and the *Kingdom* meditation lies deeper, however, than their common use of the warfare analogy. More significant is the dogmatic reality underlying the figurative expression.

It is my will to conquer the whole world and all my enemies, and thus to enter into the glory of my Father. Therefore, whoever wishes to join me in this enterprise must be willing to labor with me, that by following me in suffering, he may follow me in glory (*S.E.* 95).

Here Ignatius confronts us with the ineluctable duality in the following of Christ, the paradoxical "death-life" polarity of the Christian idea. I must die to self if I would live with Christ. To reject this condition is to desert the ranks. On the way to Emmaus, our Lord said to the two disciples, "Did not the Christ

---

[7] Because of limitations of space, confirmation has not been treated in this article. Cf. J. Danielou, S.J., *The Bible and the Liturgy* (Notre Dame, Ind.: University of Notre Dame Press, 1956), Chap. VII, "Confirmation"; also R. Howard, S.J., *Liturgical Retreat* (New York: Sheed and Ward, 1959), pp. 87–111.

[8] Danielou, *op. cit.*, p. 59. The military analogy recurs *passim* throughout the book.

have to suffer these things before entering into his glory?" (Lk 24:26). This same necessity is extended to all the faithful by St. Paul in a passage frequently used in the catechetical instruction of the Church Fathers, made familiar to the faithful today by its use in the Easter vigil at the renewal of the baptismal promises:

> Do you not know that all we who have been baptized into Christ Jesus have been baptized into his death? For we were buried with him by means of Baptism into death in order that, just as Christ has arisen from the dead through the glory of the Father, so we may also walk in newness of life (Rom 6:3-4).

In keeping with this idea there is a twofold symbolism to the baptismal water. Water is a saving, cleansing element, but it is also destructive.[9] This latter aspect is seen in the accounts of the crossing of the Red Sea, of Jona and the whale, and of Peter walking on the waters — all of which occur as types, foreshadowings, of baptism. Water is an agent both of life and of death.

The font, then, is both tomb and womb, and in some places, as St. Ambrose tells us, was even made in the shape of a tomb.[10] "At the same time," says St. Cyril, "you died and were born; and that water of salvation was at once your grave and your mother."[11] At the blessing of the font, the Church prays "that a heavenly offspring may emerge from the immaculate womb of this divine font" — a reflection of the traditional development of baptism as the gestation by *Mater Ecclesia* bringing forth sons to newness of life. In the same series of prayers, the Church employs the traditional symbolism of the blood and water flowing from Christ's side: blood signifying death, water signifying the life He would communicate to men.

But however the idea is expressed — death-life, tomb-womb, suffering-victory, cross-crown, Good Friday-Easter Sunday — it is the same radical duality which lies at the heart of both the liturgical

---

[9] *Ibid.*, p. 75 ff.

[10] *De sacramentis*, III, I, 1. PL, 16, 431 A. Trans. T. Thompson, J. H. Srawley, *St. Ambrose On the Sacraments and On the Mysteries* (London: SPCK, 1950), p. 70.

[11] *Catechesis mystagogica II*, 4. Edit. F. L. Cross, *St. Cyril of Jerusalem's Lectures on the Sacraments* (London: SPCK, 1951), p. 19.

kerygma and the *Kingdom* meditation, and which both strive to implant deep in the hearts of the faithful.

C. *The Basic Duality and the Imitation of Christ*

The closing colloquy of the *Kingdom* meditation asks our Lord for the grace "to imitate Thee in bearing all wrongs and all abuse and all poverty, both actual and spiritual, should Thy most holy majesty deign to choose and admit me to such a state of life" (S.E. 98).

Not only the subsequent stress in the *Exercises* on knowing, loving, and following Christ, but all subsequent growth, even the most exalted sanctity, is a development according to the fundamental "death-life" duality we have been considering.[12] To grow in the likeness of Christ calls for a willingness to share more fully in His sufferings.

In all of this, there is an analogy with the basic position that baptism holds in relation to all subsequent growth in the Christ-life. Baptism itself was called by the Fathers an "imitation of Christ" (*mimēsis toū Christoū*).[13] In this again, St. Paul's teaching is influential: "For if we have been united with him in the likeness of his death, we shall be so in the likeness of his resurrection also" (Rom 6:5). This likeness, this imitation of Christ, was graphically portrayed by the dramatic form of the early rite. By stepping down into the waters for the threefold immersion the neophyte imitated Christ descending into the tomb for the three-day burial; by rising again from the waters he imitated Christ rising to a new life.

But the point here is not simply that in the liturgical *kerygma*, as in the *Exercises,* the "death-life" duality holds such a fundamental place in relation to the following of Christ. It is rather that baptism is a new creation of fallen man to the image of God. By dying and rising with Christ, the Christian takes his first and

---

12 "It should be noted that the contemplation on the King . . . is the foundation of all the following meditations on the life of our Lord Jesus Christ; for it contains the substance of the imitation of Christ, in which human perfection consists." *Directorium* approved in 1582. *Mon. Hist. Soc. Jesu,* II, 1, 861.

13 Danielou, *op. cit.,* p. 44 ff.

all-important step in imitating Christ, a step that makes all the difference between "acting like" and "being like." Baptism not only strikes the doctrinal keynote for the Christian life, it generates that life.[14]

This incipient sacramental imitation retains its vitality primarily through the Mass. As memorial of both the suffering Christ and the risen Christ, the Mass keeps before the minds of the faithful the dual aspect of their baptism, but not simply as a pedagogical repetition. By reason of their participation in the priesthood of Christ, they share in the sacrificial offering of the celebrant and of the High Priest, Christ Himself (M.D. 87–90). From this liturgical imitation of the passion of Christ as from a well-spring flows that day-to-day imitation of Christ in Christian self-denial. This is what Pope Pius XII means when he says that this offering of the laity "is in fact not confined merely to the liturgical sacrifice" (M.D. 99). The other aspect comes to the fore primarily in the reception of the Eucharist. For the Mass is a celestial banquet prefiguring our eternal glory; and reception of the Eucharist is a token that as Christ rose from the dead, so shall we, His members. This is the sacramental source of our hope of final victory as seen in the Kingdom meditation (S.E. 95).

From the Mass as a constant source, this sacramental imitation of Christ overflows throughout the whole liturgical year as an annual review of His life. It is noteworthy that Pius XII in his summation of this idea returns once more to the duality of baptism and the Kingdom meditation: "The liturgical year . . . requires a serious and constant effort to imitate His mysteries, to enter willingly upon His path of sorrow and thus finally share in His glory" (M.D. 161).

---

[14] Treating of the imitation of Christ, St. Basil points out that it involves not only imitation of His virtues, "but also imitation of His death. . . . How, then, do we accomplish this descent into the depths? By imitating the burial of Christ through our baptism. . . . For there is only one death for the sake of the world, and only one resurrection from the dead; and baptism is the type (túpos) of these" (De Spiritu Sancto, XV, 35). Edit. Benoit Pruche, O.P., Basile de Césarée, Traité du Saint-Esprit (Paris: Editions du Cerf, 1945), pp. 169–170. Similarly, Ambrose calls baptism the "form of our faith." De sacramentis, I, I, 16. PL, 16, 422 B.

But there are further implications in Ignatius' teaching on the imitation of Christ which suggest a more intimate rapprochement with the liturgy. After his mystical experience on the banks of the Cardoner, Ignatius made a substantial change in the meditations on the *Kingdom* and *Two Standards*.

> Jesus Christ the Eternal Prince was no longer seen simply as an example for imitation whose loving passion saints had for sixteen centuries taken as their model. In addition to this, He was the living, acting King who has not laid aside the task committed to Him by His Father, but in order to accomplish it, seeks here and now for full-hearted co-workers and intimate friends whom He "sends on this enterprise."[15]

From this point on, the following of Christ is for Ignatius less a matter of imitation *a longe*; it is now rather a loyal allegiance in the service of a contemporary, of his Divine King still active in the world of men.

By this intuition, Ignatius took to himself a characteristic of the liturgy that is thoroughly traditional. "The liturgical year," Pius XII teaches, "is not a cold and lifeless representation of events of the past. . . . It is rather Christ Himself who is ever living in the Church" (*M.D.* 165). St. Paul, in order to emphasize this truth, coined a whole series of words with the prefix *syn-* (*con-*, with): "For we were buried *with* Him by means of baptism. . . . Our old self has been crucified *with* him" (Rom 6:4, 6). St. Paul returns to this idea 164 times. This is the here-and-now sacramental imitation of Christ by reason of which we are now "alive to God in Christ Jesus" (Rom 6:11). It is the same truth St. Leo the Great has in mind when he says: "Let no one fall back into that from which he has risen. Even if his sluggish body should urge him to lie back and yield to his weaknesses, let him strive immediately to be healed and raised up. For this is the imitation of his rising again which was begun in Christ."[16]

This dogmatic realism is visually portrayed in the opening action

---

[15] P. Leturia, S.J., "Ejercicios y fundación de la Compañía," *Arch. Hist. Soc. Jesu*, 10 (1941), p. 26.

[16] Sermo 71, 6. PL, 54, 389 C.

of the Easter vigil, the annual recapitulation of the liturgical *kerygma*. The paschal candle symbolizing Christ is inscribed with the date of the current year; meanwhile the celebrant recites: "Christ yesterday and today, the Beginning and the End, Alpha and Omega, His are the times and the ages."

As in any valid Christian spirituality, the Ignatian *Exercises* turn back constantly to the Christ of the Gospels; and in order to transport the imagination back in time as realistically as possible, brief preludes recall to mind the "history of the event" and the "representation of the place" (*S.E.* 47, 102, 103). But this is no mere exercise in ardent nostalgia. If there is not a concomitant growth in a vital awareness of the presence of Christ, the point has been missed. As J. Iturrioz writes,

> If we wish to sum up in a single formula the definitive spiritual attitude which the *Exercises* inspire in the exercitant, we can recall the words of St. Paul: "It is now no longer I that live, but Christ lives in me" (Gal 2:20). "No longer I" — here we have the conquest of self . . . "Christ lives in me" — here we have the spiritual attitude whence springs the ordering of one's life.[17]

It is not going beyond the meaning of this worthwhile observation to add that "Christ lives in me" cannot properly result in an individualistic "Christ-me" attitude. To "order your life" is not simply to put your virtues in order, like someone putting his room in order. It is an ordering *for* something, an orientation *toward* something outside yourself. This is the second profound consequence of the vision on the Cardoner. No longer is Ignatius the spiritual *caballero* setting out on his own to gain Christlike virtues as a free-lance knight would go forth in zealous quest of personal honors. From now on he is wholly committed to a cause. His idea of perfection and the following of Christ becomes explicitly apostolic, a selfless involvement in the campaign of the King, in the service of His Church.

This twofold insight of Ignatius, this profoundly significant shift of emphasis, reaches the very heart of the *Exercises*. It is a deeper explicitation of the first statement of the Foundation: "Man is

---

[17] "Fruto supremo de los Ejercicios," *Miscelanea Comillas*, 26 (1956), p. 234.

created to praise, reverence, and serve God our Lord," and of the consequent doctrine on the right use of creatures (S.E. 23). It is essential if one is to grasp what Ignatius means by the response to the call of the King (S.E. 98), by the colloquy of the *Standards* (S.E. 147), or by the unconditional self-offering in the *Contemplation for Attaining Love of God* (S.E. 234). It is, moreover, indispensable for a realization of the Ignatian ideal of "contemplation in action," contemplation, that is, of Christ present even while one is engaged in intense apostolic activity.[18] For all of these suppose a conception of the imitation of Christ as apostolic service of Christ present and acting in His Church.

Now it is above all in and through the liturgy that Christ is present in the world and active in the hearts of men. The following citation is representative of one of the major themes of *Mediator Dei:*

> Along with the Church, her Divine Founder is present at every liturgical function: Christ is present at the august sacrifice of the altar both in the person of His minister and above all under the eucharistic species. He is present in the sacraments, infusing into them the power which makes them ready instruments of sanctification. He is present, finally, in the prayer of praise and petition we direct to God, as it is written: "Where there are two or three gathered together in My Name, there am I in the midst of them" (M.D. 20; citation of Mt 18:20).

The notion of Christ's active presence, then, is basic both to the liturgy[19] and to the Ignatian *Exercises.* For our purposes here, however, the practical significance of this similarity is that it can serve to bring about a fuller integration of these two spheres of spiritual activity. For a more direct orientation of the *Exercises*

---

[18] Cf. J. F. Conwell, S.J., *Contemplation in Action* (Spokane: Gonzaga University, 1957), pp. 25, 27, 33, 96–97.

[19] "Christ acts each day to save us, in the sacraments and in His holy Sacrifice" (M.D. 29). "We might say that what the humanity of Jesus was for His contemporaries, the sacraments are for us: we can go to God only through these realities" (C. Vagaggini, O.S.B., *Theological Dimensions of the Liturgy,* trans. L. J. Doyle [Collegeville, Minn.: Liturgical Press, 1959], I, p. 167). This present action of Christ occurs not only in the reception of the sacraments, but in their abiding effects: Head in members, Vine in branches. Cf. Trent, *DB,* 809 and 843a.

toward these dynamic realities of the liturgy fosters first of all a fuller liturgical life; but at the same time it gives new dimension and vitality to a fundamental Ignatian ideal by placing it more consciously in the rich context of authentic liturgical tradition. Moreover, since the history of spirituality gives evidence that subjective piety has often verged toward excessive individualism, the communal and apostolic values of the liturgy can act as a balance against excessive introspection and preoccupation with self (cf. M.D. 35).

II. THE TWO STANDARDS

The Christian warfare is not simply a self-conquest, a sort of private duel in hand-to-hand conflict against the inner rebellion of the "old man." There is an enemy camp, powerful and resourceful, in active combat against the camp of Christ. The initial aim of the meditation on the *Standards* is to effect an awareness of the reality of this external combat. Appeal is made to the understanding, imagination, emotions and will, the effect being heightened by strong use of the device of contrast.

In all of this, there is a reflection of the didactic use in the liturgical *kerygma* of the confrontation of Moses and the Pharao, typifying not only the confrontation of Christ and Satan in the desert but the universal struggle into which every man is ineluctably drawn.[20] A new paradoxical duality comes to the fore here, but in reverse; for as man can follow Christ through the darkness of the tomb to eternal life, so he can chase the bedazzling will-o'-the-wisp of Lucifer, the "light-bearer," to eternal death.[21]

In the modern rites of baptism and the Easter vigil, there is the same approach and the same structural use of the contrast device.

[20] Cf. Danielou, *op. cit.*, Chap. V: "Types of Baptism: The Crossing of the Red Sea."

[21] C. Vagaggini, *op. cit.*, in Chapter XIII: "The Two Cities: The Struggle against Satan in the Liturgy," affords excellent traditional background material for the *Two Standards*, though he wrote without the Ignatian *Exercises* in mind. This in itself is a significant indication of the kinship between the basic ideas of the liturgy and the *Exercises*.

The ceremony of the New Fire at the very outset of the vigil serves as a dramatic lighting effect which renders visual the "light-dark" symbolism so prominent in St. John, and sets the stage for the dogmatic realities to be reviewed.[22] Through the *Exultet* and the blessing of the font, in order to stress the characteristics of the two camps, there is constant play on opposites: light-dark, servitude-freedom, grace-sin, life-death, day-night, joy-sorrow, hope-despair, truth-error, peace-discord, unity-division. All of this is summed up in the "Jerusalem-Babylon" contrast, a type which Ignatius borrows from ancient tradition and which was given classic form by Augustine, not only in his *City of God* but in his religious instructions: Jerusalem, the "vision of peace," is ruled over by Christ; Babylon, the capital of "confusion," is ruled over by Lucifer.[23]

The exorcisms of both the catechumens and the font stress the reality of the conflict. In the early practice, the catechumens were exorcized at regular intervals throughout their training, for the whole period was conceived of as a struggle on the part of the Church to win them over from the "hold" Satan had on them.[24] The renouncement of Satan as we know it today in baptism and the Easter vigil was in the early Church not only verbal, but was accompanied by dramatic action. During the renouncement, the catechumens faced toward the West, making a gesture of rejection or even spitting, "since the West is the region of sensible darkness, and [Satan] being darkness, has his dominion also in darkness."[25] Then, facing toward the East, the source of light and the region of Paradise, they made their profession of fidelity to Christ.

In both the liturgy and the *Exercises*, the imagery is rich, but

---

[22] Cf. L. Bouyer, *op. cit.*, especially Chap. XVI: "The Eucharistic Lucernarium."

[23] *De catechizandis rudibus*, edit. J. P. Christopher (Washington, D. C.: The Catholic University of America, 1926), Chaps. 19 and 21. Ignatius became acquainted with the theme of the "Two Cities" from the *Life* of Augustine in the *Golden Legend*. Cf. H. Rahner, *op. cit.*, pp. 27–28.

[24] Cf. Danielou, *op. cit.*, p. 21 ff.

[25] Cyril of Jerusalem, *Catechesis mystagogica I*, 4. Cross, p. 13.

the reality is sober. The foe is evil, but the evil is no abstraction.[26] We are in a state of war.

But the trainee needs more than this. He must be exercised in tactics, both his own and those of the enemy. Here we come closer to the real purpose of the meditation on the *Standards*. Ignatius directs the exercitant

> . . . to ask for a knowledge of the deceits of the rebel chief and help to guard myself against them; and also to ask for a knowledge of the true life exemplified in the sovereign and true Commander, and the grace to imitate Him (S.E. 139).

This almost paraphrases Chrysostom's idea of the catechumenate:

> . . . that you may perceive both the treachery of the evil demon as well as the wisdom of our Lord's efficacious dispositions.[27] . . . To understand both the kind of leader from whom they have been freed, and the kind of leader to whom they now profess allegiance.[28]

More in detail:

> [The catechumenate] is like a training ground or like sparring in the gymnasium. It is here that we must gain the skill to defeat that perverse demon. For after baptism when we strip for action, it is he whom we shall have to fight. While we are still here we must learn in advance the tricks he uses, the root of his viciousness, and the source of his most telling attacks . . . so that having mastered his strategems, we may engage him in conflict with full confidence.[29]

The development of thought in these passages, suggestive of a

---

[26] For the final petition of the "Our Father" Vagaggini (*op. cit.*, I, 203, note 5) adopts the translation: "deliver us from the evil one" as being more consonant with the concrete and personal tenor of the New Testament with regard to Satan.

[27] Wenger, *Catechesis II*, 7, p. 136.

[28] *Ibid.*, 14, p. 141.

[29] *Ad illuminandos catechumenos*, I, 3. PG, 49, 228. The idea is very similar to the following: "It is not St. Ignatius's intention to present in [the *Two Standards*] a bloody and spectacular conflict between the forces of good and evil. . . . Unquestionably there is such a struggle, and the exercitant will take part in it on the side of Christ, perhaps even to the literal shedding of his blood on the field of battle. But that will come later, when he goes forth at the end of the Exercises. For the present, the point to be considered is the efforts on the part of both standards to gain recruits" (L. Font, S.J., "Dos Banderas," *Manresa*, 24 [1952] pp. 447–448).

modern commentary on the *Exercises,* is not peculiar to Chrysostom. It is thoroughly characteristic of the catecheses that have come down to us, and representative of the traditional background of such expressions as "diabolical deceit" (*fraus*), "snares" (*laquei*), and "viciousness" (*nequitia*) familiar to us in the modern rites of baptism and blessing of the font.

This whole panoply of deceits was usually treated with detailed enumeration in explaining the "pomps and works" of the devil. *Pompa,* strictly understood, refers to a pagan religious procession, but in the catechetical instructions of the Fathers it embraced the whole gamut of delusive worldly allurements — "pomps of the devil and all his other tricky methods," as Chrysostom sums it up.[30] In the *Two Standards* Ignatius formulates the characteristic tactic of Satan into three steps: "The first step will be riches, the second honor, the third pride. From these three steps the evil one leads to all other vices" (S.E. 142). This comes close to Augustine's characterization of those who dwell in the "City of the Wicked":

> All men who love pride and temporal dominion together with empty vanity and display of presumption, and all spirits who set their affections on such things and seek their own glory. . . .[31]

In similar vein, Chrysostom lists "riches or power or glory or bodily beauty or any other attraction of this life."[32]

The key strategem is pride in its various forms.

Opposed to these tactics of deceit are the tactics of Christ. In the early Church, the wall decorations of the baptistries represented Christ the Good Shepherd surrounded by His sheep on an attractive field of flowers, trees, and fountains — an apt visualization for the prelude in the *Standards* depicting Christ on the plain outside Jerusalem. The characteristic tactics of Christ are described by Ignatius as follows:

> There will be three steps: the first, poverty as opposed to riches; the second, insults or contempt as opposed to the honor of this

---

30 Wenger, *Catechesis IV,* 33, p. 199. On the traditional exegesis of *pompa,* cf. Danielou, *op. cit.,* pp. 28–29.

31 *Op. cit.,* Chap. 19, p. 80.

32 Wenger, *Catechesis VII,* 13, p. 235.

world; the third, humility as opposed to pride. From these three steps, let them lead men to all other virtues (S.E. 146).

The *Two Standards* cannot be rightly understood except in relation to the *Rules for the Discernment of Spirits* (S.E. 313–336). No one can ascend these three steps except by humble submission to the direction of the "good spirit." We can call this the "right counsel" which the modern baptism rite asks for to counteract the "snares of Satan." In line with the treatment of this positive tactic, St. Cyril asks his catechumens:

> How many men of influence living in palaces have thrown wealth and honor aside at the suggestion of the Holy Spirit! . . . Avarice is rampant in the world, yet many Christians willingly give up all their goods. Why? Because they are attentive to the teaching of the Holy Spirit.[33]

In opposition to diabolical pride, the key strategem is Christian humility, resignation of self to the designs of God — the characteristic virtue, according to Augustine's catechesis, of those who dwell in the "City of the Just": "All men and all spirits who humbly seek God's glory, not their own, and who follow Him in godliness, belong to one fellowship."[34]

Training in discernment of spirits was an essential discipline in the early liturgical *kerygma;* those more advanced in perfection (*hoi teleoteroi*) are described as "those who are experienced in the discernment of good and evil."[35] But the danger is not only moral evil but also doctrinal: heresy, superstition, idolatry. For one of the faithful, this would be pride at its worst, for it rejects the word of God. It is the most devastating tactic of Satan, for it can destroy all at one stroke.

The countertactic, of course, is orthodoxy of faith. In the baptism rite, as in the modern rite and Easter vigil, the renouncement of Satan was followed by the profession of faith by recitation of the Creed. Here is the solid foundation of all discernment. "You have been taught the Creed," writes Quodvultdeus. "She [the

---

[33] *Catechesis XVI*, 19. PG, 33, 945 A.
[34] *Op. cit.*, 19, p. 82.
[35] Cyril of Jerusalem, *Catechesis IV*, 3. PG, 33, 457 A.

Church] who now brings you forth to new life and gives this protection against the poisons of the serpent."[36] But the profession of faith is not merely acceptance of a body of doctrine. It is, as we have seen, the military oath, the "joining up" with this living Body, the Church. Here, then, is the ultimate norm of discernment, the living *magisterium*.

With similar traditional emphasis, Ignatius responds to the attacks on the Church of his time with his *Rules for Thinking with the Church*, the first of which reads as follows:

> We must put aside all judgment of our own, and keep the mind ever ready and prompt to obey in all things the true Spouse of Jesus Christ, our Mother, the Hierarchical Church (S.E. 353).

Even those interior motions of the soul which seem to give every indication that they come from God must yield to this exterior norm.[37] This is the loyal service and humility of the *Kingdom* and the *Two Standards* reduced to practice in an essential area. For the "grace not to be deaf to His call" (S.E. 91) refers not only to our initial response but to an abiding attitude, that we may be "prompt and diligent to accomplish His holy will" (*ibid.*).

The same truth and the same imagery are contained in the baptismal rite of the *apertio aurium* — "that thine ears may be opened," as St. Ambrose explains it, "to the discourse and address of the priest."[38] But this need of an ear receptive to authentic teaching does not end with the assent given at baptism. "With the external word," writes Fr. Davis, "we offer the light of faith. Notice that the need for grace does not apply only to the unbeliever hearing the word for the first time."[39] This brings us back to St. Paul: "Faith depends on hearing, and hearing on the word of Christ" (Rom. 10:7).

In the course of this brief sketch frequent reference has been made to antiquity, both because modern liturgical usage has roots

---

[36] *De symbolo ad catechumenos. PL*, 40, 661.
[37] Cf. letter of Ignatius to Teresa Rejadella, *Monum. Hist. Soc. Jesu*, I, 1, 105.
[38] *De Sacramentis*, I, 1, 2. T. Thompson-J. H. Srawley, *op. cit.*, p. 48.
[39] C. Davis, "A Theology of Preaching," *Clergy Review*, 45 (1960), p. 536.

in the distant past, and because, as Fr. H. Rahner states, "the substance of the *Spiritual Exercises* belongs to early Christianity."[40] The point here has been to throw light on a kinship between two realities. In an actual retreat, however, time does not allow the use of much historical detail. But what is involved here basically is a realistic correlation between sacramental theology and the *Exercises.* For instance, two of the main ideas in the *Contemplation for Attaining Love* (S.E. 230–237) are *gratitude* for the manifold natural and supernatural gifts of God, and complete *self-offering* motivated by the love of God for His own sake. The gratitude can be aptly treated in relation to the full theological implications of the "eucharistic" theme of the Mass; the self-offering, in relation to participation in the sacrificial reality of the Mass.

Much, it seems, is to be gained by such an approach. It means, first of all, a more explicit carry-over of the ideas of the retreat into daily sacramental life, extending the *ex opere operantis* activity into the sphere of *ex opere operantis Ecclesiae,* and thereby effecting a more conscious and immediate orientation toward greater fruit *ex opere operato.* At the same time, a more habitual participation in the Mass according to its central themes will serve to keep alive the key ideas emphasized during the retreat. There is also the pedagogical advantage during the retreat itself of being able to relate the central truths and principles of the *Exercises* to the familiar experience, the sacramental life, of the retreatant. The *Suscipe* (S.E. 234) comes closer to home when it is allied to my participation in the Offertory — just as does the "suffering-victory" duality of the *Kingdom* when allied to the supernatural realities of my own baptism, or to the renewal of baptismal promises at the Easter vigil. Finally, a fuller orientation of the *Exercises* toward Christ as acting in His sacraments should tend to foster a greater realization of the Ignatian ideal of the service of Christ present and active in His Church.

Per ipsum et cum ipso et in ipso

---

[40] *Op. cit.,* p. 71.

...6...

Reflections on the Mass and Blessing of Chrism

MATTHEW J. O'CONNELL, S.J.

I

THE religious instruction or catechesis connected with baptism in the early Church was one for the whole of Christian life. In baptism the substance of redemption — death to sin, the divinization — was communicated to the believer, but only as the seed that must grow and flower. The neophyte had, then, to understand what it was that came into his life at baptism; he had to know his own new being, in order to work out in his life the imperatives contained in the baptismal event: in order to become what he was. For baptism was his commitment to life in Christ upon the foundation of faith, to the working out of sacramental rebirth in the personal dimension of life in Christ.

Consequently the baptismal catechesis, as contained in the liturgy itself (the ceremonies and prayers of the catechumenate and of the baptismal rite) and in the further development through sermons of ideas contained in this liturgy, was a catechesis for the already baptized Christian no less than for the neophyte. It was an annual renewal of understanding of his Christian commitment.

Such is the purpose today of the teaching of catechism to the adult or the grown child who has been baptized as an infant. But this catechesis is generally not connected with the liturgy. It serves undoubtedly an important and indispensable purpose (so, too, there was nonliturgical catechesis aplenty in the early Church). But it achieves its end in its own proper way, and cannot supplant

55

either the liturgy or catechesis directly liturgical. The liturgy is, potentially at least, a more efficacious type of catechesis: efficacious by its annual repetition, by its variety (affording many vantage points from which to come at the central mystery of baptism and Christian life itself), by its symbolic and imagistic character (such that it opens ever new depths of meaning, ever new possibilities of illumination and inspiration).

It has often enough been pointed out that "baptismal liturgy" cannot be restricted to the *ordo baptismi*. It includes a number of other rites which were intercalated between the various stages of the old catechumenate and which provided, and must still provide, the context for the climactic events of the *ordo*. Thus the blessing of the font explains more fully the act of baptism; in fact, of the two the blessing alone shows, for example, the relation of baptism to the Church. In similar fashion, the Mass and blessing of chrism on Holy Thursday provide the context which brings to full light the meaning of the postbaptismal anointing with chrism. It is these chrismal texts which concern us here.[1]

---

[1] We cannot enter here into the thorny problem of the postbaptismal anointing in the early Church. But some brief explanation is appropriate of why we look to the Mass and blessing of chrism for an understanding of our present postbaptismal anointing. Two problems have to be distinguished: (1) a theological problem: Does the sharing in Christ's priesthood come only through confirmation [i.e., in the early Church, only through the imposition of hands, perhaps accompanied by chrismation, of the bishop]? The answer in Christian tradition seems clearly to be, No. This gift is first given in baptism. The theology of confirmation is difficult, but the resolution of its difficulties ought not to be sought in an attribution (arbitrary in the light of tradition) of the gift of Christian priesthood to the second sacrament of initiation. Confirmation is, according to the Fathers generally, the *perfectio baptismi*. It is the complement of baptism; it perfects, through the special gift of the sevenfold Spirit, the work begun in baptism; it fits man further for the office of royal and prophetic priesthood that is his through baptism. (2) A liturgical problem: Was the gift of priesthood expressed liturgically in the baptismal liturgy proper, i.e., as distinct from the second part of the initiation rite (confirmation)? Was the single chrismation, which (apparently) was alone used in a number of Churches and with which the gift of priesthood was associated, a baptismal anointing, or was it part of confirmation? These are much-discussed questions, and it would be foolhardy to take a stand on them here. This much, however, is clear. In the Roman tradition (Hippolytus, Gelasian Sacramentary) there has been a double chrismation. It seems justified to say that the blessing of chrism looks simply to the use of chrism in the initiation rite as a whole. That is: in the light of the Mass and blessing of chrism, the postbaptismal anointing is a litur-

It is not easy for us today to understand these texts (I am thinking particularly of the blessing of chrism). They are succinct
and allusive. They suppose a feeling for the symbolic values of
oil and annointing, which is no longer ours by cultural inheritance.
They suppose a universe of ideas and representations built upon
anointing, and a view of the history of salvation which we are
today recovering only with difficulty.

Because of these barriers to understanding, our tendency is to
bypass this world of symbols and its accompanying ideas and representations. We prefer to move immediately onto the apparently
more solid ground of "theological" expression. In discussing, for
example, the anointing with chrism, we tend to reduce its significance to a simple "participation in the kingly, priestly and prophetic
role of Christ." It seems clear that this is what our postbaptismal
anointing centrally expresses. But to pass over the Mass and blessing of chrism in the conviction that the meaning of the rite (and
consequently of baptism itself) is fully understood independently
of them, is to deprive ourselves of a richer understanding of this
anointing and of baptism as a whole.

One result of thus oversimplifying the meaning of the anointing has been to divide up the baptismal rite too much according
to "negative" and "positive" effects. Thus, to the baptismal immersion or infusion is attributed (in terms of liturgical expression,
not of theological meaning) a simply negative effect: cleansing
or the remission of sins. To the postbaptismal anointing is attributed a purely positive effect: the gift of the sanctifying Spirit and
of priesthood in Christ.

This view of things arises chiefly from not reading the texts
themselves. The latter do not justify so sharp and radical a distinction of stages. Due to the exploitation of the immediate
"natural" and cultural sense, as well as the salvation-history background of each symbolic action, there is indeed an emphasis in
the baptismal immersion on cleansing, in the anointing on a

---

gical expression of the fact that in the total baptismal event man receives a
share in Christ's priesthood, while in the confirmation chrismation this same
gift is perfected by the further gift of the sevenfold Spirit.

sanctifying gift. But a reading of the blessing of the font shows that the baptismal purification is far from being conceived as simply negative, and the blessing of the chrism shows that anointing is also purifying. To divide negative and positive effects as we tend to do is to schematize the texts in a way alien to their nature. The various moments in the total baptismal rite do not each express only a single aspect of the mystery. Each rather expresses the total mystery, but from a different point of view. This characteristic of the texts has to be respected if they are to yield fuller insight into the mystery.

Another characteristic that must be respected is that these prayers are not statements of doctrinal theology, using language that is purified as much as possible of images and strives for the utmost of conceptualization. These prayers rather express the relationship of fallen and redeemed man to the living redeeming God in language proper to the sacramental order, that is, to the encounter of man with God through the material cosmos, through the human cosmos, and through the history of both as the place where God intervenes to save man. This is obvious enough. To respect this fact, however, means that in reading the texts one must recognize them for what they are. And, as Romano Guardini has pointed out:

> To understand images is not simply a matter of extracting concepts from them. We must also take them for what they are: images. We must bring them before our interior gaze, get inside of them, fill ourselves with them: only then do we receive their message. But this is not possible when he who reads [the Psalms] runs through them as quickly as possible. He must go slowly, stopping continually.[2]

What we are here implicitly touching on is a problem of large dimensions: the presence in the liturgy of a number of literary genres, none of them that of formal theological statement (theological in the scholastic mode).[3] If the orations of the Roman

---

[2] Romano Guardini, *Psaumes et fêtes* (Paris, 1961), p. 61.

[3] Even the creeds used in the liturgy are, apart from the first section of the Mass creed, simply recitals of the events of our redemption or, in the last section of the creeds, a listing of the blessings of redemption in us.

liturgy, for all their sobriety, pointed simplicity, and doctrinal richness, are not that kind of theological statement, then much less
are many of the old prayers of the Holy Week liturgy. These are
often quite lyrical in character: they try to create a mood, to
activate a many-leveled sense of the paschal and baptismal mystery. Our conclusion from this is that we ought not to be content
to remain always within these prayers, satisfied with this mood,
with this confused and shimmering world of interwoven images.
There is need for reflection: for the theologian's work of concep-
tualizing the mystery, and for the attempt which every believer
must make at setting off more sharply the contours of the mystery
and of its varied aspects, in order thereby to make it more viable
for his own life. But both sorts of reflection need to be carried
on in the climate proper to the mystery and in the consciousness
of its inexhaustibility, its overflowing richness. The believer (a
fortiori the theologian!) needs continually to return to Scripture
and liturgy. For in these sources there already exists that "connection of the mysteries" (Vatican Council I) which is to be the
chief aid to the understanding of faith and whose reconstitution
on the level of properly theological intelligence is the ultimate goal
of theology.

Such general considerations surely justify our examining more
closely the Mass and blessing of chrism and endeavoring to glimpse
something of the rich context into which the bare idea of "sharing
in Christ's royal and prophetic priesthood" is put, something of the
picture of Christian existence that is there presented. The following reflections may seem to fall, indeed, between two stools: they
are not an attempt at the detailed theological transposition spoken
of above, yet neither do they engage in a phrase-by-phrase clarification of the texts in themselves and in their historical development. They attempt simply to bring to light the major images and
ideas and to show their development within the texts. But even
this more elementary approach to the texts can be instructive.

II

In these remarks the following order will be observed in pre-

senting the texts. First, a word about the postcommunion of the
Mass, which situates the baptismal and confirmational anointings
within the redemptive mystery as a whole. Next will be discussed
the psalmody of the Mass, which gives the Old Testament texts
to be understood as types of Christ and the Christian. Finally,
the preface of the Mass and, even more, the prayers of the blessing
will unfold the christological meaning of anointing and the neophyte's participation in it.[4]

The broadest perspective within which the Mass and blessing
of chrism are situated is given by the closing prayer. Here there
is evoked the theme of *vetustas-novitas,* in which the very essence
of redemption's meaning for man is summed up.[5] It is a baptismal
theme common in St. Paul under the form of the contrast between the "old man" cast off in baptism (though he needs daily
to be prevented from overcoming us anew) and the "new man"
put on as one entered into the life-giving sphere of influence of
Christ, the New Man (Eph 2:15).

> Grant, we pray, O Lord, that as we have passed from our former
> state to newness, so we may put off our ancient selves and be
> renewed in holiness of heart.

In this prayer it is not only the Eucharistic sacrifice that is being
considered in its present effectiveness in helping the Christian to
fend off the inroads of the "old man" and to achieve the daily
renewal which is our baptismal commitment. There is the recall,
too, of the event in which man first passes from the state of sin

---

[4] Some parts of the chrismal Mass will not be touched on in this essay, because
they refer exclusively to the oil of the sick: the lesson, the gospel, the communion
verse. As for the oration and secret prayer: the oration is phrased in quite general terms, alluding simply to the baptizands and to the hierarchical priesthood
which administers the sacraments; the secret prayer enuntiates the *vetustas-
novitas* theme, but only in the perspective of the present Eucharistic sacrifice.

[5] This theme is found in the Roman Missal almost exclusively in the context
either of Christmas, where the redemptive Incarnation is shown as the source
for mankind of saving "newness" (cf. second oration of Ember Saturday in
Advent; the postcommunion of the second, and the oration of the third Christmas
Masses); or of the paschal mystery, which is indissolubly the mystery of redemption by Christ and of its communication through baptism (cf. the *oratio super
populum* of Tuesday of Holy Week; the oration of the Holy Thursday evening
Mass and of the Good Friday Mass; the postcommunion of Easter Wednesday).

(our former state) to a state of radical newness, and in which chrismal anointing plays its part.[6]

The special symbolic role of postbaptismal anointing within the one total regenerative process of baptism was noted long ago by Tertullian in a statement which will, equivalently, be developed by our present Mass and blessing of chrism.

> On coming from the bath [of baptism] we receive an anointing with blessed oil, in accordance with ancient practice. In this practice it was customary to elevate a man to the priesthood by an anointing with oil poured from the phial, ever since the time when Moses anointed Aaron. Therefore we are called "christ-ians" from chrism, which signifies anointing. It was an anointing likewise that gave the Lord His name [Christ], but the anointing in this instance was spiritual, for the Father anointed Him with the Spirit, as *Acts* points out: "For they have conspired in this city against Your Holy Son whom You anointed" [4:27]. So, in our anointing, the oil flows over our bodies but it profits us spiritually, just as the rite of baptism is a bodily thing since we are immersed in the water, but the effect is spiritual since we are freed of our sins (*De baptismo* 7:1-2).

In this passage and in the liturgy the center of interest is not the natural symbolism of anointing. It is rather the salvation-history dimension of the ritual act: anointing with the accumulated weight of significance and of historical overtones that it has acquired as one of the primary symbolic gestures used by God under the old covenant to manifest and interpret and mediate His

---

[6] The chrismal Mass as found in the *Gelasianum Vetus* (ed. Mohlberg – Eizenhöfer – Siffrin [Rome, 1960], nn. 375–390) has no postcommunion. The *oratio super populum* of the Gelasian Holy Thursday evening Mass (*ibid.*, n. 394) becomes in some eighth-century Gelasians the *oratio super populum* of the chrismal Mass, e.g., the Sacramentary of Gellone (cf. P. de Puniet, "Le sacramentaire romain de Gellone," *Ephemerides liturgicae* 48 [1934] 190) or the Sacramentary of Sankt-Gall (ed. Mohlberg [Münster, 1918 and 1939], n. 511). It is this prayer that has become the postcommunion of the chrismal Mass in the restored Holy Week Order. But before appearing on Holy Thursday at all the prayer is already found in the Leonine Sacramentary in a definitely baptismal context: as the postcommunion of the third Mass for the Nativity of St. John the Baptist and, in a slightly variant form, as the postcommunion of the fourth Mass, which is transcribed under the rubric *Ad fontem* (ed. Mohlberg – Eizenhöfer – Siffrin [Rome, 1956], nn. 245 and 250). On this latter Mass cf. A. Stuiber, *Libelli Sacramentorum Romani* (Bonn, 1950), p. 40; E. Bourque, *Etude sur les sacramentaires romains*, I (Rome, 1948), pp. 114–115.

relationship to men. Within this salvation-history dimension of New Testament and Christian anointing-symbolism there is always present, in addition, the pattern of type and fulfillment. The types are Old Testament personages and events. The fulfillment is primarily and perfectly in Christ, secondarily and by participation in the Christian. The Christian's participation is initial and imperfect during this life when the personal implications of sacramental configuration to Christ are a project as well as a given reality and need to be worked out slowly and painfully, in cooperation with grace, until the sacramental configuration penetrates all the levels of personal being; his participation is definitive and perfect only in the life to come. It is this historical dimension of the symbolism of anointing, with its pattern of type and double fulfillment, that the Mass and blessing of chrism primarily develop.

A. *The Psalmody of the Mass of Chrism*

The chant pieces of the Mass provide the types and the divine interventions which have their fulfillment in Christ; these pieces are allusive, presenting a phrase or image that carries with it an unspoken scriptural context and a universe of images and ideas.[7]

The first part of the Introit is Ex 30:25, 30: "You [Moses] shall make an oil for anointing, and you shall say to the sons of Israel: 'This oil of anointing is holy to me through all your generations.' " The context of these verses indicates that the oil is not to be poured out on simply anyone (verse 31) but is reserved for things to be consecrated to God which will then possess an eminent sanctity, so that whoever touches them will be holy, and for consecrating Aaron and his sons for the exercise of priesthood.[8] Here there already sounds the note that will be made explicit in Heb 5:4:

---

[7] We do not know what chant pieces were used in the Gelasian Mass of chrism. The pieces now used were selected for the restored chrismal Mass.

[8] The date of these prescriptions in Exodus and the question of whether all priests were anointed or only the high priests are not our concern. Cf. note in the *Bible de Jérusalem* on this passage; for extended discussion, E. Cothenet, "Onction," *Dictionnaire de la Bible: Supplément* 6. 722–726, or R. de Vaux, O.P., *Ancient Israel, Its Life and Institutions* (New York, 1961), pp. 103–106.

"No one takes to himself the honor . . ." and which is valid for all priesthood: for Christ's own (Heb 5:5–6) and consequently for all sharing in His priesthood. The baptismal anointing is thus the mark of election, of divine choice.

The second part of the introit is the opening verse of Ps 89(88). The psalm sings of the divine choice of the house of David and, as far as Israel could see, also of the divine rejection of this same house. The psalm has three parts. The first (2–19) is a hymn in praise of the covenant graciousness and the fidelity of God, the Creator and Ruler of the universe: graciousness shown in choosing and entering into covenant with David, fidelity to David and his house forever. Blessed is the people who walk "in the light of His face"; in God and in His saving power exercised in their behalf (His "justice") is their abiding joy; through the king, their own living symbol and incarnation, the people experience God as their radiant strength (verses 16–19).

The second part of the psalm (20–38) details the great promises made to David "my servant, whom I have anointed with my holy oil" (21), and dwells upon the gracious fidelity of God to David and his descendants, a fidelity that will be proof against all their ingratitude and infidelity. God will always be at hand to strengthen David and his posterity, will allow no enemy to deceive them, no malicious men to oppress them, will be to them always "my Father, my God, the rock of my salvation" (27). The last part of the psalm, however, shows Israel appalled before the great contradiction: the God who has sworn fidelity to Israel and David's house has not been faithful, He has rejected David's posterity and broken His covenant.

But where the Israelite, believing against all appearances, can only cry out in the darkness "God be praised forever!" (53), the Christian knows that God has not been unfaithful, that there is not contradiction but the paradox of the Cross and of triumph through failure. For Jesus is the chosen and anointed one (Lk 23:35) and the true posterity of David and of Abraham (Gal 3:16); in Him all the promises are fulfilled, but only through

His bearing in His sole person all the "shame of the anointed one" (Ps 89[88]:52).[9]

This psalm, perhaps already in the New Testament, certainly from an early date in the Church, was given a christological and ecclesiological interpretation. St. Augustine set forth the principle for understanding the psalm: Christ is the seed of David and Abraham, but He is this as Head of His Body, the Church; all His "generations" are heirs of the promise.[10] It is with this understanding that the psalm is used in the chrismal Mass and in the context of Christian initiation; the first verse, alone cited, is a recall of the whole psalm. The moment of anointing will be the moment in which the God of the new covenant encounters the neophyte; in which the fidelity and perduring love of God for His Christ embraces men to whom He gives, through the anointing that "christifies" them, a share in the royalty of the Son. The anointing is God's pledge to them of His graciousness and fidelity. It is this that will be the ever flowing fountain of their joy and strength.

The gradual verse is Ps 28(27):7b, d–8a, b, and it concentrates on the point just made at the end of the preceding paragraph: on the trust of the people in God their strength, who pledges His fidelity to His anointed one and to the people of His anointed one.[11] Through anointing, the believer enters the sphere of the

---

[9] Cf. the theme of the "shaming" of Christ in His passion (cf. K. H. Schelkle, Die Passion Jesu [Heidelberg, 1949], pp. 108–109).

[10] "Semen David quod est, nisi semen Abrahae? Quod autem semen Abrahae? 'Et semini,' inquit, 'tuo, quod est Christus' [Gal 3:16]. Sed forte ille Christus caput Ecclesiae, salvator corporis, semen est Abrahae, et ideo David; nos autem non sumus semen Abrahae? Imo vero sumus, sicut Apostolus ait: 'Si autem vos Christi, ergo semen Abrahae estis, secundum promissionem heredes' [Gal 3:29]. Sic ergo hic accipimus, fratres, 'Usque in aeternum praeparabo semen tuum': non tantum illam carnem Christi natam ex virgine Maria, sed etiam nos omnes credentes in Christum: illius enim capitis membra sumus. Non potest hoc corpus decollari: si in aeternum caput, in aeternum gloriantur et membra, ut sit ille Christus integer in aeternum" (Enarratio in Ps. 88, sermo 1, 5 [Corpus Christianorum, series latina, 39. 1222–1223 = PL 37. 1122]).

[11] The Bible de Jérusalem takes "anointed one," because of the parallelism in the verse, to refer directly to the people, and cites for the idea Ex 19:6 ("A kingdom of priests and a consecrated people") and for a similar use of the term itself Hb 3:13 (but this seems as ambiguous as Ps 28[27]:8) and Ps 105:15 (which seems clearer). But even if the "anointed one" in our present psalm

saving influence of Christ the King; God becomes his strength and shield (verse 7a), the Shepherd who watches over His heritage (9).

The offertory verse is a citation from Ps 45(44), another psalm with a long history of christological and ecclesiological interpretation, not only in the writings of the Fathers but also in the liturgy.[12] It is a marriage song for a king. It describes the king (3–10) and his bride (11–16), and closes with a wish for the king (17) and for the permanence of the song itself (18). The verse used in the Offertory is, in a measure, the central verse of the psalm. It recalls the king's ritual anointing at his enthronement and speaks more immediately of his "anointing" with joy at his marriage.[13]

It is the ideas present in the Christian interpretation of this verse (and psalm) that have largely influenced the formulation of the prayers for blessing chrism. The interpretation has two major elements. The first can be found in St. Augustine, for example, who speaks of the double espousals of the Word (of the eternal Word with flesh and of the Incarnate Word with His Church) and of a double anointing with the oil of gladness (the anointing of the humanity of Christ by the divinity, and the anointing of Christ in His members or *participes*). The second major element derives from the application of Ps 45(44):8, in Heb 1:9, to Christ at His entrance into glory, when He receives the joy and gladness which His "justice" on earth has won for

---

is the king, the essential point is that "Man kann an dieser Stelle sehr schön erkennen, wie der einzelne beständig an einer grösseren, sein Einzelschicksal umgreifenden und tragenden Heilswirklichkeit partizipiert," that there is question here of "der 'individuellen Partizipation am Mysterium der königlichen Heilssphäre'" (Hans-Joachim Kraus, *Psalmen* [Neukirchen, 1960 ff.], p. 231).

12 For the Fathers, cf. Philip King, *A Study of Psalm 45(44)* (Rome, 1959), Chap. 1, Sect. 1. For the liturgy, cf. A. Rose, "Le psaume 44: Son interprétation chrétienne," *Questions liturgiques et paroissiales*, 36 (1955), 178–189.

13 Was this a metaphorical anointing? Since oil was used not only to strengthen the body and to increase the sense of bodily well-being but also as an expression and sign of festal joy, the gift of gladness could be called an anointing, even if no bodily anointing occurred. In like fashion, the prophets (even Elisha, despite I Kgs 19:15–16?) were not ritually anointed, yet were called "anointed" because they received the Spirit of God who came upon kings through anointing. But it is also possible that at his marriage a king was again ritually anointed in a recall of his enthronement (cf. Kraus, *ibid.*, pp. 235–236).

Him and which He is to communicate to His fellowmen (cf. Heb 2:9–13).[14] In the Christian interpretation of Ps 45, then, there is the possibility of speaking of a triple anointing and a triple joy.

Two important aspects of kingly anointing in the Old Testament ought to be noted. They are not explicit in the psalms used in the Mass, but they are an intimate part of that world of ideas and images which the psalm verses are expected to evoke, and they will be made explicit in the preface of the Mass and in the blessing.

The first is the connection of the Spirit of God with royal anointing. After Saul's anointing, Samuel promises him the Spirit of Yahweh: the presence of the Spirit will be manifested in ecstatic prophesying when Saul meets the band of prophets (1 Sam 1:10), but also in the form of strength for great enterprises (11:6). More important for later Christian thinking is the gift of the Spirit to David at his consecration: for here the gift of the Spirit is immediately linked with his anointing and it is permanent (1 Sam 16:13). In the picture (Is 11:1 ff.) of the just king to come, descended from David, the Spirit of God is the source of his action and efficacy.[15]

The second point to be made is that the king was also a priest. He did not, indeed, engage in the ordinary carrying out of public cult, but he did on special occasions offer sacrifice and bless the people from the sanctuary.[16]

B. *Preface of the Chrismal Mass*

For an understanding of the preface and of the blessing to follow, it is needful to keep in mind that for the ancient world oil was a means to health and strength, and consequently a symbol of these in the corporeal and personal spheres; that it was, especially when perfumed, a sign and symbol of festive gladness (pre-

[14] On the exegesis of Heb 1:9, cf. C. Spicq, *Epître aux Hebreux*, 2 (3rd ed.; Paris, 1953), pp. 19–20.

[15] For a fuller discussion of royal anointing and the Spirit, cf. E. Cothenet, *art. cit.*, cols. 719–720.

[16] On the king as priest, cf. R. de Vaux, *op. cit.*, pp. 113–114.

supposing, ideally, the state of bodily and personal health and strength); that it sinks in and penetrates, and consequently could be symbolic of permanent consecration and office.

The preface, in the form of a prayer that God would make chrism a sacrament (a symbolic medium of spiritual effects), describes in dense phrases the double result to be hoped for from this sacrament:

> It is meet and just . . . to ask You that in Your mercy You would make this creature, chrism, an effective symbol of perfect salvation and life for those who are to be renewed in the baptism that cleanses the spirit; so that [1] when this sanctifying ointment is poured out upon them and removes the corruption that accompanies their first birth, each one's holy temple may be fragrant with the odor of innocence of a life acceptable to You; and [2] that, according to the mystery You have instituted, they may be gifted with the dignity of kings, priests, and prophets, and clad with the immortal garment of grace.

Here, contrary to what the chant pieces might lead us to expect, the center of attention is not the Old Testament types or Christ's own priesthood, but the basic symbolisms of anointing in the cultural world of the early Church and the effect of the anointing in the neophyte. It is only in the prayers of the blessing of chrism that all three stages in the divine plan of salvation — the Old Testament types of Christ and the sacraments, Christ Himself, and the members of Christ who share His dignity and office — will be gathered into one unified vision. At the same time, in the blessing the symbolisms of oil here mentioned will drop into the background and yield pride of place to oil as the symbol of joy.

Perhaps the most striking point about this short prayer is that to the anointing is attributed man's purification from original sin. Clearly, there is no room here for a sharp contrast between washing and anointing as negative and positive. It is not even accurate to say that the anointing, while symbolizing purification, also symbolizes (unlike the baptismal cleansing) positive effects, or that it symbolizes more perfect positive effects than does the baptismal cleansing. For, in the blessing of the font God is asked to sanctify the waters of baptism in order that from them may come forth a *progenies caelestis*. Rather than speak of "positive" or "more perfect" effects in an effort to distinguish baptismal immersion from anointing, we would do better to speak of each as embracing the total baptismal mystery from its own special viewpoint.

In the second effect of anointing depicted in the preface, we may legitimately see the double gift of baptismal character and baptismal grace (and, in the confirmation chrismation, of confirmation character and grace). The term *munus* seems here to mean "grace" rather than "office" (in which event the clause "clad with the immortal garment . . ." would be a rhetorical amplification of the previous clause "gifted with . . ."). This sense is suggested by the garment image with its Pauline background of "putting on Christ" or "putting on the new man," which refers to amissible grace rather than inamissible consecration (cf. the need continually to "put off the old man"). Doubtless the liturgy is not concerned, any more than the Fathers usually are, with distinguishing character and grace in the sense that it would be envisioning a possible reception of the baptismal character without the corresponding grace. But this is not to say that the realities corresponding to character and grace are unknown to the liturgy. Here the "dignity of kings . . ." and the "immortal garment of grace" correspond quite well to some of the terms in which Augustine formulated the distinction of character and sacramental sanctification: "consecration" and "grace."

One phrase in the preface has a depth of meaning that is perhaps not immediately evident. It is the phrase *secundum constitutionis tuae sacramentum*, here translated "according to the mystery You have instituted." There appears to be a double sense in the words. In the background is the "mystery" of God in the Pauline sense: the divine redemptive design in which men are called to be in Christ and to share in His sonship. In the foreground is the "mystery" in the sense of the ritual symbolic action in which the divine redemptive love here and now enters the life of one thus called.

C. The Blessing of Chrism

The blessing has three moments, the whole (together with the blessing of the oil of catechumens) being framed within the two parts of the processional hymn "O Redeemer!"

Preparation of Chrism

Phials of balsam and chrism oil are shown to the bishop and placed on the altar. The bishop blesses the balsam first. God is asked to make the balsam acceptable for His sacramental mysteries and to sanctify it with His blessing; to grant it spiritual grace and to fill it with sanctifying power. The prayer then opens out into a rhythmic sentence, amplifying the terms "spiritual grace" and "sanctifying power":

> May it be seasoned with the gladness of faith. May it be forever the oil of priestly anointing. May it be worthy to imprint the heavenly captain's banner upon the soul: so that all those reborn in sacred baptism and anointed with this liquid may receive the fullest blessing of body and soul and be forever enriched with the gift of gladdening faith.

It should be evident that we are no longer dealing with straightforward sober petition. There is a lyric impulse at work in the metaphors used, and in the strange mingling of metaphors in the third phrase (oil — to imprint — the heavenly banner). Yet the rhetorical fullness is itself restrained within the chiastic framework of the sentence as a whole (gladness of faith: priestly anointing and impress of spiritual sign :: blessing of body and soul: gladness of faith).

The consecratory preface over the chrism will be an expansion upon the "oil of gladness" theme, where the "gladness" for man will be the redemptive peace of Christ and its flowering in the joy of eternal life. Here at the beginning of the blessing the note of Christian joy is already sounded, as the symbolic action of anointing is situated, with its effects, in relation to the whole of Christian life. The baptismal transformation of man is seen under the sign of the "joy of faith" (hilaritas fidei, beata fides). In baptism one enters into a life founded on the faith that opens one's eyes and reveals the true relationship of man and all creation to God, releases the deepest well-springs of vital creative activity and generous self-oblation, and thus brings true and eternal joy. In this transformation anointing plays its specific role as the priestly anointing that sets the Christian soul forever under the banner of Christ the priest-king.

These themes of joy and priestly consecration will appear in amplified form in the consecratory preface over the chrism oil. But before that moment, to the accompaniment of a symbolic gesture, the priestly anointing of Christ Himself, which is the exemplar and source of all Christian priesthood, is described and with it the ultimate finality both of Christ's and the Christian's priesthood. On a paten or in a small vessel the bishop mixes the blessed balsam with a little chrism oil. Prayer is then made to God

> who in a wondrous disposition of His providence inseparably united the incomprehensible godhead of His co-eternal only-begotten Son to a true humanity, and, by the co-effective grace which is the Holy Spirit, anointed Him with the oil of gladness beyond His fellows, in order that man, composed of two unique elements, and destroyed by Satan's deceits, might be restored to the everlasting heritage whence he had fallen,

that He would bless these oils with the "perfecting power of the Holy Trinity" and would grant that being mingled they may become one and that whoever is outwardly anointed may also be inwardly so anointed as to be cleansed of all stain and to have the joy of sharing in the heavenly kingdom.

In this prayer it is evident once again how far the liturgy is from any artificial pairing of the great moments in the baptismal rite with isolated, sharply distinguished effects. The inward anointing both cleanses and gives the life that leads to eternal joy. Indeed, the theme of this prayer is, in a sense, man's restoration to wholeness through baptism. A parallel is drawn between the *Incarnate Word*, in whom there is a wonderful duality of divinity and humanity wherein the divinity "anoints" the humanity and makes it a sharer in the joy of God Himself, and the *chrism,* made of balsam and chrism oil whose union, blessed by God, is the symbolic medium through which the very purpose of the redemptive Incarnation is realized in man. For the chrism enables *man*, himself composed of body and spirit, to be cleansed of stain and restored to the inheritance he lost in yielding to Satan: that is, to enter into divine joy through Christ.

In this prayer, too, we are given the framework, as it were, within which the long consecratory preface over the chrism oil is to be set: that is, the starting point and the finishing point of the divine redemptive plan — the "anointing" of Christ in His Incarnation, and the anointing of the Christian in his initiation, through which he shares in Christ's own dignity and grace.

Exorcism and Consecratory Preface

The bishop and his assistant priests breathe thrice over the phial of chrism oil. The exorcism, addressed to the "creature, oil," is to dispel from it, by its Creator's power, all of Satan's influence, that so it may be effective, for those anointed with it, unto "adoptive sonship through the Holy Spirit."

In the consecratory preface, the theme of joy or, more properly, of the "oil of gladness," which has been present throughout, becomes central. With this as focus or a binding thread, a great sweeping vision is presented of the realization of the divine redemptive plan through human history: the types and prophecies of Christ, the Anointed One; Christ Himself and the revelation of His person at His baptism; the chrism which anoints us and brings us to the goal of the whole divine plan: eternal glory. This prayer with its concluding epiclesis thus forms a companion piece to the central part of the blessing of the font. Both have the same basic structure: paradigms — Christ — the Christian.

The consecratory preface can be disconcerting to the present-day reader. The images seem jumbled together, and the principle of progression, if there is one, of the whole prayer is not clear. This, however, is more of a problem to the reader in his armchair than to one praying the consecration of the oils with the bishop. A further obstacle is that the term "anointing" or its equivalent keeps shifting from one register to another, as it were. In one phrase the term refers to a purely spiritual event unaccompanied by any ritual action, in another it refers to bodily anointing. But this is a difficulty for us chiefly because we like to reduce images to univocal simple ideas, and have lost to some extent the ability and the willingness to enter into multileveled images on their own terms and to cultivate a sense of the complexity of aspects in the divine mystery of salvation. Our very criticism that "here is meant a purely spiritual reality, there a ritual action" is already a misunderstanding and oversimplification of the text. For the memory and significance of these spiritual events are evoked and conveyed to us precisely by symbolic actions used on other occasions. Thus the "anointing" of Christ's humanity by the divinity (in the previous prayer) and His "anointing" by the Spirit at the Jordan are spiritual events[17] that are understood against the Old Testament background of the anointing of kings and priests, and by analogy with such ritual anointing; and they are recalled by our sacramental anointings as being the spiritual exemplars of the present sacramental (corporeal-ritual and spiritual) events. In other phrases, the anointing is a corporeal-ritual action, but precisely as symbolic, that is, as symbolizing a spiritual process or event.

God, the Creator of the oil, is addressed. Then the antecedents which illumine the meaning of the sacramental use of oil are detailed, and finally the appropriate petition is made.

For David, knowing beforehand by the prophetic spirit the sacramental mysteries of Your grace, sang that our countenances were to be made glad with oil; and in earlier times, when the sins of the world were being wiped away by the deluge, a dove, with an olive branch that imaged forth the gift to come, announced the return of peace to the earth. This gift of peace has in these last times been made known by evident effects when the waters of baptism destroy all sin and the anointing with this oil makes our countenances joyful and serene.

Moreover, You bade Moses Your servant to have Aaron his brother purified with water and then to consecrate him priest by the infusion of this ointment.

---

[17] At the Jordan there is a visible sign, but not a visible anointing.

Greater honor still was given this oil when Your Son, our Lord Jesus Christ, asked that John baptize Him in Jordan's waters. For You wished, after sending the Holy Spirit down in a dove's form, to show by the testimony of the ensuing voice that He was Your beloved Son in whom You were well-pleased, and thereby to bear witness in the most evident way that here was fulfilled what David had foretold: that He would be anointed with the oil of gladness beyond His fellows.

We therefore pray You . . . that You would deign to sanctify this opulent creature with Your blessing and to mingle with it the efficacy of the Holy Spirit, by the cooperating power of Christ Your Son (from whose holy Name the chrism takes its name, with which You have anointed priests, kings, prophets and martyrs). May it be for those reborn of water and the Holy Spirit the chrism of salvation, and make them partakers of eternal life and sharers in heavenly glory.

If we try to order the images and make explicit the connections and the unspoken implications, the following series emerges. The dove (figure of the Holy Spirit), after the purification of a world grown evil, prefigures by an olive branch (source of oil and thereby symbol of anointing) the peace of reconciliation (an anticipation of the reconciliation of the world by Christ and His sacraments); Moses, having had Aaron purified with water, anoints him priest; David foretells the mystery of the Anointed One and the sacramental gift of joy to His members ("sacramental mysteries": "mysteries" or *sacramenta* has a triple sense: the eternal redemptive plan; its realization in time in the Incarnate Son; its prolongation in us through the sacraments); the Father fulfills the figures of the deluge and the dove, the example of Moses, and the prophecy of David, when at the baptism of His Son (which is not His purification, but His public commitment to His great "baptism," i.e., His redemptive death which would purify the world), He sends His Spirit in the form of a dove (which, because of the link with the dove of the deluge and its olive branch, is symbolic of the invisible anointing of Christ by the Spirit and of the descent of divine power upon Him for His redemptive mission), and makes known that this is He who is anointed with the oil of gladness above all others. As a second moment in the fulfillment of these figures, types, and prophecies, we too in baptism are purified and then anointed with the oil of peace and joy. This oil is a sign that in the initiation which is our rebirth we, like Christ, are invested with the office of priest, king and prophet.

This vast canvas does not include all the wealth of imagery and idea which we have seen in the various other prayers of the Mass and blessing, but it does provide a climax toward which all else moves and in whose light all the other prayers yield their full meaning. Can we say that, having come to this climactic point in the chrismal liturgy we grasp any more fully the idea of "royal and prophetic priesthood" which is the central signification of the postbaptismal anointing and of the "perfecting" of baptism in the confirmation chrismation? In terms of technical theological defini- tion, doubtlessly not; in fact, the meaning of such priesthood is not even touched on in these prayers.[18] But to an understanding of the Christian's priestly dignity and of his place in the re- deemed universe, these prayers have surely much to contribute. They help to make the Christian conscious that he is part of a great history. They bring home to him, above all, that he is called to joy: a joy paradoxically associated so intimately with the Cross of Christ but a joy, too, that is the beginning of the joy of eternity.

Final Commingling of Balsam and Chrism Oil

The final act in the blessing is to pour the small mixture of balsam and chrism oil, made earlier, into the phial of chrism oil. After the enthusiasm and broad sweep of the consecratory preface, the final prayer of the blessing is brief and sober and colorless enough: "May this mixture of liquids be unto all anointed with it a means of forgiveness and a saving guardian for eternal life. Amen." But the final exclamation, "Hail, holy chrism!", thrice sung by the bishop, is far more laden with meaning than the "holy oil for anointing" which opened the Mass of chrism.

---

[18] We say nothing about the anomalous reference to "martyrs," found only here and in the preceding blessing of oil for the sick. A discussion of the solu- tions offered for this obscure reference is found in Walter Dürig, "Die 'Salbung' der Martyrer: Ein Beitrag zur Martyrertheologie der Liturgie," Sacris erudiri, 6 (1954), 14–47.

...7...

The Community of the Faithful

SHAWN G. SHEEHAN

It has been a common practice of priests that, when they bless a person, saying, "May the blessing of almighty God, Father, Son and Holy Spirit, descend upon you and remain forever," they also add the "Amen." When the late beloved Father Michael Mathis was in his last illness he gave some of us who visited him in the Notre Dame infirmary a little lesson in liturgical participation. When we were giving him our blessing and before we could say the "Amen," he would say it, raising himself a little, weak as he was. Still showing a spark of the radiant enthusiasm we had seen so often as he gave us new insights into the liturgy, he would say, "See, you are not going to deprive me of my 'Amen'; that is all I have left."

If we were continually alert to the simple ways in which the liturgical rites themselves provide for participation, we could open up a new view of priestly ministration and of liturgy as worship by the whole community of the faithful. Liturgical rites are not simply actions to be performed by priests. Those on whom priests confer the sacraments and the various blessings are not mere recipients; they are themselves involved in the liturgical action. They are not only receiving God's favors but they are also called on to respond; they are worshipers.

BLESSINGS

If we look through the Ritual with this in mind, we see that

75

familiar blessings, for example, of children, of the sick, of homes, of wedding rings, and so on, which are generally considered simply as blessings given by priests, are in reality rites that call for active participation of at least one other person. Usually these rites open with the versicle and response, "Lord, hear my prayer. And let my cry come unto Thee," followed by the exchange of sacred greetings, "The Lord be with you. And with your spirit." No doubt we have all heard priests answering themselves even when persons who can make the responses are present. This is a failure not merely to observe properly the external form of the rite but also to understand the significance of this form. The very fact that provision is made for such an exchange shows that this is a rite for an assembly of the faithful. Moreover, the phrase, "The Lord be with you," said by a bishop, priest, or deacon in a liturgical rite, expresses the mystery that the Lord is in our midst, that this is an action of His Mystical Body.

We note also in these rites the invitation, "Let us pray." Even though a blessing is to be given and the priest is the only one who has power to give it, the Church provides that he will call on the others present to join their prayers with his in asking God to bless what is being blessed. The others are not to be mere bystanders but are to be worshipers, acknowledging God's dominion and power and expressing confidence in His goodness. Ordinarily the prayer that is said is addressed to God the Father "through Christ our Lord." Christ unites His members, both clergy and laity, with Himself in these prayers of His Mystical Body.

The participants answer "Amen" to express their assent, their union with the priest and with Christ in the prayer. Moreover, on the lips of one who is receiving a blessing the "Amen" expresses acceptance of God's gift, an openness of soul to his love and a response of gratitude. A blessing is not simply a channeling of divine gifts to people by a priest. It is a personal meeting with God; it is an event, one in which God's children approach Him in union with His beloved Son, are welcomed and blessed by Him, and respond with sentiments appropriate to the occasion.

THE SACRAMENTS

What we have said about blessings is to be said also of the sacraments and of the rites by which they are conferred. Let us start with a striking example of a sacrament that is conferred with active participation of the whole assembly of the Church, namely, the ordination of priests.

We are so used to thinking of ordination as a uniquely episcopal power that those who attend an ordination are likely to think of themselves as spectators at an action which in itself is entirely between the bishop and the men being ordained. Of course the assembled clergy and laity pray for these men and they thank God for His goodness, but they are not usually conscious of being called upon to take part in the rite. We are not referring here merely to the "Consultation of the People" and the Litanies as ways in which they have a part (although it might be well to mention that Litanies are included in the liturgy precisely in order to enlist the prayers of the whole gathering), but we are referring more particularly to the sequence of actions and prayers in that part of the rite at which the priesthood is actually conferred. The significance of this sequence as an action of the entire assembly is not clearly indicated in the Pontifical or in the booklets usually supplied to the congregation, nor is the historical development of this part of the rite entirely clear. But the fact is clear that in the sequence we have a perfect example of a rite in which the whole Church is acting, each member taking part according to his particular position.

The deacons who are to be raised to the priesthood kneel in turn before the bishop and he places his hands on the head of each of them, in this way designating them as the ones to receive the priestly powers. This is the "matter" of the sacrament. Then the priests impose hands as a sign of their union with the bishop in the priesthood, as a greeting to the men entering the priestly order and as an expression of their prayerful hope that the Holy Spirit will bless them abundantly with the graces they need. Then the bishop invites all, clergy and laity, to pray for the ordinands, saying, "Dearly beloved, let us pray to God the Father almighty, that He will shower heavenly graces on these His servants whom He has chosen for the priestly office. May they persevere by His help in this state which they are entering at His call. Through Christ our Lord." The response, "Amen," is made. Then the immediate invitation to pray is given by one of the assistants, saying, *"Flectamus genua."* All kneel for a time praying silently, until the assistant says, *"Levate."* The bishop prays in the name of all: "Hear us, we beseech Thee, Lord, our God, and shower down upon these Thy servants the blessing of the Holy Spirit and the power of priestly grace, so that they, whom we present to Thee for consecration, may always be supported by the abundance of Thy gifts. Through our Lord, Jesus Christ, Thy Son, who lives and reigns with Thee in the unity of the Holy Spirit, God, forever and ever." All answer, "Amen." It is after this that the bishop sings or recites the consecratory prayer which is the "form" of the sacrament. He says this in virtue of his priestly power and as a representative of the whole body of Catholic bishops, asking God to give them assistants endowed with priestly powers and to give these men the virtues they need to perform the work of the priesthood worthily.

The way in which this part of the ordination rite is usually conducted needs to be revised. The unity and full significance are obscured if the priests are returning to their places during or right after the invitation to prayer, if the people are not asked to stand for the invitatory, if the *"Flectamus genua"* and *"Levate"* are not said in a loud voice, and if the pause for silent prayer is not observed.

The form that is used here for enlisting the prayers of the whole gathering is an ancient form with which we are familiar especially from the Good Friday liturgy. At one time this form was used at Mass, right after the sermon (or after the dismissal of the catechumens), to pray for various intentions of the Church and of the particular congregation. The current proposals for liturgical reform reflect a widespread desire for the restoration of this "Prayer of the Faithful." The recent codification of the rubrics has restored the pause after the *"Flectamus genua,"* which occurs also on several Ember Days and in various other rites. This rubric is another simple but significant indication of the fact that the laity do not merely attend liturgical rites but have a part in them.

A study of the rites of the other sacraments can yield rather easily a knowledge of the principal ways in which the recipients and the others who are assembled can participate entirely. For a conclusive analysis of these rites one would have to consult scholarly commentaries, but many of the elements are clear enough. Versicles and responses, *"Oremus,"* and *"Amen"* stand out especially. The simple indication "R." for "Response" has been overlooked for so long or thought of as calling only for response by a server, that the Sacred Congregation of Rites in its revision of liturgical books recently, that is, in the restored Holy Week rites and in the new edition of the second part of the Pontifical, makes the congregational participation explicit with rubrics such as *"Omnes respondent."* Many booklets published in recent years for use by the laity at Baptism, Confirmation, Anointing of the Sick, and other rites, make clear the parts to be taken by the various participants.

PRAISE AND PETITION

In some instances the action of the faithful is itself the most important sign in a rite, but we are so used to thinking of liturgical rites as acts of the priests that we miss the point. This has been true generally of the ceremony with the palms at the beginning of Holy Week, which in most places was reduced to an early morning blessing by a priest and their distribution during the day to the people. The revised Holy Week rites have emphasized the fact that the ceremony consists principally of the procession in which clergy and laity together give public testimony of their love and gratitude to Christ our Redeemer and King. A similar restoration is needed for the Candlemas celebration. The new code of rubrics has introduced changes to encourage processions on the Rogation Days.

Another rite in which the assembly and action of the faithful is the principal sign is the ceremony of the ashes at the beginning of Lent. It is often referred to as "getting the ashes," and at best it seems to be thought of as simply a reminder of death or as some sort of a blessing. What is the full sign in this ceremony? First the faithful assemble to begin the holy season of penance. The choir sings on their behalf a plea for divine mercy. The priest blesses some ashes, asking God that they may be a remedy "for all who humbly implore Thee, conscious of their sins, accusing themselves, deploring their crimes in Thy sight, earnestly beseeching Thy great mercy." Then those who are repentant and seeking God's mercy are to come forward. This is the principal part of the sign. It is a public profession that they are sinners, that they intend to amend their lives and do penance, that they are going to observe the Lenten discipline, and that they have confidence in God's mercy dispensed in His Church. As they come forward to have the ashes put on their heads by the priest, the choir sings a series of antiphons which express what should be in their minds and hearts. Even when the full ceremony is not carried out, that is, without a choir and using ashes already blessed, it should not be a matter merely of people lining up to get something. It is a sacred event, an encounter with God, an act of worship, and here specifically a public act of penance.

These last examples we have considered — various processions and the ceremony of the ashes — are rites that are meant simply to praise God or to invoke His mercy. There is a rather general lack of appreciation of such rites, at least in their full meaning. A similar lack of a full liturgical sense is seen in the attitude of many to the burial of an infant. In many places the rite provided by the Church is not even performed. People say, "What need has the child for prayers?" Actually the purpose of the rite is to gather the faithful to praise God. We join our voices with those of the angels, singing psalms of adoration, and we thank God for having admitted this child to the heavenly choirs. While inevitably there is sorrow on such an occasion, for those with vital faith it has much of the significance of a canonization.

EASTER VIGIL

For some rites very special planning is required to give the participants a sense of involvement. It is clear now that such planning may be needed to make the Easter Vigil the important event it should be in the life of each parish. After the first enthusiasm for the revised rite, interest has tended to decline in many places. In the search for a solution it has been pointed out that in the early centuries practically all of the faithful in each community were involved in preparing for the Vigil, that is, in helping and encouraging the catechumens; at the very least they knew them and were praying for them. Do we need some such way of getting the faithful involved today? It is not essential, for improved preaching on the Redemption throughout the year and especially during Lent, with special reference to the Holy Week themes, could provide the appreciation of the basic mysteries of the Christian life that is so desirable and that would lead to an enthusiastic celebration of the Vigil as the climactic event of the year. Still, it would help a great deal if parishes worked out some ways of getting large numbers personally involved in activities that would culminate in the Vigil celebration, for example, inquiry and convert classes, the effort to bring lapsed Catholics back to the sacraments, and a general renewal of parish life. Many could also be involved in the preparation of children for First Communion and Confirmation and this work could be related to the Vigil celebration even though these sacraments would not be conferred just at that time. If all these efforts were brought to a climax at Easter, then the hailing of Christ's victory over the darkness, the recalling of God's leading His people out of slavery to the Promised Land, the Baptisms and renewal of baptismal vows, the singing of the *Gloria* and the first *Alleluias*, the corporate offering of the Holy Sacrifice, and the Communion at the holy table would be a wholehearted celebration by the whole parish, a truly corporate act of faith and gratitude.

HOLY MASS

The Holy Sacrifice of the Mass is a community action, as has been made abundantly clear in papal documents and in countless books and articles in recent years. The Instruction on participation in the liturgy issued by the Holy See in September, 1959, states it concisely: "The Mass by its nature calls for participation by all who attend, each in the way proper to him." There are two aspects to this statement, one ritual and the other strictly liturgical. On the ritual side, different roles are assigned to the various participants, that is, to the celebrant, to the deacon and subdeacon if it is a solemn Mass, to the servers, the choir, and the congregation. Each has particular actions and words proper to him. There is also the strictly liturgical side. We use this term for want of a better way to refer to the Mass in terms of the definition of the liturgy given in *Mediator Dei*, as "the public worship which our Redeemer as Head of the Church gives to the Father, as well as the worship which the community of the faithful gives to its Founder and through Him to the heavenly Father." Looking at the Mass from this viewpoint we see that it is the offering of Christ's Sacrifice to the Father by the whole Church, that is, by Christ the Head and His members. Each member participates "in the way proper to him." The celebrant acts in the person of Christ as head of the assembled faithful; he effects the change of the bread and wine into the Body and Blood of Christ, and he serves as Christ's minister in the corporate offering and in the sacred banquet. The celebrant and all the rest of the faithful are co-victims and co-offerers with Christ in His Sacrifice.

Keeping in mind both the ritual and the strictly liturgical aspects, we shall consider some of the ways in which the corporate nature of the Mass may be learned. The starting point is very important. The Mass must be identified immediately as an action in which the laity are involved and not as an object outside them. The best place to start is with the gathering of the people. The liturgy is made up of signs; and the first sign is the assembly, even though it be only two or three gathered together in Christ's name. This is the *ecclesia*, the assembly of those called together by God. Not only is this starting point good psychology, to give the laity a sense of involvement right off, but it is also good doctrine, making clear the fact that their coming together is in response to God's call. Why are we Christians? Why are we Catholics? Why do we go to Mass? The most fundamental answer is that we are God's people, called by Him and formed by Him. The Old Testament preparations for the Church and her worship in the *Qahal Yahweh*, as described, for example, by Father Louis Bouyer in the third chapter of his *Liturgical Piety*, can serve as good preliminary lessons in this matter.

The taking of holy water as we enter the church (or the *Asperges*) is another liturgical sign, and it can serve as a starting point for considering the life of grace that makes our gathering a Christian assembly. Baptized in water, with the invocation of the Holy Trinity, we were conformed to Christ, crucified and risen, and we entered into a new life. The congregation of the baptized is itself a sign. Looking at it with the eyes of faith, we see it as a living body, in which the Holy Spirit dwells, uniting the members with each other and with Christ their Head.

The church building can be seen as a sign if we use the metaphor given us by the Apostles, that the Church is built on the foundation of the Apostles and Prophets with Christ as the cornerstone and the faithful as living stones, "built thereon into a spiritual house." In various ways the architectural arrangement can provide understanding of the liturgy as a corporate action. At least the impression should be removed that the interior arrangement has the same functional purpose as a theater, with a raised platform in front for the action that is to be viewed and seats placed in rows for the audience. One of the elements that entered into the development of church architecture is especially helpful, namely, that in the earliest days the faithful came together for a community meal that culminated in the Eucharistic meal. We still have the "head table," in front of which we gather for the sacrificial offering and meal. The altar rail may distract us from seeing this, as it seems to separate the laity from the altar. Actually it is not a necessary furnishing in a church, and where it is found, its purpose is to contribute toward a more orderly conduct of the sacred action by the whole community, marking off the space in which the clergy perform most of their functions and also providing for an orderly procedure when the laity come up to receive the sacred Bread from the priest.

UNITY OF MINDS AND HEARTS

The assembly of the faithful is a sign of their unity with each other in Christ. This fact imposes an obligation on them to strive for constant growth in charity, in both love of God and love of each other. In *Mediator Dei* there is repeated insistence on the need for ascetical effort along with liturgical participation. There is a lengthy treatment of the matter in the first part of the encyclical, and from the way in which it is presented some might take it only as a refutation of those who would say that liturgy is sufficient. In the full context, however, it is seen as a lesson on the interior aspect of the liturgy and on the ways in which we can be rightly disposed for sincere, devout, and fruitful participation in the liturgy. The encyclical sums it up in words from the Epistle to the Hebrews: "Since then, brethren, we have confidence to enter the Holies in virtue of the blood of Christ, a new and living way which He inaugurated for us through the veil (that is, His flesh), and since we have a high priest over the house of God, let us draw near with a true heart in fullness of faith, having our hearts cleansed from an evil conscience by sprinkling, and the body washed with clean water. Let us hold fast the confession of our hope without wavering. . . . And let us consider how to incite one another to charity and good works."

As we assemble for Mass, the familiar lesson from St. Paul's letter to Corinth is a pertinent warning. Although we do not gather first for a community meal, we have the same obligation to be concerned about each other's needs, and by our failures in this we could become just as unworthy of the Eucharistic meal as those to whom St. Paul wrote. At the very least it is required for our sincere coming together that we have been striving to remove from our hearts any hatred, anger, or prejudice and from our actions any dissension, discrimination, or other injustices. In a positive way, we should be striving to strengthen the bonds of charity, to make more vital the life of the community in which we live. Even more clearly than our coming together, our praying together imposes this obligation on us. We are seeing today a growth of active participation through dialogue Mass and congregational singing. Praying together is a clear sign of oneness of minds and hearts. If we are not trying to attain that oneness it would be a dishonest sign.

Much has been written about the relationship of the social apostolate to the liturgy. At times social action is presented as one of the fruits of our union with Christ and with each other at Mass. This can be true, but there is another way of relating them, namely, to see social action as one of the ways in which we are properly disposed for sincere participation in the Mass. In the same section of Mediator Dei in which Pope Pius XII spoke of the necessity of exercises of piety, he also spoke of the social apostolate as a preparation for being united with Christ in His Sacrifice. He referred to the efforts of the Church "to permeate with this same spirit (of Christ) the life and labors of men, their private and family life, their social, even economic and political life," and he stated, "Such action on the part of individual Christians, along with the ascetic effort prompting them to purify their hearts, actually stimulates in the faithful those energies which enable them to participate in the august Sacrifice of the altar with better dispositions."

A priest could come to see the relationship of the liturgy to the rest of his pastoral work and thus find the unifying principle in his life by meditating on the gathering together of the people for Mass. His various sacramental ministrations and blessings, his teaching, spiritual direction, conduct of parish societies, formation of apostolic groups, and so on, are directed toward forming the parishioners into a "holy people" whom he will lead into the Holy of Holies.

The priest himself is a sign. He represents Christ. He is a man set apart. But we must understand this correctly. He is not set apart from the community of the faithful; he is set apart within that community; he is its head. He is rightly called "another Christ," but this too must be understood correctly. It does not mean that the laity are not "other Christs." The priest is "another Christ" in a special way. He represents Christ as Head of the Body, exercising unique powers as the instrument of Christ to sanctify the members, whom he unites with Christ in the worship of the Father.

It would be well for writers and preachers to make these things clear in vocation literature, First Mass sermons, and so on. It is not right to separate the priest from the community. Such an approach may well discourage vocations; it downgrades the dignity of the laity, and it obscures the meaning of the Christian life as the life of the Mystical Body of Christ. Not only the terms "set apart" and "other Christs" should be qualified but also such terms as "leaving the world," "called by God," "following Christ," "vocation," etc. There might also be less emphasis on the priest as one "who brings God down upon the altar" (not an accurate description of the Consecration anyway) and more emphasis on him as one who leads the people into the Holy of Holies with Christ our High Priest, there to offer a perfect Sacrifice to God.

ACTIVE PARTICIPATION

In the actual rite of Holy Mass it is obvious that the congregation has a part, or rather it is becoming obvious since the liturgical apostolate has drawn our attention to what was there all along. The fact that the Mass is a community action with a distribution of roles had become obscured through a series of developments, such as the choir's taking over the congregation's parts and the celebrant's having to say all the parts even when the others are fulfilling their roles. It was the decline in congregational participation that brought on these developments. That decline was caused by shifts in devotional attitudes and practices as a result of necessary emphases in the Church's preaching when particular doctrines were attacked by heretics. An undesirable by-product of the necessary clarification and defense of these doctrines was that Christ's mediation and the laity's participation in His worship of the Father ceased to be vital factors in the devotional life of the faithful. Although most of the prayers said by the celebrant at Mass are phrased, "We beseech Thee . . ." or "We offer Thee, O heavenly Father . . . through Jesus Christ, Thy Son, our Lord," the full meaning of these words was being overlooked. In restoring active participation to the laity it is helpful to give them a sketch of the reasons for its decline and for the present revival. It is essential to teach them Christ's headship and mediation.

We shall not go into the doctrinal instruction that is necessary in fostering participation in the liturgy as corporate worship. We have touched on various aspects of it in passing. We shall consider some further pedagogical and pastoral steps that would help to make such instruction practical and vital.

The fact that the Mass is a community action is often overlooked in making visual aids to teach its meaning. How many books and sets of slides giving pictures of the successive actions in the Mass include even a hint of the congregation's part? What we said about the best starting point applies here. The Mass should not be presented to people as something outside them, an action going on "up there." The same error should be avoided in giving demonstrations of the Mass rite. Through the commentary or through enlisting some participation, the corporate nature of the action should be made clear. Likewise, when Mass is celebrated to be viewed on television, the cameras should not concentrate on the actions of the priest, but should show the whole action, and it is certainly preferable that the congregation be participating actively. In all these instances one small but significant detail is usually overlooked, along with the larger one of the presence of a congregation, and that is to have a ciborium on the altar. Pius XII recommended that, where it is feasible, hosts be consecrated at each Mass for the participants, so that "all the actions at the altar may manifest more clearly the living unity of the Mystical Body."

For active participation in sung Mass a simple form of congregational singing is necessary. When Gregorian chant is discussed this reason for it is often overlooked. It is frequently discussed simply as an art form and is compared with other types of music from an aesthetic point of view. Moreover it is often discussed only in reference to its rendition by choirs and its impression on hearers. These considerations are not irrelevant, but they are not the primary issues. The decline and restoration of Gregorian chant does not belong in the history of musical forms but in the history of liturgical participation. When the congregations ceased to participate and their parts were taken over by choirs, more elaborate music was developed. The Gregorian chant is being restored now because active participation is being restored and not because of any decision based merely on musical taste. This is the music that is available for simple, unison singing by the people. Other forms are being developed which may eventually replace the Gregorian if they become more popular and if they have the requisite qualities of holiness, beauty of form, and appropriateness for the texts to be sung. The ultimate purpose is to make possible for all the faithful the fulfillment of the Church's wish for them, expressed as follows by Pope Pius XII: "Let the full harmonious singing of our people rise to heaven . . . and let them testify by the melody of their song to the unity of their minds and hearts, as becomes brothers, children of the same Father."

The doctrines basic to lay participation must be taught. This does not mean that they have to be expounded in a series of lessons before the people are taught the responses and some of the other prayers that are theirs in the Mass. The theological and liturgical teaching can be correlated. We have already indicated at the beginning of this article the mysteries that are contained in the liturgical use of the form of prayer: *"Dominus vobiscum. Et cum spiritu tuo," "Oremus,"* the prayer of the celebrant in the name of all to the Father, through Christ our Lord, and the *"Amen"* of the congregation.

In the Mass this form is even more significant than in the other rites, and the recovery of its significance calls for a reorientation of devotion at Mass. Even more clearly than in the other rites there is here a corporate action and not just a receiving of a blessing. The devotion of the people at Mass has tended to focus on Christ becoming present at the Consecration. This is not wrong, and in fact such devotion has produced great saints and heroic generations. However, it is bound up with a temporary necessity in the Church's defense of particular doctrines, as we have already indicated, and now the popes are calling for the realization that the faithful have a more active, dynamic union with Christ at Mass. Christ is present from the beginning of Mass, uniting all with Himself in worship of the Father.

In the very first part of the action the priest addresses the people with the words, *"Dominus vobiscum,"* and he prays in their name, *"per Christum Dominum nostrum."* They hail Christ as *"Kyrios,"* their Lord, the one who makes them a people. When His word is proclaimed they address Him as present: *"Gloria tibi, Domine"* and *"Laus tibi, Christe."*

In the dialogue before the preface the priest calls on them to join with him and with Christ in giving thanks to the Father, as Christ did at the Last Supper. They are to join in offering Christ's Sacrifice, the Eucharistic Sacrifice. As the sacrificial action begins and they "have confidence to enter the Holies in virtue of the blood of Christ," the celebrant invites them to join their voices with those of the angels in the divine presence, saying, *"Sanctus, Sanctus, Sanctus."* Entering in with their High Priest, they turn to Him also and say, *"Benedictus qui venit in nomine Domini."*

The word "Amen" is a simple one, but to teach the meaning of "the great Amen" at the end of the Canon is to teach many things: how the faithful are co-victims and co-offerers with Christ in His Sacrifice, the distinct roles of the priest and the laity, the ways in which the Canon expresses all this, especially in the *"Unde et memores,"* and various doctrines related to these matters, such as the laity's union with Christ in His priestly acts by virtue of their Baptism and the baptismal character.

The culmination of our union with each other and with Christ comes in Holy Communion. Repeated statements by recent popes, especially Pius XII, as well as a reexamination of St. Thomas Aquinas' teaching on the ultimate meaning of the Eucharist, have shown us that this is the sacrament of the Church's unity, of our unity with each other in Christ. An interesting note here is the correct etymology of the word "communion." Usually people seem to take it for granted that it comes from a compound of *cum* and *union*, so that it would mean "union with," and they think especially of the union of the individual with Christ in this sacrament. But the proper division of the word is "commun-ion," and the root is *mun*, as in *munire*, meaning "to build a wall," that is, to construct a city, to form a community.

The Communion rite in the Mass starts with our praying together to our Father in the words taught us by the eternal Son. The breaking of bread follows and this is to be seen as a typical action of the head of a family at table. We go up to the holy table in procession. It is obvious that many people do not think of it as a procession. It is true that there should not be regimentation, with one row after another being ushered into line, but once the communicants have left their places to approach the altar it would be well for them to form a procession and in doing so to be conscious that what they are about to do is to eat together at the family table. After all have received Communion, the celebrant invites them again to pray together and he prays in their name for the graces they seek from their reception of the Sacrament.

We have considered many actions in the sacred liturgy as it is defined in *Mediator Dei*, with special attention to the fact that it is worship by "the community of the faithful." It is "the public worship which our Redeemer as Head of the Church gives to the Father, as well as the worship which the community of the faithful gives to its Founder and through Him to the heavenly Father. It is, in short, the worship offered by the Mystical Body of Christ, Head and members."

...8...

The Language of Prayer

C. J. MC NASPY, S.J.

As LONG as the liturgy was thought of within a Baroque frame-work — as something to be wondered at from afar, a kingly cere-monial, an awesome hierophany, with little part actively taken by the people — the matter of language caused slight concern.[1] Indeed, the more remote, hieratic, and mystifying the sacred words sounded, the better. Moreover, against the backdrop of aggressive Protestantism, with its disavowal of everything but the preaching of the word and its consequent stress on the unique validity of prayer and hymnody in the vernacular, for a number of centuries it was axiomatic that no change could be made that might be interpreted as a surrender.[2]

Today, of course, when post-Reformation polemics are giving way to a vigorous dialogue, the question of a functional liturgical language is openly discussed. Hardly an article, volume, or con-gress dealing with social worship fails to note the problem, with a growing consensus among the faithful that something urgently needs to be done.[3] Many eminent faculties of sacred theology

---

[1] Fr. Louis Bouyer discusses the Baroque attitudes toward liturgy in Chapter 1 of his *Liturgical Piety* (Notre Dame, Ind.: University of Notre Dame Press, 1954). See also I. H. Dalmais, O.P., *Introduction to the Liturgy* (Baltimore: Helicon, 1961), p. 170.

[2] For the background of Trent, where a very moderate position was taken, despite certain extreme notions of some of the Fathers of the Council, see H. Schmidt, *Liturgie et Langue Vulgaire* (Rome: Gregorian University, 1950) and Fr. Angelus A. De Marco's excellent synopsis, Chapter 5 of his *Rome and the Vernacular* (Westminster, Md.: The Newman Press, 1961).

[3] The congresses of Lugano (1953), of Assisi (1956), of Uden (1959), and of Eichstätt (1960) all show the feeling of liturgists and catechists. See *La Maison-Dieu*, Nos. 37, 44, and 47. Paul Winninger's new book, *Langues*

have addressed petitions to the preparatory commissions of Vatican II, imploring the wider use of living languages in the liturgy, and there is every indication that the Fathers of the Council will formulate some decrees on the liturgy at the second session of the Council. Meanwhile, repeated papal emphasis on the need for lay participation has focused attention to other needs. Who has ever attempted to teach entire parishes the high Mass or the dialogue Mass without seriously wondering whether a great deal of this energy was being misplaced? For all our heroic efforts, can we ever achieve widespread, intelligent participation in a language that hardly anyone understands? The rare exceptions, accomplished after tremendous investment of time and energy, and with groups usually not typical, only reinforce the argument.[4]

It need hardly be said once again that today's vernacular "movement" (which, to my surprise, I found as earnestly favored, if less openly, in Latin countries as in others) has nothing whatever to do with the centrifugal, Los von Rom mood which the Council of Trent had to cope with. This is no eccentric or ethereal disturbance spawned by malcontents in their restlessness or by mere lovers of novelty; it is deeply pastoral and Catholic.

LIVING LATIN

In the sixteenth century, Latin was still a living language among educated men of Western Europe and enjoyed a privilege of dignity among all classes — those who understood it and those who did not. The modern languages were just reaching a peak of form and flexibility, and printing was beginning to help them achieve the stable, classical shape they still possess. Soon, within a generation of the Council of Trent, Shakespeare, Cervantes, Camoens, and a number of the French masters would give their

---

Vivantes et Liturgie (Paris: Editions du Cerf, 1961), with a preface by the Bishop of Strasbourg, is the deepest and best documented study of the problem to date.

[4] Accounts published in Worship, under rubrics like "It Can Be Done," are edifying and distressing. When one reflects on the number of lives that could be more apostolically spent, if only our language paradox were resolved, it is disquieting, to say the least.

languages a status comparable to Latin and Greek. But, on the whole, even the major Protestant theologians continued to write in Latin, and in universities all over Europe Latin remained an international medium of communication. Even in our own time (at least in some areas) Latin has been rather widely, if decreasingly, used in the academic world. True, the use has become vestigial — limited to inscriptions, diplomas, formal citations — and, on occasion, quaintly humorous, somewhat like costumes from a forgotten past.[5] But as a vehicle of real communication among learned men it has virtually disappeared. It should be remembered, on the other hand, that when the Council of Trent decided on its retention, Latin was still a living language throughout the literate world.

I personally observed, after several trips throughout Europe, that among priests of various countries Latin is hardly ever used for communication. Some modern language, even badly spoken, always manages to win out. (This came as something of a disappointment to one who had done graduate studies in Latin and spent many years teaching it.)

What is perhaps more noteworthy is the demise of Latin even as a written language. It is hard to name any major work of theology or philosophy that has appeared in Latin since De La Taille's *Mysterium Fidei.*[6] Almost all the respected international journals of Catholic thought are today published in modern languages.[7]

---

[5] I found it amusing to quiz friends who proudly displayed copies of *Winnie Ille Pu.* The Columbia University 1961 valedictory was a witty Latin "tsk-tsk" addressed to Harvard for dropping its Latin diplomas. Translations were, of course, provided for the learned audience, as they still are at Oxford when honorary degrees are conferred. Even Oxford and Cambridge, those last bastions of classical lore, have abandoned the Latin requisite.

[6] This was finished in 1915. Most of Fr. De La Taille's other work was published in the vernacular, and, needless to say, even the *Mysterium Fidei* is now little read except in translation. This remark about "major works" does not apply to a number of very meritorious textbooks, which are still required to be presented in Latin.

[7] To mention just a few, we think of *Nouvelle Revue Théologique, Theologie und Glaube, Theological Studies, Zeitschrift für Katholische Theologie, Teologia y Vida, Revue d'Ascétique et de Mystique, Vita e Pensiero, Theology Digest, Lumière et Vie, Recherches de Science Religieuse, Theologie der Gegenwart, The Heythrop Journal, Estudios Bíblicos, Revue Biblique,* and the like. Even

This is not, of course, to suggest that Latin has no place in ecclesiastical documents. Everyone will grant that there are advantages in having official texts published in some neutral language like Latin. However, the advantages are not unmixed, and the fact that fully half of the contents of *Acta Apostolicae Sedis* appear nowadays in the vernacular should keep us from exaggerating the advantages of Latin. Moreover, much of the recent controversy about the encyclical *Mater et Magistra* came from the obscurity of the Latin text. A number of passages which were quite clear in Italian (in which the encyclical was originally drawn up) and in several translations based on the Italian, became very difficult when put into Latin. Those of us who spent hours working over single Latin paragraphs when preparing translations for publication will testify to the greater clarity of the Italian and other modern versions.[8]

Again, we should not bypass another serious disadvantage of Latin as an official language: the fact that Catholics of non-Latin rites are thereby made to feel somewhat less than first-class Catholics.[9] I do not suggest that Greek (or possibly Esperanto or Interlingua) be adopted as the official language of the Church — though a good case could be made for them — but only that we should not lose sight of the real problems involved in treating Latin in a privileged way.

Despite these difficulties, it is hard to question that an official text for ecclesiastical, dogmatic, and other pronouncements does make for security of doctrine and unchangeableness. But, on reflection, it seems that the significant question to be asked is: Pre-

the *Gregorianum*, published in Rome, now has the large majority of its contents in modern languages.

[8] In the case of *Mater et Magistra*, we were advised to "keep one eye on the Latin and two on the Italian." When making other translations of Roman documents I received similar admonitions. This is not, of course, to minimize the stylistic accomplishment of the Latinists who translate such documents *into* Latin from some vernacular text.

[9] To treat them as marginal Catholics and their liturgy as somehow less than the Latin is bizarre, particularly when we recall that Greek and two Semitic languages were used by God in Holy Scripture, and not Latin.

THE LANGUAGE OF PRAYER

cisely how can this official text be *best put to use?* The problem is
not how to preserve these texts on paper. It is rather how to make
sure that they are correctly understood.

Moreover, the problems of a liturgical language and an official
language for ecclesiastical documents need clear distinction.

Every Latin teacher knows how difficult accurate translation is.
The argument used by some antivernacularists (that it is hard to
find good translations) is really topsy-turvy. Precisely because Latin
is hard to understand, we need to insure accurate translations. If
we leave it to the individual priest or layman to try to understand as
he reads along, we have no assurance that he will be accurate.[10] On
the other hand, if translations are authoritatively made by trained
experts and checked by others and then given the official approval
of Rome, then precisely we can be sure that the true meaning has
been kept. Latin, unless it is translated, can easily become a means
of disunity.

What about translations becoming archaic? It is a well-known
fact among philologists that since the invention of printing, languages have tended to become stabilized and now do change very
little. (This is not to overlook that exuberant and ephemeral
phenomenon, slang, which is really not germane to the discussion.) Does anyone have trouble understanding the Declaration
of Independence after almost two centuries? Our common prayers
too (like the Our Father and the Hail Mary) are still quite intelligible after many centuries of use. In any case, new translations
can profitably and easily be made every century or oftener. This
we do with regard to Holy Scripture, which is God's own word.
Should we hesitate to do it with the man-made part of the
sacred liturgy?

---

[10] How many busy priests have time to keep reviewing their Latin to the
degree needed for spontaneous devotion in their breviary? How many, for example, do not black out or stumble over lines like *gliscens fert animus promere
cantibus* or *sunt multa fucis illita?* How many can tell you, without probing
their linguistic depths, what *jugiter* means, even though they use the word every
time they give Benediction? My point is: should one have to *translate* one's
prayer?

MODERN COMMUNICATIONS

At the time of the Council of Trent, communications were difficult. Today, at least in the free world, it is easy to reach almost any spot instantly. Telephone, air mail, plane travel, radio have made communication between Rome and any bishop a matter of seconds or, at most, days, where months used to be required. Moreover, the visual media — television, movies, pictorial press — have made it possible for everyone to know the Pope as never before. Before the invention of photography (I have mentioned this in a previous article[11] but believe it bears repetition) hardly anyone knew the Pope or even what he looked like. Today, Catholic homes and schools treasure his photograph, honoring it symbolically near the image of Christ and His Blessed Mother. Whatever advantages Latin may have had (and may still have for some people), as a symbol of unity, are certainly made less important by our superior communications today.

THE ARGUMENT FROM TOURISM

With the spread of travel and the opportunity of most Americans to visit foreign countries, we sometimes still hear Latin extolled as a link with home. Surely it is a comfort for a traveling priest to be able to say Mass in the familiar Latin wherever he may be. However little the server may understand what he is saying, he does answer the same words that one hears at home. Yet what does the priest do at the end of the Mass, with the Hail Mary and other prayers? Does it matter so much that the answers are given in another tongue, and could not this dialogue be carried on during the Mass? In any case, it would seem that priests when traveling could manage to serve each other (they usually travel in company) or to continue saying Mass in Latin, if they prefer. In any case, too, the Mass is not principally for the priest's benefit.

[11] "The Vernacular Re-Viewed," *Worship*, March, 1961, pp. 241–250. This is reprinted in pamphlet form by The Liturgical Press, Collegeville, Minn., together with an interesting letter by the Right Rev. John Bresingham, Archimandrite.

Some lay people too are consoled to hear the same familiar if half-grasped sound of Latin abroad as at home. But can anyone seriously maintain that the liturgy should be geared to the artificial conditions of travel? Besides, tourists would be even more comforted, it seems, if together with the familiar rites and gestures they heard words which meant something to them, since they had known them at home. The mere change of sound, from English to German, for example, would matter little, compared to the joy of discovering the unity of the Mass. But, more important, tourists expect some language problems when they go abroad. When they are at home, however, it is strange that they are asked to be foreigners in their Father's house — having to hear an archaic, unintelligible tongue.[12]

WHAT ABOUT GREGORIAN CHANT?

An argument against the vernacular that one continues to hear is rather subtle and involves only a few, highly cultivated people. It is this: if we give up Latin in favor of the vernacular, we destroy the beauty of Gregorian Chant.

Here I must be a bit personal, since I myself feel the argument acutely and know that it deeply disturbs some of my fellow musicians. The chant, I quickly avow, offers an ideal sacred music to many trained monks and some others (including myself). For those who have spent years in daily contact, it is a sort of musical vernacular (as it was during a large part of the Middle Ages). But for the great majority of the Church, it presents difficulties which appear, on honest examination, insuperable.

I must emphasize that for monasteries and for professional musicologists and other persons with musical culture, chant is more than acceptable — it is one of the great, authentic art forms, comparable to the Romanesque style with which it grew up. However, the problem here is not whether the chant is excellent

---

[12] The *argumentum ex turismo* receives a deathblow from Paul Winninger, *op. cit.*, pp. 66–70 and 82–85.

sacred music, but how well it fulfills its function of being ideal *liturgical* music.[13]

Since the liturgy is the worship of the whole Mystical Body, what is ideally liturgical is whatever is best adapted to the needs of God's holy people in their public, social worship. For one thing, the modalities and rhythm of Gregorian Chant are so strange that most people find them bizarre and foreign, rather than really prayerful. To expect the *people* (again, I am not speaking of monks or seminarians, who have a steady diet of chant) to respond and "resonate" to a style of music that was living and vital a thousand years ago, without undergoing the arduous training of musicians or seminarians, is to misunderstand the psychology of music. Further, to expect them to be able to use it effectively — to participate in it, not simply to admire it from afar as visitors do at Solesmes and elsewhere — is utterly unrealistic.

In fact, only the tiniest fraction of parishes in Europe, North and Latin America, where I have made extensive inquiries, are able to perform Gregorian Chant in a way that could be judged beautiful or even tolerable. That we can point to admirable exceptions is owing to the extraordinary efforts of a few talented and courageous musicians. But we wonder whether these exertions have been most usefully directed. Is there not another way that could be more effective? Had this same energy and talent been spent in the development of a true vernacular music — a music geared to the real needs of the normal parish — we would be closer to the solution of a serious problem. Many of us who have devoted thousands of hours to teaching the Latin Gregorian Chant are honestly troubled and ask ourselves whether something more practical might not have been done for the help of God's people.[14]

---

[13] The principles concerning liturgical music are wonderfully set forth by St. Pius X in his *Motu Proprio*. After almost sixty years of subsequent experience, liturgical musicians do not question the principles, but rather certain points of practical application. Today, in the Church at large (not in monasteries, seminaries, or great basilicas — where problems are different), is chant a workable solution? See Dom Gregory Murray, O.S.B., in *Downside Review* (*passim*, especially Vol. 74) and Alec Robertson's new volume, *Christian Music* (New York: Hawthorne, 1961).

[14] It is common to hear the complaint that people have not really tried chant.

Let us grant, for the sake of argument, that Gregorian Chant may possess some quasi-sacramental power to move souls — to incarnate or translate the words of the liturgy into a musical language that is more meaningful than any vernacular — is the chant so unchangeable and fixed as the argument supposes? (I hesitate to mention such a fantastic argument, but have on occasion heard it offered in all seriousness.) In the first place, recent musicology has established the fact that the chant did not arise in connection with the Latin liturgy or language.[15] Many Gregorian melodies, and the general style itself, are Latin only by adoption.

Second, and perhaps more important, it is well known to all students of chant that many of the greatest compositions are used with different sets of words, often words as unalike as possible. This suggests that we should not be too confident when we identify a melody with certain words (or even with a certain language, since, once again, the same melodies have been used in several languages). Take, for example, the thrilling melody used in the gradual of the Requiem Mass. Who has not been shocked on discovering that the same melody is used at the Nuptial Mass? Was, he wonders, some humorous monk at work here? Further, the same melody occurs in still other liturgical settings, where the words are quite remote from each other: Christmas Eve, the Mass of a Confessor, some Ember Days, the vigils of several Apostles, the First Sunday of Lent, the Twenty-First Sunday After Pentecost, and elsewhere. And take the great melody associated with the *Christus Factus Est* in Holy Week. How dismaying to discover it used in the Mass of St. John the Evangelist, the Second Sunday After the Epiphany, the Mass of a Confessor Bishop, and the like.

Actually, I believe, this is not the problem. An enormous amount of expense and honest effort have been invested, which should have brought spectacular results if spent on something more feasible. In a very moving note Paul Winninger (*op. cit.*, p. 177) cites his own experience of fifteen years as chant director in a seminary. Like many another priest musician, "he loves the chant, but has suffered much under its tyranny."

15 See Egon Wellesz' work in general, and especially Eric Werner's monumental study, *The Sacred Bridge* (New York: Columbia University Press, 1959), with Eugene J. Leahy's scholarly review in *Journal of the American Musicological Society*, Fall, 1961, pp. 394–398.

Dom Paolo Ferretti, O.S.B., in his authoritative work on Gregorian aesthetics, has an entire chapter dealing with what he calls "Type-Melodies."[16] He goes to great lengths, with charts, showing how differently the same melodies are used and adjusted to different words. In another chapter he explains precisely that Gregorian melodies are *not* rigidly set to particular words or meanings, but keep only a "vague and indefinite expression," in such a way that we "can imagine expressed and almost described many different sentiments."[17]

Perhaps Dom Ferretti's great study has not become sufficiently known to Gregorian students because it has not been translated into English. But there is surely no excuse for them to go on maintaining that the wedding of words and melody in Gregorian Chant is indissoluble and sacrosanct.

Thus it is evident that to sing Gregorian Chant, adapted to other languages, can hardly be the outrage that some partisans of Latin maintain. In many instances, indeed, greater changes are made with the melodies when adapting different Latin texts to the same melodies than would be necessary in adapting the same melody to other languages.

Another point needs to be made. Many chant masters who follow the Solesmes method of interpreting Gregorian rhythm seem to forget that this theory is musicologically suspect.[18] We really do not know — and it may be that we shall never know — how chant was sung during its great creative period. I mention this with some reluctance, since the fact is a commonplace among professional musicologists. The differences between the Solesmes method and any of a dozen other methods, in the actual performance of

---

[16] *Estetica Gregoriana* (Rome, 1934).

[17] Chapter 5 of Section 3, Part 1, pp. 131–135.

[18] See G. Vollaerts, *Rhythmic Proportions in Early Medieval Ecclesiastical Chant* (Brill, 1958), Willi Apel, *Gregorian Chant* (Bloomington, Ind.: Indiana University Press, 1957) and Gustave Reese, *Music in the Middle Ages* (New York: Norton, 1940), where he sums up impartial scholarly opinion: "Nevertheless, while admiring the beauty of the Solesmes interpretations, one should not overlook the fact that they are historically suspect" (p. 148). In a burst of confidence, one of the world's leading musicologists expressed it more graphically in private: "Those monks invented that damned ictus!"

a given chant, are far greater than the differences between the same chant performed in Latin and in a good English translation. True, anyone trained in a single system will naturally complain that a change does not do justice to the original (we resent being jarred out of what is familiar). But does this complaint really touch the center of the problem? Are the *people* disturbed?

Moreover, should we be too concerned about certain niceties that belong to one or other (doubtful) system? From a musical viewpoint, this may make some difference and be of interest. But, from a *liturgical* viewpoint, the question should not be whether it sounds to our ears like Solesmes or Beuron or other styles, but whether the music is prayerful and helpful to God's people. Moreover, if in translation some of the beauty is lost, the subtle loss can hardly be comparable to the enormous gain in intelligibility.[19]

Thus, two points seem significant regarding Gregorian Chant: (1) there are reasons for seriously questioning its suitability for ordinary parochial liturgy; (2) in any case, it constitutes no serious argument against the vernacular, since the chant melodies have already been adapted to different words and even to different languages.

WHY THE VERNACULAR?

The basic argument for the vernacular in all prayer, public as well as private, is so evident as to need no formal statement. As Fr. André Godin, S.J., the eminent psychologist, put it, "We don't need laboratory proof of the fact that one can pray adequately only in his native language. Common sense is argument enough."[20]

----

[19] St. Augustine touched the nub of the problem when he asked: *"Quis movetur si nescit quod dictur?"* Again he put it effectively: *"In verbis verum amare non verba. Quid enim prodest clavis aurea, si aperire quod volumus non potest?"* (*De Doctrina Christiana, passim.*)

[20] Fr. Godin is editor of *Lumen Vitae,* the journal of Christian education published in Brussels; as a sort of model of modern communications, this journal is published simultaneously in several languages. The *International Journal of Philosophy* (Fordham and Louvain) is also published in more than one language. In private conversations with a number of eminent Catholic psychologists I have heard Fr. Godin's opinion emphatically endorsed.

It is no secret that we think in words. To put a language veil between our prayer and our inmost thought is to damage our prayer. Further, liturgical prayer is social prayer, and it is certainly a devious procedure to try to become united by means of a language that is obscure if not opaque. What should join us actually adds to our isolation.[21]

The most insidious peril to our faith today is secularism, which maintains that religion is irrelevant. If we shroud our public worship in a language that seems dead and without full meaning to us, we strongly suggest (even to ourselves) that the faith itself is, if not altogether dead, at least unmeaningful. Students of cultural history point out that there are several cultures in competition today (the scientific, for example, and the literary-artistic); if we seem to ally Christian life and worship too rigidly with the forms of an antique Latin culture which is no longer considered vital, do we not invite the charge of being out of date?[22]

The original liturgical language of our Lord was not the imperial language of Rome. It was the vernacular. The first Christians of Rome spoke Greek, and the first Roman liturgy was accordingly Greek. When their common vernacular became Latin, their liturgical language naturally became Latin. For special reasons, which no longer seem to apply, Latin was retained in liturgical use even when it had become the vernacular only of clerics and the learned. Today, in a totally different cultural situation, its prolonged use seems to many students of the liturgy

---

[21] See Francis Vandenbroucke, O.S.B., "Aux origines du malaise liturgique," in *Les Questions Liturgiques et Paroissiales*, 40 (1959), pp. 252–270; also in précis form, "At the Roots of Our Liturgical Malaise," in *Theology Digest*, Autumn, 1961, pp. 131–136. Fr. Vandenbroucke concludes: "Latin separates the people from the clergy more completely today than in the Middle Ages, and it has become the major obstacle to the pastoral efficacy of the liturgy."

[22] A golden sentence of Pope John XXIII ought to be made the point of much prayerful meditation: "When the Catholic Church will appear sanely modernized, rejuvenated, it will be able to say to the separated brethren: Come to us." The separated brethren are not only those of Eastern rites. If we are to heal the schizophrenia within the West it can hardly be by appearing to belong to the past. A liturgy that uses a dead language is bound to appear dead.

to be positively harmful.[23] Many of us, accordingly, petition the
Holy See to reexamine the problem of a liturgical language.

---

[23] While the problem of the vernacular affects mainly the laity, priests too
are personally concerned. When, in 1945, Pope Pius XII, despite much conservative criticism, broke with the ancient custom of using St. Jerome's psalms
in the Divine Office, he did it in the name of *intelligibility*. Since, apart from
Italians, to whom Latin is more of an ancient vernacular than a really strange
tongue, priests all over the world find Latin an encumbrance to prayer, many
hope that the principle of intelligibility will be extended.

...9...

The Schola Cantorum and the Parish School*

THEODORE N. MARIER

THAT the term "liturgy" has in recent years achieved what in America is commonly known as "status" is evidenced by many factors. Not the least of these is the occasion of the appearance of this commemorative volume, issued in honor of a man whose life has been identified in a unique way with the liturgy. But the cause for which Father Ellard labored for a half century has not always enjoyed its present position of esteem. One remembers, for example, the time, not more than 15 years ago, when Father Leonard announced the first sessions of his School of Social Worship at Boston College. He purposely chose not to use the term "liturgy" in the opening announcement of his workshop because at that time this word was either not known at all or, and this was perhaps more important, those associated with it in the so-called liturgical movement were held suspect. For these reasons the words "social worship" were substituted. As his principal lecturer and discussion leader he invited Father Ellard. An editor in the office of the *Pilot*, the weekly paper of the Archdiocese of Boston, thinking that the announcement as submitted by Father Leonard contained a glaring error, saw fit to change the banner line of the paid advertisement to read: Boston College School of Social Service. Apparently the concept of social worship had not penetrated into the consciousness of the editor, nor did the presence of Father Ellard as key man on the staff of the faculty of the session have meaning for him. Obviously, the substitution of "social worship" for "liturgy" did nothing to further the cause.

---

* Since this essay was written, Mr. Marier has been placed in charge of just such a school as he describes. It will open in September, 1963 at St. Paul's Parish in Cambridge, Mass. and will be known as "The St. Paul Choir School, Archdiocese of Boston."

It is doubtful that such a mistake in editorial judgment would occur today, for even to the most casual observer the progress through the liturgy toward the "restoration of all things in Christ," St. Pius X's motto, is in evidence all around us. Moreover, one impressive aspect of the restoration is the dynamic character of its most recent growth. Witness, for example, the volume and indeed the quality of the literature on the subject of the liturgy now available that surely did not exist in those not-so-distant but dim early days when men like Father Ellard were valiantly lighting candles to illumine the darkness that enveloped liturgical pursuits. In the past decade alone, the annual output has progressed at such a pace that no sooner is a cataloguer's list issued and it becomes obsolete. Included among recent publications are numerous and inspiring commentaries on the liturgy, scholarly articles on Scripture and liturgy, sacramental theology, biblical studies, and classroom texts with an orientation toward the liturgy, together with numerous daily and weekly missals in an unending variety of formats. Clearly such an abundant supply is an answer to a need.

There is sufficient cause to be optimistic, therefore, from the point of view of the diffusion of information on the theory of the liturgy and the extent to which it is being read. There is, however, another view of this stained-glass window through which not so much rosy light radiates. It is at the point where the principles of the liturgy are translated on the parish level into terms of action, or more particularly, the moment when the people are called upon to give exterior expression to their interior dispositions of religious devotion. Here new sets of problems have arisen, the general attitude toward which is perhaps anything but optimistic in spite of the detailed help and encouragement given in the most recent papal instructions pertaining to this very problem.

Experiments have recently brought to light the fact that among the impediments to successful and widespread liturgical participation on the part of the people, are the alleged difficulties found in the language of the liturgy, namely, Latin, and those latent in the music of the liturgy, namely, Gregorian Chant. The reaction of some zealous and well-informed liturgists, when confronted with the so-called barriers of Latin and Chant, is to bypass both. In such instances the "most noble form of eucharistic celebration," as Pius XII termed the Solemn Mass, is either regularly avoided on the parish level as a matter of principle, or, in the place of Latin and the Chant, linguistic and musical improvisations are substituted and affixed to the Low Mass where broader permissions than those given in the Sung Mass make such substitutions legal.

It is not the purpose of this discussion to refute or defend the validity of the Church's position with regard to Latin as the official language of the liturgy or Gregorian Chant as its ideal music. It is rather to suggest that in the wake of the current renaissance in the liturgy, and in order that progress in music might keep abreast of the pace being set by liturgical studies, a second look be given to the position held by music in the Church, and, at the same time, to propose a program of action which in principle has been frequently recommended by the Church, though all but ignored in this country — a program which, if woven into the educational fabric of our Catholic life, will inevitably lessen the magnitude of the musical barrier now being faced in the transition from liturgical theory to liturgical practice on the parish level. Furthermore, this educational program will tend to obviate the superficial need of dismissing the Chant summarily, together with the language proper to it, as some champions of "participation at all costs" would seem to recommend without reservations. It is contended here that the alleged problems of singing and understanding the Chant do not lie in the difficulty of the music and its text, but in an absence of adequate teaching and preparation. It is further contended that strong, vital, artistic leadership and example in liturgical music can render negligible the difficulties of implanting Chant as the basis for participation in the Church's liturgical observances. There is no need to wonder that this music is meeting with opposition and, in some quarters, with open resistance. How, indeed, can the Chant and other liturgical music treasures of the Church be sought and performed if they are not known? How can liturgical practices be implemented by competently wrought and artistically rendered music if composers and choirs are not adequately trained for this end and if congregations are never exposed to the finest spiritual expression of which music is capable? How can the enriching, unifying, and uplifting power of the finest liturgical music be exercised and participated in by all, if steps are not taken by those responsible in the Church to create the environment where such latent power in music can be made operative?

With these thoughts in mind and in the hope that liturgists and church musicians might find concurrence of interest here, the present topic was decided upon. Although it touches only one aspect of the liturgical music restoration, it is believed — and the Church has given strong support on more than a few occasions to the principle involved here — that the implantation of such a program as the one proposed would resonate far into the future of the Church's liturgical life in the United States.

Some may wonder at the reason for establishing the geographical limits of our country as the area that might benefit most from the establishment of *scholae cantorum*. Several irrefutable factors prompt our taking this position. In the first place, the secular musical environment in which we live in the United States is perhaps unique in the world for the sheer density of its saturation. The floodtide of musical output in performance and composition, satisfying the daily demands of the theater, concert hall, radio, and television, is higher nowhere in the world. Our music conservatories and the music departments of our nonsectarian colleges are training more young people than anywhere in the world for careers in the music profession. Yet the Church in the United States seems to be deriving little from the qualitative and quantitative musical effort that is everywhere being exerted in our land. In fact, there is no observable evidence that the Church is even actively engaged in the competition for musical talent here. Until recently, with some exceptions, the subject of music itself — not to speak of Church music — was not admitted into the regular curriculum of our Catholic elementary schools. The study of music, and with it that of Church music, is still absent from the curriculum of the majority of Catholic high schools (except for such extracurricular activities as bands and glee clubs), and music is conspicuously absent from the list of accredited courses available to students in most of our Catholic colleges. From these facts it becomes clear that the musical leaders of tomorrow are neither being formed nor motivated by the Church for specialization in the field of Church music, and that the leakage from the Church's own reservoir of potential musical talent increases day by day with the proportional increase of the overall Catholic population.

It is our contention that the soil of America is fertile and ready to receive the Church's seeds of future musical leadership, for indeed not only is the air we breathe filled with the sounds of music, but our vast and complex network of parochial schools serving the cause of Catholic education from the kindergarten through graduate schools is vigorously operative in these times. Now is undoubtedly the propitious moment to recapitulate a particular theme played so eloquently and so frequently by the popes of our century. It is a well-known tune, worth rehearing, and it is closely related to the problems being met in the liturgical restoration. Listen:

> Let care be taken to restore, at least in the principal churches, the ancient *Scholae Cantorum,* as has been done with excellent fruit in a great many places. It is not difficult for a zealous clergy to institute such *Scholae,* even in the minor and country churches, nay, in them they will find easy means for gathering around them both children and adults, to their own profit and the edification of the people.[1]

> With this intention the Reverend Parish Priests, Rectors, and Superiors, especially of the principal churches, should employ the greatest zeal, making use of the assistance of competent and capable persons to found their own *Scholae Cantorum. . . .*[2]

> It was in the Lateran Palace that Gregory the Great having made his famous collection of the traditional treasures of plainsong, editing them with additions of his own, had wisely founded his great *Schola* in order to perpetuate the true interpretation of the liturgical chant.[3]

---

[1] *MP,* para. 27, p. 263. *Cf.* Bibliography, p. 119, for abbreviations.
[2] *LCR,* para. 17, p. 277.
[3] *DC,* para. 6, pp. 287–288.

Choir schools for boys should be established not only for the greater churches and cathedrals, but also for the smaller parishes. . . .[4]

That Gregorian Chant be diligently and zealously promoted . . . and that moreover the old *Scholae Cantorum* be restored, at least in principal churches.[5]

First of all see to it that there is a *good school of singers* in the cathedral itself and, as far as possible, in other major churches of your dioceses. This *school* should serve as an example to others and influence them to carefully develop and perfect the sacred chant.[6]

Still more important to sacred and religious singing is that institution called a "boys' choir" which has several times been praised by the Holy See. It is to be desired and striven for that every church have a boys' choir and that its members be instructed in the sacred liturgy and particularly in the art of singing well and piously.[7]

We have said that the soil of the United States is fertile. We have just seen that the sower has surely sown the seed. What is the hoped-for harvest? The sower himself has told us that too many times, as a few random passages will show:

Sacred Music, being a complementary part of the solemn liturgy, participates in the general scope of liturgy, which is the glory of God and the sanctification and edification of the faithful. It contributes to the decorum and the splendour of the ecclesiastical ceremonies, and since its principal office is to clothe with suitable melody the liturgical text proposed for the understanding of the faithful, its proper aim is to add greater efficacy to the text, in order that through it the faithful may be the more easily moved to devotion and better disposed for the reception of the fruits of grace belonging to the celebration of the most holy mysteries.[8]

Wherever the regulations on this subject (music) have been carefully observed, a new life has been given to this delightful art, and the spirit of religion has prospered; the faithful have gained a deeper understanding of the sacred liturgy, and have taken part with greater zest in the ceremonies of the Mass, in the singing of the psalms and the public prayers.[9]

---

[4] *DC*, para. VI, p. 290.
[5] *MD*, para. 191.
[6] *MSD*, para. 73.
[7] *SMSL*, para. 114.
[8] *MP*, para. 1, p. 255.
[9] *DC*, para. 4, pp. 286–287.

It (i.e., the Chant) makes the celebration of the Sacred Mysteries not only more dignified and solemn but helps very much to increase the faith and devotion of the congregation.[10]

Thus the Church Militant, faithful as well as clergy, joins in the hymns of the Church Triumphant and with the choirs of angels, and all together sing a wondrous and eternal hymn of praise to the most Holy Trinity in keeping the words of the Preface: with whom our voices, too, thou wouldst bid to be admitted.[11]

Let the harmonious singing of our people rise to heaven like the bursting of a thunderous sea, and let them testify by the melody of their song to the unity of their hearts and minds, as becomes brothers and the children of the same Father.[12]

The most noble form of the eucharistic celebration is found in the Solemn Mass, in which the combined solemnity of the ceremonies, the ministers and the sacred music manifests the magnificence of the divine mysteries and prompts the minds of those present to the pious contemplation of these mysteries.[13]

Music is among the many and great gifts of nature with which God, in Whom is the harmony of the most perfect concord and the most perfect order, has enriched men, whom He created in His image and likeness. Together with the other liberal arts, music contributes to the spiritual joy and the delight of the soul.[14]

Hence, We hope that this most noble art (i.e., music), which has been so greatly esteemed throughout the Church's history and which today has been brought to real heights of holiness and beauty, will be developed and continually perfected and that on its own account it will happily work to bring the children of the Church to give due praise, expressed in worthy melodies and sweet harmonies, to the Triune God with stronger faith, more flourishing hope and more ardent charity.[15]

"To our God be joyful and comely praise (Ps 146, 1)." With these words of the psalmist resounding in Our mind and in Our ears, certain familiar interests are reawakened, namely, the increase with every diligence of all that may render divine worship more splendid and pure. We are convinced that divine worship and sacred music are intimately connected and every day We have oc-

[10] MD, para. 191, p. 64.
[11] Ibid., para. 192, p. 65.
[12] Ibid., para. 194, p. 65.
[13] SMSL, para. 24, p. 9.
[14] MSD, para. 4, p. 1.
[15] Ibid., para. 83, p. 18.

casion to appreciate more the sublimeness and effectiveness of that connection.[16]

Nor has the choice of words on the part of Popes been merely a pious exercise in observance of verbal religio-cultural niceties. We listen again:

> We do, therefore, publish, *motu proprio* and with certain knowledge, Our present Instruction, to which, as to a juridical code of sacred music, We will with the fulness of Our Apostolic Authority that the force of law be given, and We do by Our present handwriting impose its scrupulous observance on all.[17]

> These things We command, declare and sanction, decreeing that this Apostolic Constitution be now and in future firm, valid and efficacious, that it obtain full and complete effect, all things to the contrary notwithstanding. Let no man therefore infringe this Constitution by Us promulgated, nor dare to contravene it.[18]

> This Instruction on sacred music and the sacred liturgy was submitted to His Holiness Pope Pius XII by the undersigned Cardinal. His Holiness deigned to approve in a special way the whole and the single parts and ordered that it be promulgated and that it be exactly observed by all to whom it applies.[19]

By means of this recapitulation of significant quotes from the papal documents which have dealt specifically with music in the twentieth century, we have tried to establish a basis for the claim of liturgical music to our serious attention. It is further hoped that by reminding ourselves of the force of law which has been given to these instructions pertaining to music, the institution known as the *schola cantorum*, which holds so high a place of esteem in the Church, will be founded and functioning in many places and soon. The present and future of the liturgical restoration in its practical fulfillment on the parochial level is and will be largely dependent on such educational programs as the one implied in the setting up of a *schola cantorum*.

In ecclesiastical circles and among Church musicians, the term *schola cantorum* is most frequently interpreted as "boys' choir."

---

[16] *PISM*, para. 1.   [18] *DC*, para. XI, p. 293.
[17] *MP*, Introduction, p. 255.   [19] *SMSL*, p. 34.

There is another interpretation, however, one that was more common in earlier epochs of Church music history, and it is "choir school." While there is a difference between what we commonly call merely a boys' choir and what the popes have called a choir school, in actuality one ought not to exist without the other. The boys' choir is the end product, so to speak, achieved by means of a thorough and systematic program of instruction pursued in a choir school. The true interpretation of *schola cantorum* is, therefore, that of a school of singers. It is a place where there is an educational program through which training is offered in liturgical music to numbers of talented boys as part of their Christian formation. The immediate end toward which this program is directed is participation in the parish activity we call the boys' choir, wherein boys are expected to fulfill their musical assignments in the liturgy with competence, artistic skill, and understanding. The remote end of the choir school is the early formation of liturgically oriented musicians who can, later on in life, assist in the formation of others or contribute, each in his own way, to the energetic growth and sustenance of the Church's musical flowering.

It is difficult to understand how a boys' choir can be expected to fulfill its duties with competence and skill (indispensable requisites) without the benefit of an in-school training program. And yet such is the situation that prevails among those parishes in some dioceses of the United States where boys' choirs have been organized. Of the total number of boys' choirs that do sing regularly in our churches, there is only the most extraordinary exception that receives anything amounting to adequate in-school training in music. If at all, the boys' choir in the average United States parish receives its full instruction during out-of-school hours, for example, during recess, before and/or after school. The choir activity is treated simply as an extracurricular activity. Under such conditions, and even assuming a high degree of competence on the part of the choirmaster, the pursuit of a systematic program of training in matters pertaining to music and liturgy is virtually impossible. That some choirs under this type of pressure have achieved even a minimal competence is a tribute to their own self-sacrifice and to the director's powers of hypnosis. By giving up recreational time to which they are entitled, the choir boys logically come to the conclusion that only they and the director think the work of preparing for the solemn liturgical observances is important, that actually the choir is extracurricular to the real work of learning and growing in the Christian life. If it were otherwise, they think, there would be time in school for the study of church music. In other words, they evaluate the situation from the evidence at hand: since there is no time in school for the study of choir music, it cannot be important.

The director's plight when faced with a lunchtime choir rehearsal is equally depressing. Neither the art of "singing piously" nor the art of singing chant and polyphony correctly can be taught to boys indoors while their friends are enjoying the freedom of out-of-doors. The system that requires the director to "steal" practice time after or before school imposes on him also a less than ideal method of imparting musical repertory, namely, rote teaching. As a result of resorting to the rote method, the rehearsal period often becomes a time of poll-parrot repetition when pages of music of varying degrees of difficulty and significance are dinned into the ears of the boys without so much as passing through their channels of understanding and appreciation. The residual effect in the actual performance being prepared and ultimately in the adult life of the boys thus processed is nil. And yet personal contact with choirmasters from various parts of the United States at summer sessions in Church music reveals the recess-time practice period and rote-teaching methods to be the normal structure of the boy-choir program in our country, that is, wherever boys' choirs have been organized. Surely this kind of situation does not reflect the true interpretation of the term *schola cantorum*.

In pursuing this line of thought it becomes more and more apparent that a boys' choir worthy of the name *schola cantorum*, which the popes have so often and so urgently requested, cannot do for the liturgical life of the parish, nor for the singers themselves, nor the Church as a whole, unless the requisite means be also adopted, namely, in-curriculum time for liturgical music and a systematic, thorough program of training. No one who is sincerely concerned about safeguarding the solemnity and beauty of the liturgy can condone the prevailing conditions under which our boys' choirs are being trained in the United States. At best, our present process is an improvisation that leads to and perpetuates musical mediocrity.

The solution to the problem seems to lie in two directions. In the first place, the Church can begin immediately to take advantage of the rich musical and educational resources that surround us in the United States. From this environment can come high standards of musical excellence in techniques and creativity, modern scientific and pedagogical methods, and a prestige status for those immediately and enthusiastically engaged in the study and performance of music. This last, especially, will be reflected in parental and parochial support of the proposed choir school program. In addition, the Church can make use here and now of the present buildings, teaching and administrative staff, physical equipment, and financial resources of her well-established parochial schools by founding within their educational framework such scholae cantorum as would be consonant with the mind of the Church in this matter.

In the light of these two considerations, the transition from the recess-time boys' choir (or no boys' choir at all, which is perhaps a more prevalent situation) to a full-fledged schola cantorum can be made smoothly and efficiently. The practical procedure through which this can be accomplished is to consider the boys of the schola cantorum as belonging to an "honors course" and to model their curriculum after that of the collegiate counterpart. Because of the need for daily music periods, the schedule would have to be organized as an independent curriculum, running parallel with that of the other classes from Grades 4 through 8, and even further, through Grade 12. Because choirboys have special talents and in virtue of them perform a special function in the Church, it would seem to be the responsibility of Catholic educators to provide the required opportunities for their development and exploitation. If the "honors course" treatment can be given to special students in languages and sciences, why not for music? Furthermore, does not this program, which could become operative immediately where the goodwill and the enthusiastic leadership are present, ring harmoniously with the same theme proposed by the popes?

A quick glance at an overall plan for integrating the *schola cantorum* into the existing framework of the parish school points up a few factors worth noting with regard to the personnel and equipment needed, the curriculum itself, the function of the parish *schola cantorum,* and, finally, the selection of the boys for the choir. These points, selected and developed at random, are suggested to show how the principles under discussion might be given particular application.

Personnel. The key person in the operation is, of course, the music director who is engaged for this program on a full-time basis. He should be one whose competence in the matter of teaching children the rudiments of music, especially Church music, has been established. Though not essential, it would be helpful if he were an organist. His work would include the planning, rehearsing, and directing all of the music for the parish in which the *schola* would be involved. During the academic year he would teach several music classes daily, including those from the fourth to the eighth grades.

In addition to instruction in music from the music specialist, the boys would receive full instruction in other academic subjects from regular classroom teachers on the faculty of the school. While the fourth-graders could remain regular members of their class, with special time out for advanced music training during the regular classroom music period, in the other grades, namely, fifth through eighth, a special curriculum would become effective that would require at least two separate teachers, one for the fifth- and sixth- grade choirboys, and a second for the seventh- and eighth-grade choirboys.

Besides the full-time music director and two classroom teachers, it would be desirable also to assign the spiritual direction of the *schola cantorum* to one of the priests of the parish. Because of the special study of the liturgy, of Latin, and of altar-boy rubrics (it would be expected that all choirboys could also serve Mass) and the opportunity for individual guidance, the group would benefit greatly from such direction.

Physical Equipment. One large, well-heated, and ventilated room with a reasonable amount of acoustical resonance, that is, hard plaster walls, ceiling, and hardwood floor, situated if possible within the church building itself or at least in a building that permits covered access to the church building, would be ideal though not indispensable. Such a room ought to be at the exclusive disposal of the choir so that music, cassocks and surplices, suit coats, etc., could be left there, all instruction take place there, and the immediate preparation for the liturgical services be held there. This room should have blackboards, a good grand piano (or, better still, a small pipe organ), a tape recorder, equipment for playing records, a record library, and benches to accommodate 75 people arranged in the "U" shape on risers.

Curriculum. The academic curriculum of the school need not be altered radically in order to make room for the *schola cantorum* program. The regular 15-minute music period in the fourth grade need only be expanded to 30 minutes; from the fifth through eighth grades, the music period need only be extended to 40 minutes. Because of the need for a full daily music period the *schola* boys ought to be provided with an independent horarium.

The music classes would be devoted at the outset to the development of the skills of note reading, especially for the correct and intelligent reading and interpretation of the notation of chant and polyphony; learning to sing with well-placed tones and accurate pitch; preparing a broad repertoire of liturgical music to supply the full needs of the parish for the liturgical year; stressing the meaning of sung prayer and understanding the basic terms of the ecclesiastical Latin vocabulary; making frequent contact with the finest recreational music through singing and listening; studying music theory, history, and participating in creative musical activity; and, as far as time allows, receiving instruction in the playing of an instrument, especially the piano, as preparation for study in organ playing.

There is no reason why the choir boys could not also take full advantage of the athletic, art and science programs of the school so long as these do not in any way interfere with the work of the choir.

Function. Among the duties of the *schola* would be the preparation of the music for the Sunday High Mass and for the High Masses of the principal feasts of the liturgical year and, on occasion, one or more of the hours of the Divine Office, such as Vespers, Compline, or Terce. Alternating with the congregation at the Sung or Dialogue Masses, they would set the tone, pace, and style for the proper rendition of the hymns, psalms, and Mass ordinaries. The singing of Votive Masses, such as Requiems, funerals, and weddings, could easily be assigned to teams of boys who could alternate from week to week so that the standard of the singing could be maintained at a high level of excellence without suffering from the deteriorating effects of excessive routine repetition. Special parish music programs at Christmas and in the spring in cooperation with the rest of the school would be a normal part of the *schola's* program. It is understood, of course, that where men are available, the boys would be expected to join with them in the singing of part-music and the chants at least for the Sunday High Mass.

Selection of Boys for the Choir. The mine of musical talent among boys in the age group of 9 to 14 years is almost limitless. The gift of music is a free one from God and it behooves us to find it and shape it. The larger the group of applicants for membership in the choir, the stricter should be the process of elimination. In making a selection the first year, preference might be given to the younger boys because these will be members for the longer period of time and thus will benefit most from the systematic course of instruction. Among the tests used for selecting the voices are those of musical memory, imagination, and rhythmic response. The severity of the tests can be gauged according to the number of openings there are in the choir. A group of 50 boys more or less evenly distributed over the five years of the grammar school should be large enough for the musical needs of any parish, large or small.

The extension of this integrated program of music into high school would lead to further specialization in music and the development of such more immediate musical skills as would be needed in the formation of organists and choir directors. The daily music period could continue with special emphasis on music theory, instrumental techniques, music literature and appreciation, liturgy and Latin during the period of voice change. In the eleventh and twelfth grades, the boys would normally be ready to sing the tenor and bass parts of polyphonic music and to sing the chants at the pitch level of mature men's voices. As for the academic subjects, all those ordinarily taught in these grades could be offered so that no boy need be deprived of adequate preparation for college or the minor seminary.

If music is to serve the liturgy effectively it must keep pace with its dynamic growth. One way of achieving this is to provide a training ground for leadership in the field. The *schola cantorum* integrated with the present parish school would seem to a simple, obvious, and immediately accessible means of training leaders for the future in the United States. Other countries have seen the foundation of completely independent Catholic choir schools, such as those at Westminster Cathedral in London and St. Michael's Cathedral in Toronto. But this type of school, though ideal, is expensive to build, staff, and maintain, and is perhaps not altogether necessary for the Church in America.

The training of leaders must begin early in their formative years and continue over a long period of time. The Palestrina, Josquin Des Pres, Guido D'Arezzo or even St. Gregory of tomorrow is perhaps today in a parochial school third grade, waiting to be led, encouraged, and motivated by the Church to a life of fruitful creativity in her service. If the opportunity of training him is not seized now, the Church will sit by and watch him spill out his musical talents in the service of the theater or a television network, instead of in the fully dedicated service of her liturgical music.

BIBLIOGRAPHY

ABBREVIATION	TITLE
DC	Apostolic Constitution, *Divini Cultus et Sancti-tatem* of His Holiness Pope Pius XI, December 20, 1928. Quoted in its entirety in Sir Richard R. Terry, *The Music of the Roman Rite* (London: Burns, Oates and Washbourne Ltd., 1931), Appendix E, pp. 285–293.
LCR	"Letter to the Clergy of Rome" from Pietro, Cardinal Vicar, February 2, 1912. Quoted in its entirety in Terry, *op. cit.*, Appendix C, pp. 270–281.
MD	*Mediator Dei*, Encyclical Letter of His Holiness Pope Pius XII on the Sacred Liturgy, November 20, 1947 (Washington, D. C.: National Catholic Welfare Conference).
MP	*Motu Proprio* of His Holiness St. Pius X on Sacred Music, November 22, 1903. Quoted in its entirety in Terry, *op. cit.*, Appendix B, pp. 253–269.
MSD	*Musicae Sacrae Disciplina*, Encyclical Letter of His Holiness Pope Pius XII on Sacred Music, December 25, 1955 (Washington, D. C.: National Catholic Welfare Conference).
PISM	Letter to the Pontifical Institute of Sacred Music of His Holiness Pope John XXIII, December 8, 1961. Quoted in Boston *Pilot*, issue of January 13, 1962.
SMSL	Sacred Music and Sacred Liturgy, Instruction of the Sacred Congregation of Rites, September 3, 1958 (Washington, D. C.: National Catholic Welfare Conference).

... 10 ...

But What About the Chant?

CLIFFORD HOWELL, S.J.

IN THE Foreword to his book *The Mass in Transition* Fr. Ellard explained that he did not consider it worthwhile to revise and publish a new edition of his *Mass of the Future* because "it was shortly overtaken by the rapid march of liturgical changes following the wake of the Encyclical on Corporate Worship of 1947." No doubt a wise and practical decision; but it would be a grievous mistake to weed the unrevised book out of one's library because parts of it are now out of date. Its first two sections remain — at least in my opinion — as a permanently valuable contribution to the progress of the liturgical movement — perhaps more valuable in this respect than anything else he has written.

The reason is this: in all Fr. Ellard's works we find wide and exact scholarship, and in all those wherein the subject calls for it we find also a concern for the pastoral aspects of liturgy. But in none is this pastoral concern more explicit or the analysis of pastoral needs more penetrating than in the pages of this ever interesting book. His diagnosis of our present liturgical ills in Section II, and his discussion of their origin in Section I remain — at least in my opinion — unsurpassed. It is always a rewarding experience to take this book down from its honored place on the shelf and to read through one or two of its chapters. It sets one's mind working.

A particularly illuminating chapter is the eighth, "Disruptive Singing in the Choir Loft." If this be followed up with the twentieth, "Not All at Ease With Latin," one is reminded that a solution to this problem would have tremendous repercussions not only in the choir loft but also in the nave. For the question arises: When the Church solves the problem of an unintelligible liturgy by allowing the use of living languages in her worship, what is going to happen to the chant?

No doubt many writers far more competent than I have discussed this in the past and will do so in the future. But it is a subject on which I do happen to have some ideas, and since not a few of them have been influenced by Fr. Ellard's writings (both in this book and elsewhere) a symposium written in his honor would seem to be a suitable place in which to set them forth.

It looks as if this generation is about to witness, in the sphere of liturgy, a spectacle sometimes fancifully imagined in the sphere of mechanics — namely, the impact of an irresistible force upon an immovable obstacle. The upshot proves, of course, that if a force is truly irresistible no obstacle can be truly immovable — or the converse. Now what looks like an irresistible force in liturgical development is the drive toward intelligibility — which means the admission of vernacular into the official liturgy. And what looks like an immovable obstacle is the passionate attachment of many church musicians to the Gregorian chant. For many centuries the obstacle has successfully resisted the force because this had not attained its full strength. But all the signs are that it is now building up to a point where it will be irresistible. When this happens there will inevitably be a head-on collision; then we shall know whether the immovable obstacle is, after all, quite so immovable as it appears now. The crash may come during the Second Vatican Council; personally I am of the opinion that the vernacular will there breach the walls of the hitherto impregnable Latin fortress. But if it does not do so then, it is bound to do so later. For the idea that the Church will retain, until the very Parousia, a liturgy unintelligible to all but a few of its most highly cultured members is so improbable that I am amazed that anyone can hold it. Vernacular is bound to come — if not sooner, then later; but it will come.

Why has it not come already? All kinds of things have held it back, and one of these, beyond doubt, is the implacable opposition of those whose prime interest is the Gregorian chant. Let us be fair to them and acknowledge our debt: in the early stages of the liturgical movement their interest and devotion to their cause was invaluable. It was they who rescued the liturgy from its centuries-long condition of suspended animation during which it had been mummified in the enswathing red bands of the rubrics. They showed it to be beautiful and rich in spiritual nourishment, something to be loved and lived, not merely performed. They made the Church as a whole conscious of the great value of the treasure hidden so long in her field, labored manfully in the digging, and truly deserve a major part of the credit for bringing the liturgy up again to the light of day. But for the aesthetic and archaeological zeal and the reverent piety of such men as Dom Guéranger, Dom Pothier, and Dom Mocquereau we might never have had a Dom Beauduin; and but for the *Motu Proprio* of 1903 occasioned by the plainchant movement we might not have had *Mediator Dei* of 1947 to guide the liturgical movement.

But the aesthetic enthusiasm so valuable in early days has now been superseded by pastoral considerations; while Gregorian chant remains important it cannot be given pride of place. A living liturgy is more vital to the welfare of souls than a beautiful liturgy; if a choice has to be made between one and the other, then surely beauty must be sacrificed. Experts in Gregorian chant tell us that the admission of living languages into the Mass would sound the death knell of the chant. If they are right we cannot but grieve while making our inevitable choice of living language essential for living liturgy. But are they right? And how far are they right? Is it not possible to save the chant — at least in some form — and yet have an intelligible and pastorally effective liturgy?

Much depends on the extent to which the vernacular will, at some future date, be admitted into the Mass liturgy. Some Latin is sure to be retained — even until the Parousia! My guess is that the day will come when no Latin at all will be used among those nations who have a non-European civilization of their own, such as the Indians, Africans, and Chinese. But among peoples whose civilizations have developed from European roots Latin will never, I think, be displaced from the short greetings and responses of the Mass. These would be a permanent reminder of the past history of our rite.

Perhaps far more Latin than this will survive through the evolution of two forms of liturgy — the monastic and the parochial. Our present troubles are largely due to the fact that we have only one form of liturgy, which, while parochial in basic content (prayer, instruction, sacrifice, communion) is monastic in dress (Latin, plainsong). If the future gives us two forms, the Mass as celebrated in monasteries might well remain in Latin adorned with all the beauties of Gregorian chant undiminished. There is, after all, no difficulty in Latin for those who understand it, nor in plainsong for those who have learned to sing it and appreciate it. Monks, for whom the *opus Dei* is the main task in life, possess (or are situated to acquire) the linguistic and musical culture needed for such a liturgy which, in fact, was notably shaped by themselves. Among them Gregorian chant with Latin words could flourish in the future as well as in the past. It was they who developed the chant to its artistic perfection; it is they who have preserved it so far, and they alone make any considerable use of it now. If they continue its use then the future situation of Gregorian chant will differ *in fact* hardly at all from that which it has occupied up until now. For it is undeniable that in practice Gregorian (apart from the simplest syllabic chant) has been confined to monasteries for the past thousand years. The *Liber Usualis* is by nature and origin a monastic songbook; for the Church at large it is an unsingable songbook and will ever remain such. In monasteries it need not die; in parishes it cannot live for it has never lived, and all the efforts which enthusiasts may make, and all the decrees which they may induce higher authority to hand down will never breathe life into it for parochial use. Any parish wherein the *Liber* is habitually used is now, and will ever be, an astonishing exception.

But if a genuinely parochial liturgy ever develops it will have to be largely in the vernacular. What scope will there be then for the chant? It will still have some place in the short greetings and responses which would remain in Latin. As things are, the Latin Epistles are monotoned or, like the Latin Gospels, are sung on one note varied at cadences. There seems no compelling reason why this rudimentary form of chant should not survive with English words, for here we are dealing with mere melodic formulae rather than genuine melodies. The same may be said about Collects and Postcommunions (and also Secrets which, I hope and pray, may some day be sung aloud as they once were).

American readers may be surprised when I say that I am one of those who would favor the retention of Latin for the people's chants, *Kyrie, Gloria, Credo, Sanctus-Benedictus,* and *Agnus Dei.* I am fully aware of the arguments for having them in the vernacular, but am not yet convinced that in countries with a European civilization these arguments outweigh the contrary reasons based on tradition, quasi-universality, manifestation of unity, usefulness to travelers, and all the rest. I hold that the people can say or sing these in Latin and can learn what they mean because they are always the same; these items are not necessarily meaningless noises. Their retention in Latin certainly involves difficulties, but I hold that these difficulties can be and should be overcome. There is no space to expound this matter further beyond saying that if these parts remained in Latin the Gregorian chants to which they are set would also be saved. If they do eventually come in the vernacular their chants would then become involved in the exceedingly difficult problem I shall now discuss, namely, those chants which are not mere melodic formulae but are genuine melodies.

Such melodies are used for many parts of the Mass. Some are of the type called "syllabic"; that is, they have (more or less) one note per syllable. Examples would be the Preface and *Pater noster* of the priest, *Gloria* VIII, *Credo* III, and *Sanctus* XVIII of the people. Other chants are of the type called "melismatic"; that is, they often include a series of many notes to be sung on one syllable. Examples of this type abound in almost every Introit, Gradual, Offertory and many Communions and in many "Masses" of the *Kyriale.*

If these are to be sung in English (or in any other living tongue) they raise a formidable issue bound up with the very genius of the Gregorian chant itself. It is this fundamental point which is the main rock of offense for those who oppose the use of the vernacular on musical grounds. Unfortunately it is somewhat technical; and because it is not likely that all who read these pages will be musicians I feel that I ought to attempt some explanation of it. With the minimum of technical terms and the maximum of generalizations it amounts to this:

There are certain characteristics which make a melody "Gregorian chant" and not just "ordinary music." It may suffice to list three of them:

1. Ordinary music is composed by using notes out of just two kinds of scale — major and minor. But Gregorian music is composed by using notes out of eight different kinds of scale, called the Gregorian modes.

2. Ordinary music has a regular rhythm, being built up of "bars" of the same length having so many "beats" each. But Gregorian music has "free rhythm" with no regularly recurring beats.

3. Ordinary vocal music, while it may try to express the mood of the words (joy, sorrow, pathos, and the like), has little or nothing to do with the actual *sound* of the words. But Gregorian music (apart from the formula type) is most intimately connected with the actual sound of the words. It grows, as it were, out of the sounds of the words themselves. This is true mainly of syllabic chant, but applies to some extent also to melismatic chant.

It is this third point which raises the greatest problem concerning living languages in the liturgy. It is also the most difficult of the three points for the ordinary nonmusical reader to understand and for the writer to explain intelligibly. But let us see what we can make of it.

The natural way of speaking any language involves variations in the pitch of the voice. People just do not talk "all on one note," but their voices go up and down. They make some words or syllables higher in pitch than others. But though this happens in all languages, it does not happen in the same way in each. Every language has a kind of "singsong" typical of itself. If you listen to a German reading out of a book, and then listen to an Italian doing likewise, you will easily recognize that the two languages sound utterly different, even if you do not understand a word of either. Each has a typical sort of "tune" or lilt called its "intonation"; and it would be just as unnatural for an Italian to read his language with a German intonation as it would be for a German to read his language with an Italian intonation.

For the intonation is an intrinsic quality of the language; the language is distorted if spoken with any intonation other than its own. Sometimes you may meet a foreigner who has mastered English grammar, syntax, and pronunciation perfectly. And yet there remains something about his speech which still tells you he is a foreigner. That "something" is his intonation. His voice goes up and down in the wrong places, and this gives him away.

Now intonation is very closely connected with (and is largely determined by) what is called "accent." Accent is a quality which brings some syllable into prominence. In English the prominence is achieved by stress — that is, by increased loudness. Take that word "prominence" as an example. The syllable "prom-" is spoken with just a little more force than the syllables "-in-" and "-ence." But in Latin it is not so. If we say the words *Pater noster* in such a way as to make the syllables *Pa-* and *nos-* a bit louder than those which follow we are pronouncing Latin with an English accent. The French, whose accents usually fall on the last syllables of their words, would make the syllables *-ter* and *-ter* a shade louder than those which precede them. They would be pronouncing Latin with a French accent. As they normally do this, their Latin sounds as queer to us as ours does to them. And both of us are wrong. For we are pronouncing Latin according to the accent and intonation of our own language, whereas we ought to pronounce it according to the accent and intonation of the Latin language. And in Latin this does not consist in laying stress on any syllables as compared with other syllables. All syllables ought to be equally loud. But the syllable bearing the accent ought, in

Latin, to be at a *higher pitch* (though no louder) or else a little *longer* (though no louder) than the unaccented syllables. It is these distinctions of pitch and of length which give to Latin its own proper intonation.

Now one of the peculiar characteristics of a Gregorian melody is that it brings out this typically Latin accent and intonation — or, at least, it does so very frequently, especially on the accents of the most important words in any phrase. An example: think of the Latin words and Gregorian melody for the *Salve Regina*. Almost everybody knows them. I will print the most important accents in capitals, thus: *Salve reGIna, Mater miseriCORdiae, VIta, dulCEdo et spes NOStra SALve.* Now sing those words to the tune, and you will find that the tune goes *up* to the syllables -GI, -COR, VI- and NOS-, while it allots a longer note (or a pair of notes) to the syllables -CE- and SAL-. Thus it brings out each accent, and *does it in the Latin way* by rise of pitch or increase of length, *not in the English way* by increase of loudness.

So also the Gregorian melodies used in the Mass have taken their shape and intonation according to the accentual principles of the Latin language. That is why they are so closely wedded to the Latin tongue. Any other language with different accentual principles cannot possibly fit those melodies as well as the Latin does. They were built for Latin and for nothing else. How could one fit English to such melodies?

There are two possible ways of tackling the problem; both have been tried and both are moderately successful as applied to syllabic chants, though both fail dismally when applied to melismatic chants. One is a partial solution which, of its nature, can never attain artistic perfection. The other is a radical solution which, of its nature, is capable of attaining artistic excellence. But the first retains the melodies as they are, while the second abolishes them completely. Let me explain.

First Solution. Keep the chants as they are, but fit under them English words which have precisely the same rhythm as the present Latin words. This is far from easy to do, and the resulting English cannot be a precise translation of the Latin but only a paraphrase of it. However, when the adaptation is well done the result is not at all bad and is quite worth singing. Its musical inferiority, as compared with the original, is so slight that it goes unperceived by all who are not themselves plainsong experts.

As an example take the setting of the *Salve Regina* devised by the monks of St. John's Abbey, Collegeville, Minn. "Mary we greet thee, Mother and Queen all merciful; our life, our sweetness, and our hope, we hail thee!" These words are not identical with "Hail Holy Queen, Mother of Mercy, hail our life, our sweetness, and our hope," but they do mean the same thing. And because they have exactly the same rhythm as the Latin words they will fit the original melody note for note. To the ordinary person the music sounds exactly the same whether sung with English or Latin words; but he vastly prefers to sing it to the English words because they mean something to him, whereas the Latin is mere sound. For the ordinary person (and, after all, the Church is largely made up of ordinary persons) the adaptation is entirely successful.

The musically cultured ear, however, is not quite satisfied. For something has happened to the tune which robs it of its artistic perfection. True enough, not a single note has been altered; but now accents in terms of stress have been introduced by the English words which, by the nature of the English language, are accented by stresses. Formerly these stresses were not there; the melody had a different accentuation which was not in terms of stress but only in terms of "liftings" in pitch and prolongations in length derived from the Latin words. To express it otherwise, a tune with Latin-type accentuation has been wedded to words with English-type accentuation; and the two cannot suit each other with absolute artistic perfection. Hence the musically cultured ear judges the melody to be better music when it is sung with Latin words.

Second Solution. Translate the Latin into the best possible English and thus have a new text. For this new text compose new melodies which will fit the English words as perfectly as the old melodies used to fit the Latin words. This can be done by applying to the English the very same Gregorian principles that were applied to the Latin; that is, use the Gregorian modes, use free rhythm, and arrange its melody so that its accents bring out the accents of the English words.

Such a plan has already been tried by some German composers for the German language; they have produced highly artistic chants completely Gregorian in character. For they have all the distinguishing characteristics of Gregorian — they have grown out of the very sounds of the spoken words, are in Gregorian modes, and have free rhythm. But, of course, they are completely *new tunes*; they are not the tunes hitherto printed in the Church's liturgical books. They are (or can be) perfectly satisfying from the artistic point of view, but their adoption would necessarily displace our present Gregorian heritage.

It would take too long to explain why neither of these solutions would work in the case of melismatic chants. I must content myself with saying that the English language (as also the German, though perhaps not the Italian) sounds utterly deformed and unnatural if some of its syllables are set to melismas (many notes on one syllable). I have studied not a few Anglican attempts to fit English words to melismatic chants and think many of them are quite revolting! And I believe that even the ordinary musically uncultured Catholic would find them so odd that he could not tolerate them.

After all this we are in a better position to answer the question: "What would happen to the chant if we get vernacular into the liturgy?"

I would say:

a) Those parts of the Mass that are sung to mere Gregorian formulae (Epistles, Gospels, Collects) could remain as they are.

b) Those parts sung to syllabic chants would have to be treated according to one of the two plans described above.

c) Those sung to melismatic chants could be treated only according to the second plan, for with them the first will not work at all. The present melismatic chants could, however, be retained for words not translated, such as *Alleluia, Hosanna,* and so forth.

We must conclude (and concede to the musicians) that if the vernacular gains official entrance into the parochial liturgy there is bound to be some aesthetic loss. If the present Gregorian melodies are kept but adapted to vernacular words (according to Plan A) their beauty is marred. But, one may add, this would be apparent only to musicians provided the adaptation is well made. On the other hand, if new chants are composed on Gregorian principles to fit vernacular words all the ancient Gregorian melodies would be lost to the parishes. And to this, one may add that the loss would hardly be apparent to ordinary Catholics since so few of these melodies are ever used in parishes. People do not miss what they have not had.

To comfort the musicians one may also point out that there is no intrinsic reason why new chants could not be as artistically satisfying as the old ones. Nobody could expect them to come into being in a perfected form — it would take time. But the same applied, a long while ago, to the Latin chants. We are told that Pope Gregory rewrote heaps of them; we are quite sure that the medieval monks did the same in later days. Generations passed before the Latin chants attained their present perfection. It may be that generations would have to pass before vernacular chants could attain a similar perfection. But they might do it much more quickly than the Latin chants did since our composers know far more about the science and art of music than did the men of old.

Be this as it may, it is certain that somebody has got to forego something in any case. There are three desiderata at stake: (1) intelligibility of the liturgy, (2) artistic perfection of the liturgy, (3) the existing chant repertoire. It is quite impossible to have all three of them simultaneously. The attainment of any two excludes the other. At present we have (2) and (3); and if both are retained (1) is impossible. If we chose (1) and (3) according to the first solution suggested, then (2) is impossible. If we chose (1) and (2) according to the second solution, then (3) is impossible. Hence somebody has got to go without something.

Those whose prime concern is a pastorally effective and living liturgy are convinced that this necessarily involves the use of living languages in worship, and they will never desist until they have obtained their object. It is then up to the musicians whether they sacrifice existing melodies or artistic perfection. Those whose prime concern is to retain the existing melodies together with their artistic perfection are convinced that this necessarily involves the retention of Latin, and will fight for this to the last ditch. On their principles (that the beauty of music is more important than the pastoral effectiveness of the liturgy) they cannot logically do anything else. Wherefore a head-on collision is inevitable.

For the very nature of the problem renders it impossible to find a solution satisfactory to both parties. If the musicians prevail it means that music, which should be the handmaid of liturgy, has become the mistress. If the liturgists prevail it means that in parish churches the musicians must suffer the loss of artistic perfection or else the loss of their ancient melodies (though they could retain these in monasteries). And since worship in parish churches is for parishioners, the conclusion should be obvious.

... 11 ...

The Church Composer and the Liturgical Challenge

REMBERT WEAKLAND, O.S.B.

THE quickened pace of the liturgical reform has presented un-precedented challenges to the Catholic composer, challenges that he must face with clarity of vision and sincerity of purpose if Church music is to progress. From among the recent trends one could single out the repeated emphasis on lay participation as the most exacting of the new demands. Although all the Protestant sects were forced to face the same problem in the sixteenth century, a similar situation has not arisen in the history of Catholic Church music since the Patristic age. In addition to contributing to a more active lay participation, the composer must face the added task of integrating such participation with the traditional role of the choir.

But one can perceive among liturgists a certain dissatisfaction with the way Catholic composers are meeting this challenge. Writers and lecturers have sometimes pictured the composer as an enemy of lay participation, insinuating that he fears that he would be deprived of his freedom of artistic expression if the choir lost its traditional position. The lack of sympathetic understanding by the liturgists, I feel, comes from an unawareness of the depth of the problems the composer must confront. It may be difficult to comprehend the specifically technical features with which the Church composer must grapple, but one can certainly understand the basic cultural milieu out of which the composer comes and in which he works, as well as the internal struggles that he, as artist, undergoes, even before he wishes to channel his talents to liturgical fields.

The lack of adequate response to the musical challenge cannot be studied apart from our general cultural background. The starting point is a survey of the state of the creative arts in the Church, especially in this country, to see who is available to take up the work. This is not enough, however. To help and encourage the first-rate composer to dedicate himself to liturgical music the liturgist will have to enter into the difficulties that all contemporary Church artists face in reconciling their talent with liturgical demands. These internal struggles must be appreciated and understood as realities to the artist. Since the Catholic artist's problems are not limited to music, they can be dealt with in more general terms. In addition to these, however, the composer faces difficulties specific to his field which the liturgist may be unable to grasp in their entirety. This does not make them less real to the composer, and they must be recognized as such by the liturgist. It is hoped that the latter, by searching for a clearer insight into the general and specific problems of the composer, even though finding himself unable to solve them, will be ready to exercise more Christian patience and charity toward his musical collaborator.

THE COMPOSER'S MILIEU

Liturgical art can be demanded only of great religious artists. The case of music is no different from that of painting, sculpture, and architecture. In surveying the culture of our day, we should begin by asking ourselves whether the Church has competent religious artists whom she can draw upon at this moment and to whom she can entrust the task she desires. Unfortunately, the liturgical reforms that we are witnessing today come at an unpropitious moment in the history of music in general and of Catholic Church music in particular. They come at a time when there are so few exceptional Church composers, almost none in truth in this country.

In the past few years Monsignor John Tracy Ellis has assumed the role of the devil's advocate in the lively debate on the state of our Catholic intellectual life. In this public discussion attention has been focused primarily on intellectual pursuits. What of the creative arts? If the picture drawn of the intellectual ghetto that has characterized our Catholic society in this country must be painted in somber colors, should not the canvas of the creative arts be left totally blank? If there is visible now the emergence of a new intellectual class in the Catholic Chuch, we can also say that there is the glimmer of hope for such an emergence in the creative arts. But because it is not simple to find a solution to the problems of the creative arts in the Catholic Church, there is more reason to be pessimistic about the future. I feel, moreover, that music, of all arts, is in the worst state in this country, and the picture in Europe is only somewhat brighter.

The deficiency must lie in the artist, not in the values to be communicated, not in the source of his inspiration. Art, one can assume, should deal with eternally significant problems and do so with insight and understanding. We can further postulate quite logically that the more significant the value communicated, the more profound the work of art. It follows that an artist whose whole life is saturated with what is true of God, man, and the mutual relations between these two, should produce the most significant art. The true Catholic (I dislike the qualifying adjective but it excludes the nominal or Sunday Catholic) must indeed possess that awareness of what is true of God, the universe, and human nature — not just human nature in itself, but human nature as raised to a new state of being and given a new purpose and meaning by Christ's redemptive act. Therefore, should not the Catholic be the best artist? And let me add: would it be possible for the truly Catholic artist to treat of any subject without seeing it in the new light of the restored order of creation that results from Christ's redemptive act? We return to our original question: Why do we not have first-rate religious artists — in our case, composers — to call upon in this moment of need? Where are the Bach and Schuetz Passions of our day? or the Mozart and Haydn Masses? or the Brucker and Verdi *Te Deum's*?

In answer we can say that no single individual can contain within himself the whole of truth about the universe and man in their relationship to God. We acknowledge this. A Dante and a Shakespeare may have come close to totality in their comprehension of human existence, but such beings are rare indeed. That combination of religious sensitivity and artistic skill which produced a Fra Angelico and a Palestrina is not an ordinary phenomenon in the history of art. The dilemma still remains if we seek, not the artist or musician of total comprehension, but one of at least partial comprehension. If the syllogism was correct, then, making allowances for human limitations, we can still ask why the Catholic is not first in the field of creative arts and music, and, more specifically, where the failure lies if the American Catholic is not the leader in the creative arts.

For the American Catholic the answer lies partly in his reaction to values, in his reaction to the inspirational sources, and partly in training. To say that our American Catholic art is lacking in inspiration is to say that it lacks religious maturity; it lacks that living, existential quality that true religious expression must have. We find it more readily in converts to Catholicism than in the so-called "born Catholics." Perhaps it is an inhibition that grows out of a false concept of tradition, or an inability to think out thoroughly a vital reality because it is merely "accepted." How refreshing the *Missa Luba* sounds to our ears! When we hear the loud beating of the drums and the crying out of the *Miserere nobis,* how different it seems to us — and also how genuine — in comparison with the hush-hush of our stereotyped *Misereres* that are found in every Catholic Mass setting since the Renaissance!

If, on the other hand, the deficiency in this country is one of training, it too can be attributed to a general cultural cause. Our Catholic colleges and universities in the past were inadequate in the arts. Only in the past few years has more and more attention been given to the need for such departments, but even now few schools are permitted the budget needed for exceptional departments in art, music, drama, sculpture, and so on. Few Catholics with talent, on the other hand, had the money required for study at the great secular universities and conservatories or to study abroad. If training is a deficiency, the remedy, we can hope, will be forthcoming in the next generation.

Unfortunately, since we have so few first-rate Catholic artists, both in religious depth and in the technical mastery of their art, we are plagued with the work of second-rate, hardly better than amateur craftsmen. The better artists have left the field of Church music to the mediocre. From these latter the liturgist can expect very little.

ARTISTIC PROBLEMS OF THE COMPOSER

If we ask why the better artist, both in this country and abroad, has been reluctant to enter the field of liturgical art, it is because of certain vital questions he must answer about his art and its relationship to the liturgy. The most difficult of these centers on the personal versus the collective, or the subjective versus the objective. The artist worries about this problem even before he enters the field of liturgy, but it is accentuated whenever he thinks of the liturgical demands. He will find among liturgical writers statements such as the following that will cause him to probe deeply into the whole rationale of his compositional processes.

> Whoever wants to take part in liturgical prayer must attune his personal individuality to the proper subject of public prayer, which . . . is no other than the Church. He will have to enter into the mind and the will of the praying Church, therefore, adapting his own mind and his own will to the Church's to bring them into definite conformity with the objective norm of liturgical prayer.[1]

The struggle to achieve such an attitude is not just a theoretical matter discussed by estheticians; it is a practical one which the artist must face within himself. He is reacting to the highly overpersonalized art of the Romantic period, while seeking some sort of objectivity or universalism. From the psycho-historical and sociological histories of art he is hearing more and more of his

---

[1] Gabriel M. Braso, O.S.B., *Liturgy and Spirituality*, trans. Leonard J. Doyle (Collegeville, Minn.: The Liturgical Press, 1960), p. 131.

role as the projector of collective thinking. Recent studies wish to make the artist think that he is like a prophet in his age, pointing out its tensions, sometimes subconsciously, and revealing them in symbolical form. To find the tension that his contemporary society is experiencing he must constantly be turning within himself — into his very depth, he is told — to bring out what is to be the expression of society.

The problem, then, is one of the artist's relation to society. In seeking to become its messenger he is actually succumbing to an even greater personalization than the Romantics espoused. The Catholic artist finds himself in somewhat of a dilemma before all this; he fears that if he does not acquire objectivity he is not being truly Catholic, truly universal in his art. He wishes to be a spokesman for his people, but he must also capture the quality of universalism which transcends time and place and which permits his art to endure.

In the field of music the esthetics of objectivity has had a strong influence on Stravinsky and Hindemith, but one wonders if this cannot lead to dryness and sterility rather than detachment. The effect of esthetics of this type on mediocre artists is appalling and ends in pseudo-chant, pseudo-sixteenth century polyphony, and other hideous imitations of past arts. Witness in the field of painting the sterility of the schools of Beuron, Maria Laach, and other pseudo-Byzantine attempts. Much of the neo-Gothic Church music written today, with its open parallelisms, Landini cadences, and harsh sonorities, although it sounds fresh to one unacquainted with the history of music, will seem but a passing fad to the next generations. Living in an age of excessive psychic analysis and concern, working under the prism of Freudian perspectives, can the artist ignore self and concentrate only on the representation of the object for its own sake?

Recently Brother Antoninus, O.P., summed up the picture in the history of Church art this way:

> Most of sacred art as it has come down to us, due to the historical conditions of Christianity, has been a kind of collective art. The major instances of sacred art which are commonly listed — Gregorian

Chant, mosaics, cathedrals — these three examples are all collective art. They reveal the ability of a religious movement or community to consolidate itself in terms of collective performances, probably over against the secular world, in order to insure the permanency of registration of its value. It was in modern times that that collective mould was broken at the Renaissance. Out of this new order emerged the individual ego freed from the collective. The problem became different. It is not possible for us to revive at this time anything like a liturgical art of collective authenticity.[2]

Must the artist look for this objectivity totally outside of self and the environment in which he is living? Must he totally efface self to find it? I think not. The longing for a medieval collective art is unrealistic and could only be satisfied if we Catholics were living in an artistic and cultural vacuum. The objectivity the artist is to express should be the outcome of the struggle between — or at least confrontation of — the living redemptive act of Christ operating in the Church and within himself and the contrary forces of the society in which he is living. If it were not so, all the periods of religious art would be alike. At times, as in the works of Palestrina and Fra Angelico, we are not aware of conflict; at other periods, as in the work of Monteverdi and El Greco, we feel deep tension. At all times the artist must realize within himself the true depth of the Christian transformation. If God dwells within him, then all searching into his own depth takes on new color, for he is searching not self but God in him. He need have no fear of self nor anxiety for objectivity in his art-product.

This leads us to another aspect of the general problems faced by the artist today, particularly when he wishes to create religious and liturgical art. In many aspects it is another side of the problem of objectivity. It is the problem of originality. All artists seek originality; they must be dissatisfied with the vulgar, the conventional, the commonplace. They seek new modes of expression, new techniques, new content. Here the Catholic artist frequently reaches a psychological impasse. The old themes seem

---

[2] Brother Antoninus, O.P., "The Artist and Religious Life," *The American Benedictine Review,* XI (1960), 234–235.

worn out; what new insights can he bring to them? In the works of many artists this leads to empty imitations of past art or to emotional frustration and the avoidance of religious themes. The artist without personal values preserves this struggle within him, is unable to solve it, and leaves us with the feeling that his work is never complete. It merely presents evil and does not bring it face to face with redemption. The frustration in the works of art of such moderns comes from the lack of resolution of tensions. The frustration of the Catholic artist, if he has within himself values needed for the resolution of the tensions, is his inability to give the old values new resonances in the face of the power, fascination, and oppressive beauty of the destructive forces.

Perhaps the solution to this lies in the ability of the Catholic artist in our day to face head-on the problem of Christian suffering. Much of the conflict comes from the search for false sublimations that are always found to be wanting. It is the attempt to avoid suffering and to find relief in false remedies that causes unresolved conflicts. To present suffering that is both human and genuine and at the same time triumphant is not easy for any artist. Perhaps Rouault has done so in his *Miserere* series, Claudel in *The Poet at the Foot of the Cross*. To present the cross as true suffering but always with the glorified figure of Christ shining through is a great, if not overwhelming, challenge to the modern creator. If he can learn this approach to the tensions of his age and add to it the full picture of Christian joy and dignity, he will not be afraid of lacking originality.

MUSICAL CHALLENGES

One might feel that in discussing the problems of the Church composer this long introduction on the general problems of the creative artist today is unimportant. The problems may be unimportant to the second-rate composer because he is oblivious to their existence, but they are important — vitally so — to the real composer. He must cope with them if he is to maintain his artistic sincerity and be true to his artistic instincts. The liturgist is dealing with a creative artist, not a hack who turns out mechanically something thought through by someone else.

In the light of these general themes we can take up the specific problems of the composer. When we say that the Church is least well equipped at this time to meet the problem of music for the liturgical reform, we do not mean that it is only because of a lack of numbers. The problem is much deeper; it strikes at the very concept of Church music and the relationship between Church music and musical composition in general. It also involves the relationship between the composer and his audience.

The first problem is immediately bound up with the question of objectivity and originality expressed earlier. The composer must decide at once whether he will write in the Romantic idiom or not. If he chooses to write in a modern style, will his music be labeled at once as secular? The reason for this dilemma is that the composer has inherited from the Baroque period a rift between the Church style and the secular style. The very concept of a *stilo antico* to designate Church music and a *stilo moderno* to designate non-Church music would have been unintelligible to a Renaissance composer such as Palestrina. But even to the Baroque composer these terms were only technical distinctions, not functional. He wrote Church music in both styles, but by associating the term *old* with *Church* he laid the groundwork for a split musical idiom that has continued to our own day. There has always been a difference between religious and nonreligious music even in the Middle Ages and the Renaissance. The difference, however, was not one of technique and style but of spirit, text, and function. The Baroque distinction has resulted in the notion that certain specifically technical features are characteristic of Church music. There developed a pseudo-Palestrina style that reached its height in the eighteenth and nineteenth centuries and that became more and more identified with Church music. I say pseudo-Palestrina style since it had long since lost contact with the purity of line and consummate vocal form which characterized that master and became a shell into which the typical Romantic melody was poured. The Church composer today inherits this idea that Church music must be technically and stylistically different from secular music, not just esthetically. This has left him very often in the camp of the ultraconservative and has forced him into a sterile and academic idiom.

Because he is working in a medium that demands audience contact, the Church composer finds himself at another, even greater disadvantage. Since the time of Beethoven, there has been an ever widening gap between audience and composer. This does not mean that the pre-Beethoven composer wrote for the masses, but rather that he wrote for a limited patronage audience that understood and appreciated his artistic communication. The rise of the large concert audience presented a new phenomenon in the early Romantic period and saw at the same time the growing distance between composer and public. This lag has continued to grow until in our day it has reached its maximum distance. Such a lag presents an additional problem to the Church composer who must worry about both the exigencies of his art and its communication to the masses. If he compromises by retaining the Romantic idiom, he fails to meet the challenge of his art, consigns his music to the refuse pile of banality, and will soon be forgotten. No composer today can write significant music, religious or secular, in the Romantic tonal idiom, even though this is the music that is still consumed by the masses. He must be of the twentieth century. If he loses touch with contemporary existence, he condemns himself to artistic futility and barrenness.

It would seem that the crux of the problem of technique goes deeper, however, for the modern Church composer. It is one of separating technique from esthetics. So frequently Catholics have fallen into a correlation of these two elements in a way that has been not only injurious to their work but annihilating. It is this confusion that restrains the composer from attempting to use new techniques in Church music and makes him feel irrevocably bound to the Romantic or pseudo-Palestrina idiom. Much of this comes from a false interpretation of the *Motu proprio* of Pius X.

The passage in question is the esthetic judgment Pius X makes concerning Gregorian Chant — a judgment that for its time can be considered as nothing but the extraordinary insight of an enlightened and divinely guided pontiff — and his judgment of the manner in which the sixteenth-century polyphony resembles the Chant. *"The more closely a composition for church approaches in its movement, inspiration, and spirit the Gregorian melody, the more sacred and liturgical it becomes; and the more it is at variance with that supreme model, the less worthy it is of the temple."*[3] In the next paragraph he added: "The above-mentioned qualities are also possessed in a very high degree by classical polyphony, especially of the Roman School, which reached its greatest perfection in the sixteenth century in the works of Pierluigi da Palestrina."

The phrase "approaches in its movement, inspiration, and spirit the Gregorian melody" has been interpreted by some to mean "as long as it is based on a Gregorian theme." Composers have too readily assumed that by using as a basis for their compositions a Gregorian theme they will make their music liturgical. Such an assumption is far from true. The number of compositions in the history of music that have been based on Gregorian Chant themes is legion, and the presence of such themes does not make a composition by, let us say, Rachmaninoff more, nor less, liturgical than one by Tournemire. Much of the insipid music that is heard in our churches today is considered appropriate simply because it is based on Gregorian themes, but it is far removed from the inspiration and spirit of Chant. What must be sought here is not an imitation of the technical aspects of Chant, nor necessarily a borrowing of its melodies and encrusting them in a Romantic, or, more frequently, an Impressionistic, frame, but rather the Chant's simplicity and balance.

I would not risk the statement that all pieces based on Chant themes are bad music. Far from it. I am only pointing out that because a piece is based on a chant theme it does not of necessity thereby participate in the inspiration and spirit of the Chant and

---

[3] This passage has been translated from the official Italian text (*Acta Sanctae Sedis,* XXXVI, p. 329). The Latin translation that is printed on page 390 of the same volume is less explicit.

become liturgically appropriate. I would say, however, that most of the contemporary pieces based on Chant themes tend to be academic and artificial. It takes a genius to avoid such sterility.

Under the influence of the same esthetic judgment of St. Pius X, other composers have returned to the modal system in search of a technical feature that will make their compositions liturgical. This too can only be an illusion, a confusion of technical features with esthetics. What makes a sixteenth-century composition by Palestrina participate in the spirit of the Chant is not that it is modal, since the music of the thirteenth, fourteenth, and fifteenth centuries, secular and sacred alike, used the modal system. Modality should not be taken as a synonym for Church music. It is true that some modern writers have used the greater possibilities of the modal system, in comparison with the minor-major, to advantage, and have produced works of some originality, ingenuity, and artistry. Yet one cannot help feel that the modal system has seen its day.

Still others have accepted the postulate that what makes sixteenth-century polyphony good Church music is certain imitative and contrapuntal stylistic traits of Palestrina, Victoria, and others of that period. This has already been alluded to. Few composers adhere to a slavish imitation of the Palestrina style as codified in the works of such a modern scholar as Knud Jeppesen, but they continue to write a kind of sham counterpoint based on an harmonic structure that would be worthy of the pen of Tschaikovsky or Verdi. No composer today can ignore the trend toward contrapuntal thinking, but he must avoid the idea that his counterpoint should be technically similar to that of Palestrina in order for it to be suitable for the Church.

If composers have too readily assumed that their music will resemble the movement, inspiration, and spirit of Chant if they use its themes and its technical features, or those of sixteenth-century polyphony, they also have assumed too readily that certain technical features have no place in Church music because they have been associated with a different, although not necessarily secular, esthetic. I am referring to the use of serial technics. The first uses of the tone row in Schoenberg, Berg, and Webern connected it with the fragmentation and discontinuity of Expressionism. But just as the tonal system could produce compositions as esthetically diversified as Bach's *St. Matthew's Passion*, Beethoven's *Ninth Symphony*, and Wagner's *Parsifal*, so too the serial technique has within it a variety of possibilities that are as yet hardly explored. It is the idiom that is the furthest away from the masses but the most challenging and enticing to a modern composer. In many respects such a system can bring us esthetically closer to the objectivity of Chant than its Romantic antecedents could, for it can be more intellectual than emotional, more compact and unified than overpowering and extreme in contrasts, more purely musical than sentimental. This does not change the fact that it will remain for some time misunderstood and unappreciated, even by many musicians. Nor should we exclude from possible future Church use all electronic music and *musique concrète*, if these areas become means of valid musical communication and not mere gadgets for experimentation by mathematicians and physicists.

The answer to the stylistic problems the Church composer faces cannot be stated in oversimplified terms. He cannot be told merely to write music that the people will understand, to write in a style they are accustomed to, and to disregard more advanced techniques. Most of the new *populo* Masses written with such a criterion in mind will soon be obnoxious to the people themselves and, we can be certain, will be unknown to the next generation of Catholics. Nor is the answer to tell the composer to write in the old style but somewhat "spiced up" with an occasional dissonance. The market is crowded with this kind of pseudo-modernism. Neither of these solutions can be propounded to a *bona fide* artist.

Some may ask why the modern composer, in looking for a basic idiom for lay participation, does not draw upon the folk-song repertoire. Such a solution sounds deceptively easy. In this country at least, there is no folk-song tradition with which one could work. American jazz is not folk music; it is a recent, cultivated

phenomenon that is admired by but a small portion of the population, and considered as conducive to prayer by almost no one.
The Negro spiritual comes closest to the folk-song category, but
here too we know the spirituals in their developed art form. They
did not, moreover, spring out of the roots of a whole nation, but
of a small ethnic group within it; they have been more listened
to than sung by all of us; they were not taught to us by our mother
as she in turn had learned them from her parents; they are not
traditional airs we sing at weddings, funerals, feasts, and so on.

The only solution that will have lasting effect is to work toward
a closing of the gap between the composer and the masses, but
without forcing the composer to compromise on artistic standards.
Since he is working in a period of great fermentation and experimentation in musical styles, we must be patient with him. We
must be willing to grow accustomed to the new sounds with which
he is working without rejecting them *a priori* because they are
foreign to us. He must be permitted to have his works reach the
people by performances that are adequate and sympathetic. In
writing for the people, whether it be hymns or *populo* Masses,
let him use the most recent developments and techniques, but
keep in mind that the Church is no place for experimentation for
its own sake and that the performance of his works must be
feasible by vast numbers and untrained ears and throats. The
fusion of artist and people can only take place in this way. It is
true that the masses will always lag behind the artist, but at least
the latter will have the privilege of seeing the compositions of his
youth and early middle age performed and loved when he has
advanced to new things.

But, above all, he must be certain that he is perfecting himself
both as artist and as saint — as artist so that every work he writes
for the liturgy will be truly great music, as saint so that he will
be able to penetrate more deeply into the liturgical movement
he is trying to bring alive by his music. In doing the former he
is following the admonition of St. Pius X that Church music must
be "true art, for otherwise it will be impossible for it to exercise
on the minds of the hearers that efficacy which the Church wishes

to obtain in admitting into her liturgy the art of musical sounds."[4] In doing the latter he is modeling his life on the words of Pope Pius XII: "But the artist who is firm in his faith and leads a life worthy of a Christian, who is motivated by the love of God and reverently uses the powers the Creator has given him, expresses and manifests the truths he holds and the piety he possesses so skillfully, beautifully and pleasingly in colors and lines or sounds and harmonies that this sacred labor or art is an act of worship and religion for him. It also effectively arouses and inspires people to profess the faith and cultivate piety. The Church has always honored and always will honor this kind of artist."[5]

---

[4] *Motu proprio,* I, 1.
[5] *Musicae Sacrae Disciplina,* II, 28–29.

...12...

The Spirit of Modern Sacred Art

DANIEL BERRIGAN, S.J.

I

HISTORIANS of art seem agreed that Christian art was created for the sake of the community, and that the idea of community is an irreplaceable clue to understanding its inner spirit. Its finality became clear, in fact, rather soon after its forms had been welcomed into early Christian temples; the purpose of sacred art was simply the conveying of insight into the destiny of man, as Christianity viewed him. Art was to teach and deepen a sense of fraternity in a community which through sacramental mysteries led men to eternal life.

Early Christian art worked toward engendering this vision of things in three ways. Through iconography, it presented certain sacred personages — Christ, Mary, the saints — exemplars of holiness in the Church. These icons invited the believer to ponder his unity with those Christians who stood for the highest ideal of holiness. Then, through narrative art, the Church recalled to memory the deeds of Christ, and the crucial events of history, in both Old and New Testaments, which had led man toward salvation. Third, through symbolism, art embodied the truth of the Church in a rather hidden and ambiguous way, which could be understood only by those who resonated with the belief of the artist.

The particular character of sacred art — its connection with a community at worship — both implied a problem and stimulated its solution. The artist had for his task the conveying of a sense

147

of mystery. He was portraying realities which could not be directly communicated in visible forms. It was impossible, for instance, to convey directly the meaning of Incarnation, or Eucharist, or Redemption. So the artist must search out methods that would penetrate appearances, and reach the meaning of the transcendent mysteries which his art served.

Methods like realism or literalism were excluded on principle. The artist has helped to realize their futility by the general climate of the sacramental worship of the Church, where, men believed, grace was communicated under symbolic and dramatic signs. The Church herself was in fact the structure which contained in principle both the artist's problem and its solution; for she was a cosmos both of symbols and realities. It was natural, then, that the believing artist would feel at home in a religious world which simultaneously veiled and revealed the divine realities.

It seems remarkable that in all these early efforts to portray the Christian mysteries, artists never fell into a contempt or suspicion of natural forms of this world. We note nothing of dualism in the early Church art; rather, it seems like one long hymn to the grandeur of creation.

Of course, it was the character of the mysteries themselves, above all the mystery of Incarnation, which helped the artist keep from veering off into the empyrean or the inhuman. Man's salvation was an act of God in time, in this world. Mystery had taken a visible form among men; God had entered the world of nature, and claimed that world, human and subhuman, for His own. In the light of this divine approval of man and his world, a double rhythm met in this early art; a strong sense of the sacred, and a humanism which was friend to man.

This art expressed the Christian sense that there was an unbreakable link between the historical coming of Christ and the visible world He came to. Christ had come as a man among men. He was bound, as is every man, to the wheel of time; He had strong organic roots in the world of man — a family, friends, subjection to bodily and mental growth. And He had *become* man, not merely in the process of being conceived and born, but in that immensely more subtle and mysterious experience by which the child becomes self-aware, and passes into psychological manhood. In all this process, He had been utterly immanent to the human scene, to such a degree, indeed, that the perennial search for an understanding of man — through anthropology and psychology — must go forward by way of Him. The mystery of Christ was in fact central to human history, to the point that in Him alone lay the solution to the mystery of man.

The mystery of Christ, the mystery of man — these were the world of sacred art. There were in the truest view, not many mysteries, but one; its name was Christ. It was encompassed by the majestic course of history, wherein God had come, had saved, and had announced His imminent return (1 Cor 2:7; Rom 16:25). Through the visible world, the artist set about portraying the height and depth and breadth of the Mystery. He avoided on principle, as unworthy of his task, images that would reflect great physical detail, anatomical exactness, or physical beauty. This Christ of early art was neither Apollo, nor a merely pitiful victim of evil, nor a humanist's ideal. He was the One, rather, whom the Gospels and the Church's consciousness recognized: Son of the Most High, passionately dedicated to the honor of His Father, passionately involved in the fate of His brethren. His love and His sense of honor had led Him to a staggering act of obedience. He had laid down His life, an act of holy altruism which at one stroke restored the broken order of moral reality, and assured the Father, in the love of His Son, of the love of all men (Jn 3:16).

Being man, Christ died, and being God, He arose from the dead. And in His victory over death, the whole universe becomes conscious; it "groans in a common travail" (Rom 8:22). It senses, however dimly and painfully, that evil has not written the last word about man; that this provisory life in time, incredibly noble and incredibly debased, is the prelude to an existence where the sorrows of the human family will be set aright, and God shall be Father at last, and we His sons (1 Cor 15; Ap 22:13–20). Early Church art achieved an ideal expression of this Christian sense of history. It could achieve this because it had the incalculable advantage of being close to its own sources of life. It had no history to unlearn or to destroy, as later ages would have. It could turn naturally to Bible and liturgy, not merely as documents and prescriptions but as evidence of living persons recently in its midst.

It was about A.D. 100 when Christians, who had previously borrowed their methods from pagan art, began to develop specific material in their own way. The methods of this art, as we have suggested, were narrative, symbolic, and iconic.

As an illustration of the three, we might consider the image of the Good Shepherd. Prior to the year 100, the image had been drawn from ideal pagan types such as Apollo. The figure was beardless and youthful, and related to the Roman country myths. But in the second century, the image began to assert itself as strongly Christian. As *narrative* art, it told the story recounted first in St. John's Gospel. The Good Shepherd is pictured tending His sheep, protecting them from harm, returning to the sheepfold with the lost sheep in His arms. Implicit in this art is a narrative sense which related the believer to his own history, as recounted in the word of God. The shepherd theme invited him into the Old Testament, in which God had often spoken of Himself as Shepherd of Israel (Gn 48:15; 49:24), of Israel as His flock (Is 41:11; 63:11), and of the multitude of shepherds, the priests and elders who held their charge from Him (2 Sm 5:2; Jer 10:21). The variants on this theme were extremely rich and suggestive. They sprang from a pastoral civilization of kings and prophets, and in one master image allowed for the widest range of personal contemplation.

Again, the shepherd theme would relate Israel to Christ Himself. And this had been His literal intention. Believers could discern, under this image, the Christ who was faithful to the charge of the Father (Jn 10:14), who knew His flock with the self-sacrificing spirit and fidelity of a Savior (Jn 10:14), and who finally sealed His consecration to men in the gift of His life (Jn 10:15). And to the image of the Shepherd, too, other themes tended to gather and cling, because of the implications of the parable: the theme of the stranger and the hireling and the despoiler, all of them distinguished from the shepherd by their defection from love and duty (Jn 19:8, 10, 12).

But it was in its relationship to the Passion that the shepherd image was most heavily charged with implication for the artist. The virile and sacrificial love of the Good Shepherd stood on its natural ground in the bloody hours of His agony — and, according to John's unitive view, in the consequent victory of the Savior. It is instructive in this regard, that although John places the shepherd narrative as an introduction to the Passion, the words of the parable relate almost as strongly to the resurrection. "If the Father loves me, it is because I lay down my life to take it up again" (Jn 10:17).

In fidelity to this rich theme of John, we note the early icons of the Shepherd, showing Him now wounded, now glorious, now uniting both themes, bearing the wounds of glory.

It was inevitable, given the method of John, that the figure of the Shepherd as narrative character should tend to merge with the figure of the Shepherd as symbol.

An art which claimed kinship with the Fourth Gospel would come almost of necessity to the symbolic world in which John habitually moves. So when the shepherd theme becomes prominent in early frescoes and mosaics, we are not surprised to note that the Figure of the Galilean hills is related to the great Protector of His Church, the governor of its unity and peace. This Shepherd of art is both sign and reality; He is both historically realized and historically present. He is the "form" which the transcendent God assumed for Incarnation; but He is also, in this art, the abiding Presence promised to mankind through all ages (Mt 28:20).

Given all these adumbrations of the Shepherd figure, the symbolic content often tended to merge with an iconic one. There arose in time, a kind of "ideal" figure, whose rhythms, stance, and surrounding symbols became a kind of sacred commonplace. The Shepherd figure became somewhat remote; it was related more and more strongly to the aura of the Apocalypse, to victory and freedom from human conflict. The Shepherd was deliberately set apart from the turmoil of human life. He was apotheosized; He shared in that transcendent Name which the Father had conferred on Him in His resurrection (Phil 2:10-11), *Kyrios,* great God, the Yahweh of the Old Testament reigning over the new. His guardianship of the Church was an absolute and invincible sovereignty. In such images, the figure of the Shepherd loses all character of labor or task. It is seated, as a sign of "eternal rest" (Heb 4:19). And the central Figure transfigures all it touches; the elements of this world are drawn into His paradise; He is surrounded by triumphant martyrs and virgins. The sheep are quietly grazing or approaching the Shepherd for nourishment; they too breathe the tranquil air of eternity.

In this development, the interrelation of art with community faith is strikingly clear. It is true to say that early Church art developed its general intuitions until these could worthily express the mystery of Christ. But this development, which we may see in the art of the third and fourth centuries, was also influenced by the development in the Christian community of a heightened sense of identity.

The statement is worth pausing over, if only as a way of suggesting that sacred art is an imaginative mode of the faith itself, that Christian faith is lacking its complete expression until its dynamic content has been gathered and projected in an artistic way.

And the faith, in order to be true to the laws of man's nature, demands a passage of time in order to arrive at its term, to change the direction of man's thought and values.

From a variety of sources, we are coming to realize that our view of the Incarnation and the Church, as data of faith, has been far too automatic. We have seen these central occurrences as abrupt divine epiphanies on man's scene; so abrupt, indeed, that one would conclude that God, in His action in history, had shown little sense of man's situation; of man's heart, of his bewilderment before the unexpected, of his fidelity to his past, his reverence for the shape, however imperfect, of his religious history.

But we are coming to realize the deep and gradual form of

God's action: to realize that the word of God won its hearing in the early Church only after a mysterious human preparation.

What had been true throughout the Old Testament remained true in the first centuries of the New. God waited on certain nodal points of human history, to bring His word to man's un-distracted attention. And art must follow an analogous law; the great art of the fourth and fifth centuries awaited an understand-ing of the insights of Paul, an understanding balanced by the view of salvation of which John had written. And these two writers, primarily mystics and symbolists, came to their view of Christian life, and offered it to the Church, only after pondering the earlier traditions about Christ.

As the Church came toward the fifth and sixth centuries, it set about engendering powerful fundamental images, types to whose fuller understanding believers were coming, under such differing influences as St. Augustine's Platonism, the Pelagian heresy, and the conversion of the Emperor of the West. It is worth noting, too, that during these great centuries, the Church was content merely to suggest symbolic forms, rather than to canonize or dictate them. The faith exerted its pressure on the mind and heart of the artist by polarizing his imagination around certain Christian images, which arose rather spontaneously from an understanding of Scripture and liturgy. But in practice, the artist was his own master; as long as he knew what he was about, and had a sense of realities, as opposed to dreams and mere vagaries of taste, he was free to move forward into his own vision of things. We have only to think of the variations of the Panto-crator image, the *chi-rho* symbol, the many centuries of the Mary-Church analogue. The faith was a ferment of these commonly understood symbolic forms — forms that freely and slowly took shape, interplayed, and nourished one another. In this way, the symbols seminated the artist's imagination, without in any sense being presented to him as final data or material for copy.

The freedom granted the artist in his use of subject materials is an extremely valuable clue to the greatness of this early art. Dictation by the Church of forms or methods would have led inevitably to suffocation of spirit, to the killing and sterile conventionality from which later centuries were to suffer.

Perhaps a distinction between convention and tradition would be helpful at this point. Historically, conventional art is typical of an age that has won its struggle, or thinks it has won. The faith and life itself cease to present themselves under the virile forms of community search, altruism, a religion strongly colored by this world's rhythms, passionately determined to be present to human history. We speak rather of an art that "has the truth" — not as a spur to further intellectual development, but in the manner of a pale and sterile possession. Such art takes its starting point, not in objective truth, the wrestling with apprehension of the sacred persons and events, but in the emotional temper of its age — whether this is good, bad, or merely irrelevant to main issues. Conventional art thus tends more and more to withdraw and dissociate itself from life; it is ill at ease before the real. And from its inner emotional poverty, it conjures up images of Christ whose only purpose, in coloring, line, and form, is the reassurance of sick men. Conventional art is primarily medicinal; it assures the ill that all is going well, as well after all as one can expect, given that Christians are forbidden to expect very great things of themselves or of their world. One thinks, in regard to such art, of the phrases of Nietzsche, which he wrote in reference to the petit bourgeois world of his time — an image "always alike, very small, very smooth, very obliging, very wearying."

Our question here has to do with the complementary value of subject and object, with the necessity of keeping a balance between these two — the artist's experience, and the world of objective mystery. In insisting on the metaphysical, real, intensely historical content of the Catholic mysteries as a starting point for sacred art, there is no intention of denying the necessity of the artist's experience, of a rich and freely ranging subjectivity. In a true sense, as Aquinas insists, art is in the artist. It will never issue from him with any substance or style until the mysteries have undergone a mysterious, living submission to his imaginative powers.

Still, artistic subjectivity cannot be the choice, in the sense that the artist is freed from obligation to elements of the world of man. In the case of the religious artist, these elements of reality would include the influences of his modes of worship, of the Bible, of sermons and devotional habits, together with the way in which these things are integrated and made a part of his sense of God.

Already formed (or deformed), this artist's sensibility comes to bear on a new artistic stimulus. He may be a liturgical man, in the sense that the mysteries have worked their renewing power within him through the rhythms of the Church year, through his understanding of the Eucharist, and his experience of it and its social consequence. Or he may be diminished as far as these resources go. He may be a worshiping fossil, his inner life stiffened in a gesture of worship which is simply a charade of reality. Whatever the case, these resources of habit and attitude are brought to bear on the artist's task — they are tools infinitely more real and crucial than the pigments that lie before him.

In the case of early Church art, we are speaking of a subjectivity that is eminently objective, in the sense that it has been formed by the real world — the real world of time and consciousness, the real world of mystery. Such a sensibility as this can now be trusted with freedom in its work; it is at home in the midst of the sacred. Having absorbed reality, and become the disciple of the truth, the artist is free; he is master of the truth, his own teacher, the one whose task is to form the imagination of the Church of God.

The lack of this true freedom is strikingly evident in conventional art. We note that in its work the free play of symbols is suffocated, until a kind of psychological fixity emerges. Artist and audience have connived to the point where they are giving their lives to a childish quest for a certain "type" of Christ or Mary or the saints. It is, generally, a type which will not be allowed to shock or disturb man's regressive tendencies. Rather than strike the believer with the truth of reality, such art will assure men that all is well. It tends to reduce the truth of Christ to a static projection of man's own immaturity and fear of growth.

We have an example of this pseudo-tradition in the religious painting of the Renaissance. Religious art of this period did not draw its inspiration from the Christian sources at all, but directly and thoughtlessly from pagan models and its own material pretensions. It was a misguided attempt, more or less conscious, to adjust the world of faith to a questionable view of worship, of human history, and indeed of the nature of the Church herself.

In the dignified and objective icons of the early Church, by way of contrast, we sense the presence of a tradition that is close to life; projecting the transcendent holiness of God, the images have no comfort to offer to childishness. They refuse to draw the community into a static, self-approving world, where the divine offers man nothing more than a projection of his unpurified hope. Instead, these images invite man to an adventure — to the summons of God. It is a summons which, in every case, had formed the sacred personages of history, had brought them through human travail and labor and crisis to the hour of their transfiguration, when they themselves became types of that living holiness which is at once the Father's gift and man's triumph.

In this early art, the artist's view of his work was a rather instinctive corollary of his view of the faith itself. For both his faith and his art forbade him to create his own world, in a dissociated sense. His faith was a free act by which he entered an order of things whose creation was the will of God. The mysteries stood free; they did not require man's approval. Entrance into their world was an exercise in creaturehood; it implied discipline, submission to reality.

So, as artist, the believer was servant of the mysteries. He was to be true to personal experience, but his loyalty was rooted in the truth of things as they were, in a world which in no sense waited upon his nod, a world whose existence God had declared in His Son. The artist was not free to assemble a world of mystery peopled with the ghosts of his own hopes, his longings, or his ideals. Elements of human consciousness which are indispensable to any art — dream life, fear, memories, and personalized symbols — these were welcome to the task, but they were to be entirely subordinated to the realities themselves. The validity and power of the artist's experience depended on the degree to which faith had submitted before reality, allowed it to be purified and elevated by both the word of God and the liturgy.

II

To come to the sacred artist of today, we find his work returning, after a long historical stalemate, to the sources we have spoken of. And the movement is by no means anything so useless as a retreat to the past; it has all the marks of a genuine revolution in its own right. Many influences and currents of thought have brought about this happy event; among these the liturgical and biblical movements must always be spoken of.

The Church is once more becoming conscious of herself as an organism of corporate worship. She is willing to admit, and to say publicly, that her full voice is neither that of a caste nor of an operatic choir. It is the voice of her people. She is also newly emphasizing that the Bible is her own — hers in authorship, hers to use.

So rude an awakening of the household has shaken the artists too. With regard to the past, it would serve no real purpose here to detail the centuries of vapid, dissociate art which have preceded our own, and which we are in process of disowning.

Since the late middle ages, religious art has been largely and progressively shunted to studio and drawing room; it has become the adjunct of the prie-dieu, instead of the impassioned flowering of a public, virile, and believing mind. It has been an art of good taste and little substance; if it served for anything, it was only to heal over the wounds by which Christians were marked, the wounds of their amputation from their greatest possessions, the altar and the word of God.

We are led, in this regard, into a deeper question than that of inferior art. The art of any period must of course be seen as a symptom of public illness or health. And since the fourteenth century, the Western Christian community has been quite simply ill — not irrecoverably, but still seriously; and its religious art is the syndrome of its illness.

The sickness we speak of reaches deep into the person. Man was sick because his living relationship to God, to his community, and to the organic world had been weakened or even excised.

If it did nothing else, the religious art of these centuries helped men live with their illness. It was an art designed quite literally to be hung in sickrooms. It kept alive Christian memories and hopes in a subjective, devotional way. But its cumulative effect was disastrous, because it beckoned men further and further into their sick reveries. It helped them forget that there had ever been realities like community, anamnesis, sanctuary action. In time, such art was so completely absorbed by the social organism that it became autogenous. It formed artists who lived in a moral world of defense, fear, emotion, and moral passivity. And the circle was now completed; sacred art eventually sprang, directly and simply, from the unrelated person. It became subject to every wind and tide of emotional climate, deprived of a communal liturgy, without the voice of the biblical word to purify and discipline it.

It goes without saying that art always has the cumulative effect we speak of; it injects into man's soul a new sense of identity. And during the periods under discussion, religious art slowly convinced man of the rightness of individuality in religious life, of subjectivity gone riot, of a religious sense centered in the pitiful or defeated or emotionally comforting aspects of religion. Subtly formed by the pressure of such art, man was pledged to a religion of the Renaissance ego; to be faithful to himself now, he must forget, in any living sense, his altar and his brethren.

So much for the past. We can turn from it with relief, grateful in a qualified way for the present situation. Sacred art today shows all the symptoms of a half-awakened person; it is slowly searching its way through a darkened dwelling, fingering good things and bad, perceiving well and poorly, speaking wisdom and nonsense. Still, in the main, its instincts are sound; it is discovering, almost by blind touch, a sense of those periods of history when art stood firmly about man's altar as the larger eloquence of the community action.

We note too that sacred art is being powerfully affected by the new look which the layman wears today. It is the astounded look of a man, used to hack work and poor returns, who has suddenly been singled out for an enterprise of great moment. One has only to reflect on the revitalizing of the lay scene brought about by Catholic thinkers since Newman — of Peguy and Maurin, Bloy, Undset, de Chardin, Greene, Jungmann, Murray. Their thought has given clear and unmistakable signs, and they all point in one way.

And this invitation to the layman to take responsibility for his Church is something more than a theme of ecclesiastical rhetoric. (It is also that, to the point where public utterances commonly feel obliged to make a rubrical gesture in a new direction.) Lay spirituality has bitten deep into many lives, and spurred the renunciations of unusual men and women in many directions — in the mission fields, in the intellectual apostolate, in an urgent sense of presence and love on the human scene. We would have perhaps to return to a golden age of lay greatness — a period like that of the Alexandria of Origen, or the Antioch of the Apostles — to find a like phenomenon.

It would seem reasonable to suppose that this focus of attention on the lay community should react strongly on the art of the Church. And this is exactly what has occurred. Men who live in the mind are beginning to produce and welcome an art of the mind. Recurrent images of modern sacred art have turned from the sentimental and the olympian, as useless to express the sensibility of man today. Art speaks now of the Mystery of Christ as one of Friendship and Brotherhood; He is the One who repairs in silence and in secret the noisy selfishness of modern life, the One whose holiness has not despised the life of man, but has rather urged Him more deeply into that life.

When this view of Christ comes to focus on the crucifixion event, the death of the Lord is freed from softness, pietism, and defeat. It speaks rather of a loving act offered on behalf of the brethren; a death which, by a paradox beyond all analysis, is also a victory for man, since it is the death of God, undergone on man's behalf.

Such art is the gift of a community in living contact with its own sources — in our case, with Bible and liturgy; the art of such a community will become uncluttered and pure. It will contemn the subtle and enervating self-approval which makes the sacred mysteries into the servant of what is essentially irreligious and inhuman.

In regard to the influence of contemporary thought on the religious artist, two areas seem especially significant.

The first of these is related to the idea of community.

Two great world communities are in fact seeking to perfect and express man's life today. To speak of modern life, men are conscious, to an impassioned degree, of a process within their hearts and minds, leading them toward world unity. At its best and noblest, this world sense of man expresses itself in the conviction that man simply cannot be himself in isolation — whether his isolation be one of culture, of political life, or an apartness from the free exchange of the world's goods. Without the experience of all men, shared on a world scale, man simply is deprived of the potential of his own nature. He may be affluent or intellectual or religious-minded, but he is still something short of human; he cannot know himself, he cannot even act as himself.

And this sense of interlife is becoming so spiritually and painfully real to a large portion of mankind that it sweeps aside the old structures that have in principle denied world unity, or which are seen now as merely preparatory to it.

It is clear what must end; it is by no means equally clear what must be brought into being. For the first time in his history, man as man finds himself without a blueprint for an immediate, brutal, and universal need. But in this search for a structure of unity, he is consoled by the sense that his hope is imperious enough to be able, in good time, to express itself in a workable way, to bring its world structure to birth. And some would not hesitate to say that on the bank of New York's East River the work is well begun.

Now this instinct for the unity of man, one would like to suggest, is a paradigm of the instinct of the Church. If her sense of unity must be called religious, the term in no sense implies a deprivation of human feeling. Her will to unity cannot in fact be understood simply in her ecumenical work, or her missionary activity, or her charity toward the underdeveloped nations. These are only the refractions of a light which sheds its radiance in all the declivities of human life. What the Church is searching out, in the final analysis, is not numbers, or the nations, in an isolated religious sense (whatever that term would mean). It is not as though the Church looked only to a day when the peoples of the world would arise in unison to say *credo* to her belief. She looks for this, but what she looks for implies much more.

What her instinct for unity is searching out is simply man himself. She wishes to learn of him and to teach him, to speculate with him, to marvel with him, to be silent with him. She wishes to make peace with his spirit and to irritate his spirit; to have access to the life of his mind and to welcome him into the life of her mind. If she wishes him well, it is not in order to hang the trophies of her victory before the door of her temple, as though in winning his allegiance she had been forced to slay him. If she wishes him well, her wish surpasses all egoism and clericalism; her wish for him is one with his noblest wish for himself, enriched beyond his capacity for hope, surpassing his longing for human greatness, for wisdom and inner harmony, even while it frees his energies from the prison of time and this world.

It must be stressed that these two currents of unity, the Church's and modern man's, are not simply juxtaposed. They, in many ways, are mutually interpenetrating. The urge of man to work out his destiny within a community of the nations has already within it the ferment of the Church's hope. She also is one. She also seeks to be more perfectly one. And this unity of hers, at once an agony of hope and a joy of achievement, goes before the unity of men, in time and in place, and lives there as the secret of man's triumph.

Now these two parallel movements, each seeking the perfection of man, each profoundly affected by the struggles of the
other, are of the greatest moment to the sacred artist. On the
one hand, the Church invites her artists to contemplate man, to
see him not as a scholastic vacuum, nor an abstraction, nor a
tourist on the scene of history, but as he is, in his present scene
and time, his mind and heart stirred by a wild hope he has never
dared entertain before. The artist must see him casting off the
impediments of the past, the illness that for eons had been in the
human bloodstream, and had assured man that he could be himself apart from his brother.

But he could not; and he knows it. He knows it, as Unamuno
would say, not as

> the legendary featherless biped of Aristotle, the social contractor of
> Rousseau, the economic man of the Manchester school . . . or if
> you like, the vertical mammal. A man neither of here nor there,
> neither of this age nor of another, who has neither sex nor country,
> who is in brief, merely an idea. That is to say, a no-man.

Man knows it, rather,

> . . . with all the body and with all the soul, with the blood, with
> the marrow of the bones, with the heart, with the lungs, with the
> belly, with all life. . . .

Men are one in origin and destiny. The believer, knowing this
in a world of torment and struggle, has something to offer men
which is simply unique. It is a capacity for understanding, an
assurance whose light he can bring to bear upon the habitual
darkness in which man struggles. His faith allows the artist, in
a sense, to stand at the end of the struggle; he knows its outcome. But, with no less strength, his faith also summons him to
stand within the struggle, to share it, to have part in its outcome.
In a way that is simply closed to the nonbeliever, the Christian
can sense both where men stand today and where his human
instincts are leading him. He can be oracle of man's hope because
he is artist and because he is believer.

So much for the contribution of the Church to the formation

of a world sense in her artists. But what of the contribution of world thought to the same imaginative life?

The Church knows that religious faith is not something so simple as a dogmatic possession of formulas. Such a Cartesian notion of revealed truth would be killing not only to art, but to all theology. Formulas of truth as such have little or no impact on man's life until they have been intensely thought through by a living mind, which has submitted to each step toward synthesis, and has cast the truth in forms which speak not only to man, but from within man, from within human life. When this process, which is one of both mind and heart, has been faithfully adhered to, religious truth becomes charged with a human incandescence. It shares in the full life of man; it is colored by his subconscious, it lights his symbolic life, his unformulated hopes. Now the sacred, calling to man from the center of his being, lends its radiance to all his life: to friendship, to the rhythms of his moods and mind, to his sexual activity, to his search for a human meaning within events.

In such a way, religious faith deals gently and respectfully with all those potential unities which underlie men's nature, and which are, in sum, his human equivalent. Faith does not come to force issues by an arbitrary law; rather, it is a search on behalf of man, joining forces gently with his best instincts, for the sake of "whatever is good, whatever honorable, whatever noble" in human life.

This will to work with man, to be true to him, not to construct formulas or to create spiritual enclaves — these things give the religious artist a sense of the human, and make him indispensable to the human scene. Dealing with his world in the way we speak of, he comes to know from within life the hope of man for his own unity, a hope at once signified and effected by the Church. And the artist, knowing man, knows that the master symbol of man's hope, the unity of the faith, must be given a variable symbolic form. The fact of religious unity cannot be generalized, or expressed once and for all, or merely summoned as a matter of a great past. Neither can it be conceived as a blunted apologetic weapon. It must rather share gently and peaceably in man's own human journey; it must be marked by a working humility which seeks not only to teach man, but to learn of him. By such a humility, the sacred gains entrance into the world of man's spirit.

Such art as we speak of draws both on the truth of the Church and the truth of man; it suggests to men, by indirection, that their hope is already realized in a sacred order of things. Pius XII spoke of this aspect of sacred art. He realized that the ancillary service of art is not restricted to its service of the sacred; rather, it serves man by enlarging the human instincts of believer and nonbeliever alike.

The second area of thought that seems relevant to the sacred artist today is that of psychology.

Perhaps no civilization in history has moved with such determination into man's inner world as has our own. Man today wishes not only to dominate his physical universe, but to explore and master his inner processes. And this determination is fruitful in many areas of his life. To speak only of art, the data of psychoanalysis and psychology have been of immeasurable importance to the art of the past fifty years, both in Europe and America.

Through these advances in speculative and experimental philosophy, the artist has a new and real source of knowledge at his disposal. And this is not all. The world of man's inner life is not so simple a thing as a new continent or planet, accessible to the tools and methods of the physical sciences. To learn the inner life of man, and the imaginative rhythms and symbols of this life, is an immensely more complicated task than any which man's prior knowledge had prepared him for.

But the difficulty of the task is matched by the rich rewards it holds out — and perhaps the richest rewards of all are offered to artists.

Through the data of experimental psychology, the artist has new knowledge to bring to bear on the spiritual processes of man. As psychology implies, it is no longer merely the visible world of nature that is at man's service in ordering and projecting his experience. The inner worlds of hope, fear, love, strife, and anguish — all are the instruments of man's experience to his community and himself.

In former ages, the mind of the artist was by and large that of an objective observer. The mind examined and interpreted its world, without itself being examined or interpreted. In this sense, the artist's mind was the instrument of the external world; it was dependent on the outer world both for its stimulus and its criterion of reality. The faculty of "art," as Thomas called it, was exercised in remaining relatively impersonal and unaffected before one's own inner processes. The mind and heart reached through their experience to a world outside them.

Now obviously we speak in a relative sense here. There have always been highly subjective artists, romanticists, artists with a dense mystical content. But such artists could not be called typical. When they appeared, it was from outside a general tendency of their age.

But, in modern times, art takes a new direction, an inward one. And this inward tendency operates in two ways. First, a highly charged subjectivism assembles the visible world before the artist, to be rearranged according to the radical meaning which his mind wishes to impose on reality. Things exist to serve his inner vision of the real.

But something more startling occurs, too, and for the first time as method of art. The phenomena of the organic world have become the instrument of man's mental processes, in the sense that the universe is seen as a parable of the spiritual state of man. The visible world does not exist for itself, even as object and ground of man's esthetic activity. It exists to be manipulated by the ordering faculties which lie within man. The world is servant of art, to the degree even that it serves its purpose only when man has imposed on it the rhythms and order of his inner life.

We are speaking here of a tension between outer and inner worlds whose balance will always be a central problem of art. In former periods, we could speak of the relationship of the artist to his world, as though in his art he were encountering the "real," a rigid and objective absolute. But now the artist is seen encountering the world as a fluid, relative, and mutable stream of phenomena, subject to his ordering powers.

The world as servant of man's vision can be dissociated, distorted, cubed, impressionized, and so on, precisely because the artist holds sovereignty over it; it exists for him; it has only the meaning he imposes on it, a meaning which his consciousness tells him is the extension of his own destiny.

Now this strong emphasis on the psychic life, as affected by and affecting man's world, is important in our discussion of religious art. It is always true, in a general sense, that no artist can remain at a distance from a strong current of sensibility around him, and hope to produce art of any value. But, more to our point, it is important to insist that certain truths of the Christian faith itself invite the religious artist into the psychological world.

One thinks, by way of example, of the subjective element in the dynamics of grace. The Christ who acts on the believer aims His action straight at the existence of man. This new life of God in man which we call sanctifying grace is not concerned with conveying fringe benefits, or with short cuts through the anguish and sorrow of life. It wishes, simply, to fulfill man by means of a gift which is altogether interior to man. Grace is designed to elevate man to a new existence; but in doing this it perfects him as man, by infusing into the radical powers of his being new ways of knowing and loving.

Now even this sketchy statement of Catholic belief would suggest that the sensibility of the artist is deeply affected by the action of God, by grace. Grace welcomes the gifts of this artist; there is simply no such thing as vacuumatic grace — grace which leads man apart from the main currents of human life. In the deepest sense, grace rather leads man more fully into the community of man; it makes him more aware of himself in his world. If his community suffers, so does the believer. If his brothers are unredeemed, without hope, at the mercy of the powers of this world, without recourse to faith, appalled by the silence of God — if these things are true of man today, the artist knows these sufferings too. He knows them by heart, because he holds man at his heart, and man's mind in his own. He has walked that way, and has shared man's chalice — so his hope is not a mean-spirited search for comfort in the midst of a famine, it tastes the despair of those around him. This faith is no arrogant sense of superiority to others; it is aware of their doubts and hesitancies. The Christian is a man of compassion. He is aware that the grace which restores and elevates his life also leads him within the life of all men. And he does not come to humanity as though to the "foul rag and bone shop of the heart." He knows that in spite of all the despair and degradation of man, human life is bathed in the inaccessible mystery of the Christian summons, in its whole majestic course — the Christian is summoned from the guilt of unregenerate Paul, through mental suffering and uncertainty, to his place in the communal destiny of mankind, in Christ. In the light of this mercy, the artist is invited to interpret and order the surface brutality and chaos of modern life. Grace in him means fidelity to the events of life, to his community experience, to a search for the meaning of reality — a meaning which is impervious to every eye except the one which sees.

...13...

Vespers and the Devotional Service

JOSEF A. JUNGMANN, S.J.
TRANSLATED FROM THE GERMAN BY HUGH M. RILEY, S.J.

In the liturgical life the Divine Office occupies a position parallel to the Mass, and of the different Hours of the Office we feel nowadays that Vespers is the most solemn. In any case Vespers is the Hour with which the people have some degree of acquaintance. Solemn Vespers on Sundays or Feast Days, sung in the ancient chant exactly according to the *Antiphonal* of the Holy Roman Church, the climax coming at the *Magnificat* amid rising clouds of incense, this is beyond doubt a very inspiring ceremony!

Actually a greater popularity, presumably in all countries, is enjoyed by Devotional Services, consisting of prayers and hymns in the vernacular. In most places these Devotions have taken the place of Vespers except on some greater Feast Days. But it is maintained that such devotions are not the prayer of the Church, that they are not the liturgy and that consequently they cannot effect grace as the liturgy can.[1] Therefore they do not enjoy the esteem of most exponents of liturgical renewal, a good deal of criticism is leveled against them, and they are at the very most tolerated. And yet they enjoy the protection of ecclesiastical authority. The encyclical *Mediator Dei* speaks of them, of the Marian Devotions in May, of the Sacred Heart Devotions in June, of the Novenas and Tridua and the like, and praises them.[2]

---

[1] Cf. G. Martimort, *L'Eglise en prière* (Paris, 1961), p. 9: "Ces *pia exercitia* ne sont pas la liturgie, n'en possèdent ni les grâces ni la garantie." Cf. also J. Miller, *Fundamentals of the Liturgy* (Notre Dame, Ind., 1960), p. 24 f.

[2] *Acta Apostolicae Sedis*, 39 (1947), 586,

Still there is a notable difference in tone between Vespers and Devotions. Where does this difference in character originate? What is the reason behind the difference in evaluation? Is it really true that in the Devotional Service it is not the Church praying, and that such a Service can be only to a limited degree a source of grace?

At one time Vespers was a popular Devotion. To understand this we must of course look back to the time before Vespers had attained the complex form of today. In the *Apostolic Tradition* of Hippolytus of Rome, written about the year 215, the course of an *Agape* is described. It took place in the evening. A cleric, where possible the bishop himself, presided. Those brethren in the faith who were especially poor or abandoned were invited. The *Agape* was linked with a Devotional Service, with the original form of what we call today Vespers. First the light was blessed (Vespers likewise often used to begin in ancient times with the so-called *Lucernarium*). The presiding cleric gave the greeting *Dominus Vobiscum*, invited to prayer, and spoke the blessing over the light. At this point, or after the *Agape* as well, psalms were sung. A deacon intoned the first psalm, the priest the second, and the bishop, should he himself be present, the third. For this purpose those psalms were to be chosen which bore the title *Alleluia*, that is, psalms to which the faithful who were present could answer with *Alleluia*. It was therefore a common and quite popular Devotional Service involving active participation of the faithful who had nothing more to do than to answer in the same way as they do today in a litany.

From the Antioch region we have the report of an actual evening service of the fourth century which was conducted as follows. First came the 140th psalm (because of the verse *"Dirigatur . . ."*), then the deacon prayed in the manner of a litany for the catechumens, for those tormented by the evil spirit, for the baptismal candidates, for the penitents, and after these had departed there were lengthier prayers for the faithful themselves. To each of these petitions the people answered with the *Kyrie Eleison*. At the end, the bishop himself spoke a prayer and a blessing over the people.[3] Quite similar to this was the structure of daily Vespers customary at this time in Jerusalem. Here the children come in for special praise for answering the individual petitions of the deacon with a resounding *Kyrie Eleison*.[4]

In the time after the fourth century, Vespers, as well as the other hours, underwent two further stages of development. The actual Vespers began with a reading from the Holy Scripture, which is known today as the *Capitulum*. After this there was singing, generally in the form of a psalm during which the people were invited to answer with a brief acclamation, as has been described above. Gradually this responsory psalm was condensed to what we call today the *Responsorium*, which became a matter for the cantors. Even today in most instances a *Responsorium* follows a liturgical reading, as is the case after the readings at Matins and after the *Capitula* of the Little Hours. In more recent times a hymn has replaced the *Responsorium* at Vespers, or, in the case of the monastic office, has been added to the *Responsorium*. It is, however, an old rule that Vespers concludes with the oration of the presiding priest.

In more recent times a preliminary step has been added to this central part, three or four or (in the Roman Vespers) five psalms, which were actually intended only as a prelude. One finds the same preliminary in oriental liturgies as well. In one place we discover a rubric that only after these psalms are finished does the clergy enter. What preceded, therefore, was for a long time simply a popular Devotional Service in a rather restricted sense. But then again, even the subsequent central part was in the true sense a celebration with the people, at least as long as the possibility remained for the people to take part in psalms sung responsorially.

Only when the people present at Vespers could no longer understand the Latin language did the change take place. In the northern, Germanic-speaking countries this was the case right from the outset. Vespers continued to remain in Latin and thereby

---

[3] *Constitutiones Apostolicae*, VIII, 35–37 (Funk, II, 544 f.).

[4] *Peregrinatio Aetheriae*, c. 24 (CSEL, 39, 72 f., Geyer).

turned into a purely clerical Hour. One cannot say that this made Vespers more liturgical. Granted that the clergy is the governing part among the Christian people, the clerical part is not of itself alone the Christian people, not of itself alone the Church, and, after all, liturgy should be the prayer of the Church.

At this point the discrepancy was resolved by this idea: the clergy prays "in the name" of the people; the entire Office even is executed "in the name" of the people. And when the changing times compelled the clergy to replace the common singing of the daily Office with private recitation, the idea was further elaborated that every individual praying the Breviary prays "in the name" of the Church and to that degree he prays liturgically. The faithful no longer participated in Vespers. (The same thing happened in the case of Matins, the morning Hour which we now call Lauds. The other Hours were always restricted to the clergy.) If the faithful were present, it was merely as hearers on the solemn occasions when Vespers were sung or even embellished with choral song. Gradually, however, a substitute began to take shape and this came from different directions.

The monastic orders early developed their Office in such a way that the 150 psalms formed the basis of the Office. Each week the whole psalter had to be sung. In this way the monks, generally speaking, came to know all the psalms by heart. But even in the monastic orders this would not be the case among the lay Brothers, much less among the simple faithful. In more ancient times the simple faithful did know individual psalms by heart, for example, a morning psalm (Psalm 62), an evening psalm (Psalm 90), or individual psalm verses, responses to which many people still know even today: *"Adjutorium nostrum in nomine Domini"; "Domine exaudi orationem meam."*

But the popularity of the psalms began to diminish. Even the monks and clergy had for the most part precious little interest in the more exact meaning of the individual psalms. This explains why they were not especially bothered by unintelligible verses. These were holy words; they were sung with reverence; they were in themselves alone the praise of God. Finally they learned how to put a New Testament meaning into the Old Testament psalms: they were the voice of Christ or the voice of the Church.[5] But why not express immediately with New Testament words what one wanted to express, at least in places where the content of the psalms could not be made meaningful without recourse to some such method? Thus, as early as the eleventh century, many monasteries made it a rule that the lay Brothers should pray one *Our Father*, which they understood, in the place of each psalm, of which they understood nothing. They prayed as many *Our Fathers* as the monks in choir prayed psalms. And so, beginning with the twelfth century that form of prayer grew up in which 150 *Our Fathers* were joined one after another, corresponding to the 150 psalms. Somewhat later, when it was felt that this hardly corresponded to the dignity due the *Lord's Prayer*, the *Our Fathers* were replaced by 150 *Hail Marys*, and the *Lord's Prayer* was placed only at the beginning of each group. Thus the Rosary came into being. And finally in recent centuries people began to pray the Rosary too in church, under the direction of the priest, in exactly the same place and with the same function that the psalms of Vespers once had. This practice is still current in many country churches in Austria and Bavaria. Again, this was prayer of the Church, at least of this local church, and in places where the custom was approved or regulated by the bishop, it was prayer of the episcopal Church, of the Church of Passau, or of the Church of Brixen, in the same way that the Vespers previously described were prayer of the Church of Antioch or of Jerusalem.

Of course such a Rosary Service had one disadvantage: the structure from the outset was not arranged for common prayer in the church, but was actually a form of private prayer. By the simple, continuous repetition of the *Angelic Salutation* the individual was to raise his heart to God through the Mother of God. The word of God was contained only in these recurring words of the prayer. The proper rounding-off was also missing, the concluding oration of the priest, for example. But even the Rosary could be worked into a larger framework. This structure could be

---

[5] P. Salmon, *Les tituli psalmorum des manuscrits latins* (Rome, 1959).

at least as successful as that of the oriental liturgies which contain
the *Kyrie Eleison* repeated 40 or 50 or even more times. It could
also be as successful as the Mozarabic liturgy was in building into
a penitential service the people's *Indulgentia* cry repeated three
hundred times on Good Friday.[6]

Yet the Rosary is only one of the many forms of evening Services to develop in different places since the late Middle Ages.
Other roots are contained in Vespers itself. It was a custom, cultivated especially by the Dominicans, to conclude individual Hours,
especially Vespers, with the *Salve Regina*. Now this was a prayer
text, or more correctly a song, which gained quick popularity and
to which further texts were soon joined. Here too people wanted
to honor the Mother of God. The devotional form became separated from the Vespers and became independent. There arose in
German dioceses the "*Salve* Devotions," in France the "*Saluts*."

The veneration of the Holy Eucharist which increased in the
later Middle Ages underwent the same development as did these
elements of Marian piety.[7] During the Hours or at the conclusion
of an Hour, especially at the end of Vespers, the Blessed Sacrament was exposed. A hymn praising the Sacrament was intoned
and Benediction concluded it. This manner of venerating the
sacrament was also made more elaborate, especially in conjunc-
tion with the Marian Devotion. Thus the term "Benediction Service" or simply "Benediction" became common. It was held on
Sundays and Feast Days, or on the evening previous, and in many
places was held even daily. That was the form in which the
Church in this place, in this congregation, in this parish prayed
in the evening hours.

The confraternities, too, which from the later Middle Ages
flourished in many places, developed their own forms of Devotional Service. To a great extent they were structured according
to the scheme of a daily Office, in the series of the five older
Hours, and were divided into five sections. Each of these sections
was composed like an Hour, beginning with "*Deus in adjutorium*"

[6] *Missale Mixtum* (PL, 85, 427–434).
[7] P. Browe, *Die Verehrung der Eucharistie im Mittelalter* (Munich, 1933).

and closing with an oration. Missing, however, were the psalms, which had simply lost their popularity.[8]

Instead, another element of the Office had increased in popularity, the alternating prayer at which the people had only to repeat the same answer: the litany. The litany belonged to the liturgy under different forms. Under the form which is current among us as the Litany of the Saints it was the most popular procession prayer, in which the ancient traditional invocation *Kyrie Eleison* could alternate with other responses. Under a briefer form the litany belonged to the Office even at the time of St. Benedict, where it came as a preliminary to the *Our Father* or to the concluding oration. In the *Rule* (Chapter 9) the conclusion of the night Hour is thus given: *"et supplicatio litaniae id est Kyrie Eleison."* Even the remaining hours had and have even today in the monastic Office such a conclusion, albeit abbreviated. And the *Roman Breviary* as well, still our official book, has the *"Kyrie Eleison, Christe Eleison, Kyrie Eleison"* at the opening of the *Preces* in all the Hours, although these, too, since 1956 have only rarely been used. These litanies have come to a certain extent to be familiar prayers and have undergone various developments. Actually the litanies in use today are approved by the Holy See and even have a place in the appendix of a liturgical book, the *Roman Breviary*. From this standpoint, then, there is no reason why their character as prayer of the Church should not be acknowledged when they are publicly recited in an evening service.

Now there is only one question that remains to be answered. From a theological point of view where precisely does the difference lie between Vespers and an evening Devotional Service? If they are held in the proper manner and by those persons who are deputed to worship, and if they are directed or conducted by a representative of the hierarchical Church, then both Vespers and evening Devotions are prayer of the Church. It can hardly be denied that the Church is more present in an evening Devotion legitimately directed by the priest and held in common in the

---

[8] Th. Schnitzler, *Stundengebet und Volksandacht: Brevierstudien* (Trier, 1958), 71–84, esp. 80 f.

Church than at Vespers as they are whispered by the priest alone out of his Breviary.

One thing is clear. According to the concept of liturgy as specified most recently by the Church,[9] the term "liturgy" cannot be applied to such evening Devotions in view of the fact that they are not contained in the books approved by the Holy See. It can also be said that their composition differs from what we usually associate with the prayer of the Church, as for example in a liturgical Hour. This, however, is not true of all devotional forms, as for example the above-mentioned Devotional Services of the confraternities, and it is also not true of the litanies. And it might also be noted that the liturgy did not and does not always have the forms we are accustomed to expect in it. In Vespers for Good Friday not only is the introductory *Deus in adjutorium* missing, but the reading and the hymn or *Responsorium* are missing as well. Even the liturgy itself has forms today whose structure leaves something to be desired, because in the course of time heterogeneous elements have worked their way into it or valuable parts have disappeared. If this were not the case, there would have been no necessity for undertaking a thorough reform of the Mass of the Presanctified for Good Friday. This was obviously undertaken because the traditional form had become weighted down by extraneous elements — a fact that critical studies had long previously established.

But there is an objection that can be raised against the value of the Devotional Services. It is the question of their content. What is frequently missing in them is the grand structure of the actual liturgy. The liturgy almost always focuses its attention on God's majesty, into whose presence we enter through Christ our Lord, and in remembrance of His mysteries, made present to us in the Church year. The Devotional Services on the other hand are often content to remain at peripheral objects. Frequently there is little concern in them for the liturgical year, as is the case with Devotions in honor of a saint or for some particular intention. It should be understood, though, that while certain Devotions like

---

[9] *Instructio*, 3 Sept., 1958, n. 1.

Novenas and Tridua come under this indictment, the essential idea of the Devotional Service itself remains unimpeached. The Devotions can have a correct composition as well as an infelicitous one, just as is the case in the forms of the liturgy. If there is need for reform in the liturgy then it should come as no surprise that the Devotional Service, which is frequently left to itself and which rightly enjoys a greater freedom, stands in need of some, perhaps even a great deal of reform. It is the office of the bishops to supervise and regulate the Devotional Service,[10] just as the liturgy in the strict sense is supervised and regulated by the Pope and the Holy See, for the Devotional Services are divine worship of episcopal right just as the liturgy is divine worship of papal right.[11]

As a matter of fact in many countries like Germany each diocese has its own book approved by the bishop, the hymnal or diocesan prayer book. In these the order of the Devotional Services, with their hymns and prayers and especially with the participation of the faithful, is set forth throughout the year. The faithful have this book, or as parish property it is placed in the pews. With the coming of the liturgical movement the numerous new editions of these diocesan hymnals and prayer books manifest a tendency to provide the Devotional Services with a structure which is suited to the essence of the Church and of the Church's divine worship and in this way to bring them to approximate more closely the form and content of the liturgy.[12] They very frequently begin with a reading from Holy Scripture; then comes a hymn and responsory prayer. The oration of the priest forms the conclusion.[13] This structure can recur more than once in a Devotional Service. When contrasted with a canonical Hour of the Roman liturgy the most significant difference lies in the absence of the psalms. In many countries, however, the psalms are beginning to be rediscovered. A real movement for psalm singing has

10 CIC, 1259.

11 J. A. Jungmann, "Liturgie und pia exercitia," *Liturgisches Jahrbuch*, 9 (1959), 79–86.

12 J. Hacker, *Die Messe in den deutschen Diözesan-Gesang-und-Gebetbüchern, von der Aufklarungszeit bis zur Gegenwart* (Munich, 1950), 25 f.

13 J. A. Jungmann, *Die Liturgische Feier* (third edition, Regensburg, 1961).

arisen. It had its origin in France and rumor has it that it has appeared on the American scene! In point of fact the psalms are not indispensable for every liturgical act. In the baptism of children, for example, they are completely absent even today. In the first two centuries the psalms were not yet the prayer book of the Church. Like the other books of the Scripture, they were used only for reading.[14] The Office of the Byzantine liturgy is still composed basically not of psalms but of hymns. Thus the use of the psalms cannot be considered an indispensable essential of an ecclesiastical Devotional Service.

It was a wise decision of the Holy See when the *Instruction* of September 3, 1958, brought all religious forms which lay outside of the liturgy in the strict sense of that word under the heading *pia exercitia*. Not only does private prayer come under this concept, but all forms of prayer which occur in common, even if held in a church under the direction of an authorized minister, as long as they are not contained in the Roman books. The encyclical *Mediator Dei* speaks of these, too. It not only extends protection to them, but considers them of such value "ut in liturgicum ordinem quodammodo inserta censeantur."[15]

Thus the essential difference between the Vespers of our liturgical books and the evening Devotions of the different dioceses and countries is simply this: that from the new arrangement of the Breviary in the year 1568 the Vespers of the liturgical books are stamped with the authority of the Supreme Shepherd, while the Devotions are subordinated to the charge of the respective bishop. In both instances we have divine worship, prayer of the Church.[16] The only difference lies in the plane on which the two are organized. In the liturgy the unity of the Church comes into clearer relief, in the Devotions greater provision is made for the capacities of the people of the Church. Where the greater religious value

---

[14] Balth. Fischer, *Die Psalmenfrömmigkeit der Martyrerkirche* (Freiburg, 1949), 3.

[15] *Acta Apostolicae Sedis,* 39 (1947), 586. The English translation weakens this idea in rendering it: ". . . to be an addition to the liturgical cult" (n. 182).

[16] Cf. Karl Rahner, "Thesen über das Gebet 'in Namen der Kirche,'" *Zeitschrift für kath. Theologie,* 83 (1961), 307–324.

lies depends upon where love and surrender to God are better realized.

Whoever grants that the individual bishop by divine right directs his diocese, his Church, will also understand that alongside of the forms which are praiseworthily established in a unified way for the most important acts of the Church's divine worship, there can and ought to be forms peculiar to the particular country, to the diocese, to the local church, which are not for this reason of inferior status. Today more than ever it is becoming clear that total uniformity cannot be the highest ideal in the organization of the Church, indeed that the Church in individual countries will flower only if it has the opportunity to unfold to some extent its own individuality. No one will deny that many problems still remain to be solved in this area. *Mediator Dei* observes that it would be a mistake to want all these Devotional Services reformed according to the pattern of the liturgy (*"ad liturgicorum rituum rationes ac modos"*).[17] This is quite understandable. The Hours of the Office developed and were cultivated for more than a thousand years as a purely clerical liturgy and contain many elements (for example the antiphons) which in this form would be ill-suited to the mentality of the ordinary faithful. On the other hand Pius XII wishes in the same place that the spirit of the liturgy (*"sacrae liturgiae afflatus"*) manifest itself in the Devotional Services. This is exactly the point we wish to make in these considerations.

The deserving pioneer of the liturgical renewal in America, to whom this book is dedicated, has also made it his constant concern that divine worship have a form whereby the people would be brought to true piety. He has also written a book, *The Mass of the Future*. It would be a most timely enterprise if some younger follower would write a book, *The Devotional Service of the Future*.

---

[17] *Acta Apostolicae Sedis*, 39 (1947), 587.

...14...

The Year of Shepherd and Flock

MARTIN B. HELLRIEGEL

I. *ITS MEANING AND AIM*

HAVE words more awe-inspiring and world-transforming ever fallen on human ears than "on the night before He died," on that blessed Thursday evening when the Lord commanded His disciples: "THIS — DO YE — IN COMMEMORATION OF ME"? Three most precious gifts were then bequeathed by the Good Shepherd to His flock: (1) His Eucharist, (2) His priesthood, and (3) His sanctifying year, that continuous "commemoration" of the life, death, and resurrection of the "Mediator between God and men" (1 Tm 2:5). And — *"currens per anni circulum"* (hymn at Christmas) — when, in the "cycle of the year," the flock gathers around the altar to "commemorate" with thanksgiving the work of the Lord's redemption, this work becomes present for the "glory of God in the highest" and for "the peace of men of good will."

In his *Foreword* to the German translation of Prosper Gueranger's *L'année Liturgique,* the then rector of the Mainz seminary, Dr. Johannes Baptist Heinrich, wrote — it was on the feast of the Sacred Heart, 1874(!) — these significant words: "The liturgical year is nothing less than the continuous renewal of the divine story of our redemption, the life of the Man-God and His Kingdom, symbolically and sacramentally enacted in the sacred cult, and presented in a mystic, yet most concrete reality, so that we may grasp it more securely and drink it in more livingly." Had men but listened to these words of wisdom, written almost a century ago, we might have less of that soft piety which delights to

179

dwell in the alley of emotionalism, and witness a more virile readiness to march on the King's highway of heroic service to Christ and His Church, doubly necessary in the crisis through which we are passing. And would not the message of Pius XII in *Mediator Dei* (1947) have received a far more cordial reception?: "The Liturgical Year, devotedly fostered and accompanied by the Church, is not a cold and lifeless representation of the events of the past, or a simple and bare record of a former age. It is rather Christ Himself who is ever living in His Church. Here He continues that journey of immense mercy which He lovingly began in His mortal life, going about doing good, with the design of bringing men to know His mysteries and in a way live by them. . . . By means of His inspiration and help and through the cooperation of our wills we can receive from Him living vitality as branches do from the tree and members from the head, thus slowly and laboriously we can transform ourselves 'unto the measure of the age of the fullness of Christ' (NCWC edition, § 165). *Sentire cum Ecclesia,* fasting and feasting, mourning and rejoicing with Mother Church as she journeys along the path of Christ's year, ought to be the motto of every one of her children.

II. GRADUAL DEVELOPMENT

a) The Lord's Day

At the Last Supper the Lord Jesus merely planted the holy "acorn" of the Church's year, leaving its growth to the good soil of His Mystical Body, the Church, in which He lives, through which He teaches, sanctifies, and leads His flock to the Father. Above all, He left its growth to that fecundating dew of the most Holy Spirit who "will glorify me, because he will receive of what is mine and will declare it to you" (Jn 16:14). One of the early "declarings" of the Spirit of the Lord is seen in the sprouting of the first shoot, the "Lord's Day," the day consecrated by the Son's glorious resurrection and the coming of the Spirit of Truth whom He sent from the Father. "And on the *first day* of the week, when we were assembled to break bread . . ." (Acts 20:7)! Already the Last Supper command is being carried out: the Eucharist is celebrated, the priesthood of Christ is functioning, and the first branch of the Church year, the Lord's Day, unites and gladdens His redeemed flock. "Christians no longer observe the Sabbath but the Lord's Day on which also our Life arose," writes Ignatius of Antioch in the first century.

b) The Pasch of the Lord

Then sprang up from the life-filled "seed" its second shoot, the Paschal Mystery, the yearly re-enactment of the Lord's world-redeeming death and triumphant resurrection, His "passover" from death to life, from the world to the Father. As in the springtide of nature, so also in the youth of Christ's year, "storms" would not be wanting, the storms of chilly controversy, until the General Council of Nicea (A.D. 325) paved the way to a final settlement of the dispute concerning "the date of Easter" by ordering that the paschal solemnity must be observed by all throughout the world in the same blessed night, and that this night and its dawning day must follow the fourteenth day of the paschal moon, that "blessed night in which all believers in Christ, delivered from the filth of this world and freed from the shadow of death, are renewed unto grace and made partakers of eternal life" (Exsultet).

c) Preparing for the Pasch

The precious "acorn" continues to assert its vital strength. Three new branches appear beneath the second shoot: first, that of Passiontide; then, that of Lent; and, finally, that of the seventeen pre-Lenten days, from Septuagesima until Ash Wednesday, all three for the purpose of "purifying God's household by the yearly observance of Lent" (Collect, First Sunday of Lent), making the faithful more faith-full, sinners again God's beloved children, and catechumens holy neophytes from the font of life "in that truly blessed night in which heavenly things are united to those of earth and things divine to those which are human" (Exsultet). It was fitting indeed that, enlightened by the Holy Spirit, the Church should arrange a season of penance preceding that most blessed night in which our "life is hidden with Christ in God" (Col 3:3); a period of fast, prayer, and almsgiving for a real *metanoia*, a sincere return to God, the Father, "who by a wonderful condescension of His mercy gave up His Son that He might redeem the slave" (*Exsultet*).

d) The "Fifty" Days

In the meantime the second, the paschal branch, grew stronger and developed into the "seven times seven days" of paschal rejoicing and paschal living, with the Pauline motto: "If you have risen with Christ, seek the things that are above where Christ is seated at the right hand of God. Mind the things that are above, not the things that are on earth" (Col 3:1–3). Our assimilation with Christ at Baptism, renewed and strengthened by a holy fast, blossoming anew in the blessed night of the resurrection of the whole Christ, Head and members, must, during these fifty pentecostal days, move toward greater maturity. "Send forth thy Spirit, and they shall be created, and thou shalt renew the face of the earth" (Ps 103:30).

e) The Advent of the Lord

The fourth century adds another branch, the mystery of Christ's Advent, the culmination of His merciful work of redemption; the expectation of "that blessed Hope and the glorious coming of our great God and Savior Jesus Christ, who gave Himself for us [in His incarnation, birth, and life], that He might redeem us from all iniquity and cleanse for Himself an acceptable people (by His death, His resurrection, and the outpouring of His Spirit), pursuing good works (Christ's redeemed members in vital union with the divine Head and His Body, the Church)." So speaks the epistle of the Christmas midnight Mass.

What a pity that all too soon — as early as the eighth century — the real meaning and aim of Advent — the mystery of His final return, His Advent in great power and majesty — was obscured or well-nigh forgotten! And the fact that Advent became a lowly "beginning" instead of a triumphant "ending" of the Church's year only added to this misunderstanding. Dr. Bouyer (in his *Liturgical Piety*) remarks: "The purpose of Advent, Christmas and the Epiphany is ceaselessly to re-animate in us that hope, that expectation. But how can they do so if we reduce their significance to a sentimental commemoration of the childhood of Jesus, especially when in it we see only what touches our heart about *all* childhood, transmuted only by some aura of divinity?" Most Advent texts of Missal and Breviary point, not to the *past*, but to the *future*, to His final Advent, His majestic Parousia, which is the fulfillment of the hopes and expectation of mankind, and of which Christmas and the Epiphany are the "background," the symbol, and the assurance. How strikingly we express this hope and expectation with each recitation of the Apostles' Creed: "From thence He shall come [Advent!] to judge the living and the dead." *Maranatha Jesu!* Come quickly, Lord Jesus!

May we not hope that the Second Vatican Council will include in its reform work also the restoration of the real purpose of Advent, assigning it to its rightful place in the Church's year? Through such reform the Christian peoples will be guided in freeing themselves more and more from that stuffy and sentimental atmosphere which unhappily surrounds and distorts the Christmas festivity with all the "pine fragrance," the "sweet Baby Jesus mentality," the crib on the floor next to the inevitable "train," the "Santa Clauses," the "big" family meal, and what not, and be directed toward a new — yet old — vision, the vision of the martyrs of the early Church who, with eyes and hearts riveted on that "blessed Hope and glorious Coming of our great God and Savior Jesus Christ," "lived soberly and justly and godly in this world" (Ti 2:13, 12), presenting a living image of Christ to the world while "awaiting the appearance of our Lord Jesus Christ, who will also keep you secure unto the end, unimpeachable in the day of the coming of our Lord Jesus Christ" (1 Cor 1:7–8).

f) "Tempus per annum"

Such is the rubrical name for that more quiet liturgical season of growth, "the season through the year," from Pentecost until

Advent, from Epiphany until Ash Wednesday, during which the Paschal and Advent branches are bearing precious fruits and the faithful, by partaking of them, "may have life more abundantly" (Jn 10:10), or in the words of Pius XII: "that the divine Head of the Mystical Body may live in all its members with the fulness of His holiness" (*Mediator Dei,* § 152).

As the sun of nature, ever the same in itself, is yet so different in the effects it produces by its life-giving rays, so is the Holy Eucharist — Sun, Center, and Wellspring of the Church's year — ever the same in Itself, yet so different as It shines upon us during the seasons of the year, imparting to us, with increasing measure, the life of the crucified and risen Lord and preparing us steadily for our final victory on that day of days when the Son of Man will come "on the clouds of heaven with great power and majesty" (Mt 24:30).

During the twenty-four Sundays "after Pentecost" and the six Sundays "after Epiphany" Mother Church forms and transforms, sacramentally and pedagogically, her sons and daughters so that the "mystery of Christ" may illuminate and fill their whole being; that the "Sun of Justice" with ever new brilliancy may shine upon them; that the Word of God, as through a "prism" may so impress them that they may "walk in a manner worthy of the calling with which (they) were called, with all humility and meekness, with patience, bearing with one another in love, careful to preserve the unity of the Spirit in the bond of peace" (Eph 4:1–5), awaiting "the Savior, our Lord Jesus Christ, who will refashion the body of our lowliness, conforming it to the body of his glory by exerting the power by which he is able also to subject all things to himself" (Phil 3:20–21) on that day "when the Lord shall come and all His saints with Him" (Antiphon, First Sunday of Advent).

g) "And All His Saints With Him"

The saints are the blossoms of the Cross, the offspring of the divine Victim, the fruit-laden branches of the blessed Vine. Under the leadership of the Most Holy Mother of God, the Church places the glorious choir of Apostles, the white-robed army of martyrs, the resplendent throng of confessors, the fragrant lilies of virgins, the assembly of valiant women before her still struggling sons and daughters as they march along the year of grace, encouraging them: Look, these are the men and women who have come forth from great tribulations and have washed their garments clean in the Blood of the Lamb. These are the loyal sheep of the Good Shepherd who knew His voice and followed Him. These are the heroes who walked on the "paths of God," ate the Bread of the strong, and tasted the Wine that brings forth virgins. These are the ones who overcame the world and themselves, made room for the Lord "in the inn" of their hearts, and, through Him and with Him and in Him, have won the eternal victory. Jubilantly each one of these conquerors exclaims in the words of Paul: "It is no longer I that lives, it is Christ who lives in me."

As we journey — year after year — over the "King's highway" we meet these bright "lanterns of God" who shed upon our feet the Christ-light which they possess so abundantly; who assure us of the power of their intercession, adding to it their encouraging example "until we all attain to the unity of the faith and of the deep knowledge of the Son of God, to perfect manhood, to the mature measure of the fulness of Christ" (Eph 4:13).

III. THE SCHOOL OF HOLINESS

"While the Liturgy calls to mind the mysteries of Jesus Christ, it strives to make all believers take their part in them so that the divine Head of the Mystical Body may live in all the members with the fulness of His Holiness" (*Mediator Dei*, § 152).

Truly great words! A program for our spiritual life from a "master of the spiritual life!" (1) It (the liturgy in the course of the year) strives to make all believers take their part in the mysteries of Jesus Christ; (2) so that the divine Head may live in all the members; (3) that they may have the fulness of His holiness. Is there a better "way" for priests, religious, and faithful to advance in wisdom and grace than to live the Christ-year, the first and foremost "way" to holiness? The mysteries of Christ — His incarnation, His life, His death and resurrection — "are shining examples of Christian perfection, as well as *sources* of divine grace, due to the merit and prayers of Christ. They still influence us because each mystery brings its own special grace for our salvation" (*Mediator Dei,* § 152).

How weak these modern methods of dividing the year into twelve months of "special devotion"! (1) December, the "month of the Holy Childhood" — in the light of the majestic Advent of the Lord. (2) January, the "month of the Holy Family" — in the light of the resplendent Epiphany. (3) March, the "month of St. Joseph" — in the light of the great Lenten *metanoia,* the forty days' "retreat of the Church." And so we could go on.

No intelligent person will question these or any other "special devotions." Most of them have their place and purpose in the spiritual lives of the faithful. If St. Pius X called the liturgy the "primary" source of the true Christian spirit, then there must also be "secondary" sources. But when "devotions" obstruct or tend to drown out the "ways and paths of the Lord" of which the Introit of the first Advent Sunday speaks — "Lord, make known to me Thy ways, and teach me Thy paths" — when they fail to lead to the "highway" of the year of the Church, then they are in danger of becoming "dead-end alleys." Pius XII says: "If they [he refers mainly to "spiritual exercises," but what he says applies to all practices not strictly liturgical] are an obstacle to the principles and norms of divine worship, or if they oppose or hinder them, one must surely conclude that they are not in keeping with prudence and enlightened zeal" (§ 181); in fact, he goes so far as to say "that the *criterion* will be the effectiveness of these exercises in making the *divine cult* loved and spread daily ever more widely" (*ibid.*).

IV. PASTORAL REFLECTIONS

1. How much does the average catechism teach about the Church's year "which fills Christ's members with the fulness of

His holiness"? The praiseworthy *Life in Christ* by Fathers Killgallon and Weber of Chicago broke the long silence. We are grateful for that. However, we may be permitted to suggest that in future editions an even greater emphasis be given to that "mighty oak tree" which sprang up from the divinely planted "acorn."

The new German *Katholischer Katechismus*, the fruit of eighteen years' research in catechetics and liturgy research (now available in fine English garb from Herder and Herder) brings us closer to the solution of this important question, a question of particular urgency in our country. How can children (or adults) come to a fuller knowledge of the liturgical year, its meaning and purpose, its fruitful observation and application to daily living, unless they be informed and formed? How can they, unless catechism and teacher show the way, the way to the "way of life"? The omission of the "Church year" in nearly all of the catechisms of the past hundred years reflects the mentality of their compilers and certainly shows the need of a catechetical-liturgical reorientation, so "that Christ's members may be filled with the fulness of His Holiness."[1]

2. It would be gratifying to hear from competent persons of seminaries and convents about what is being done toward making the Church year a living reality for our future priests and teachers who are, as Pope John says, the hope of the Church and, in days to come, God's instruments for the "incorporation of all things in Christ" (St. Pius X). The study of the liturgy (not merely of "rubrics" sometimes labeled "liturgy") in seminaries and convents must include a very thorough course "on the Church year," on "how to live it," "how to preach it," "how to teach it," for "the most pressing duty of Christians is to live the liturgical life, and increase and cherish its supernatural spirit" (*Mediator Dei*, § 197).

3. No one questions the need of meditation. And everyone knows that, as far as the subject of meditation is concerned, we may enjoy the fullest freedom. "It is the same Spirit who breatheth

---

[1] Current efforts are being made in this direction, for instance in the recent religion texts published by Bruce (*The Vine and the Branches*) and Sadlier (*God Leads Me*), but these are only beginnings. Much needs to be done, worked out in practice (ed. note).

where He will, and who with differing gifts and in different ways enlightens and guides souls to sanctity. Let their freedom and the supernatural action of the Holy Spirit be so sacrosanct that no one presume to disturb or stifle them for any reason whatsoever" (*Mediator Dei*, § 179). At the same time there is every reason why we should make our meditations in harmony with the magnificent plan unfolded by Mother Church in the course of her holy year. For example, why should one, on the feast of St. Aloysius, want to make his meditation on St. Mary Magdalene (with due regard for that noble "messenger of the resurrection"!)? Would not a meditation based on the mystery or feast dispose for their more fruitful celebration? "By these suitable ways and methods in which the Liturgy at stated times proposes the life of Jesus Christ for our meditation, the Church gives us examples to imitate, points out treasures of sanctity for us to make our own; since it is fitting that the mind believes what the lips sing, and that what the mind believes should be practiced in public and private life" (*Mediator Dei*, § 153).

4. Another important matter is the compilation of "Outlines of Sermons for the Ecclesiastical Year" used in many of our dioceses. This is a difficult and responsible undertaking and we can very well appreciate the enormous efforts of those who are asked to prepare them. Some of these "Outlines" are well done, some are too academic and stilted, and some reveal a lack of comprehension of the real purpose and spirit of the "Ecclesiastical Year." How can a priest be asked to preach "on holy relics" on the feast of Pentecost, as was suggested in one of them? The words of St. Pius X: "Do not pray IN the Mass, pray THE Mass" could very well be applied to our preaching: "Do not preach IN the year, preach THE year." It should not be too difficult to arrange "a three years' course of sermons" from the sacred texts which accompany the celebration of the Holy Eucharist during the year of grace. The deposit of Faith is contained in these texts by means of which, after prayer, meditation, and study, we guide our flock, deepen their Catholic faith, and anchor their spiritual life on the solid rock of the salvation-imparting year of the Church. The

"Sacramentum" will then shine forth through the *Verbum,* and the *Verbum* in turn will lead back to that *Sacramentum* of which He said: "If anyone eat of this Bread, he shall live forever; and the Bread that I will give, is my Flesh for the life of the world" (Jn 6:52). There will then be order, unity, and harmony, which, I believe, are "heaven's first law," but also "the first law" in proclaiming and celebrating "heaven's mysteries" on earth.

5. Among other pastoral problems of deep concern, there is one which I consider of special importance. I mean retreat work. All too often it has happened that retreats have been conducted during the greater seasons or major feasts of the year without any reference whatever to these mysteries. How is it possible, for example, that within the octave of Pentecost not a word should be said about the marvelous operation of the Holy Spirit who "will teach you all things, and bring to your mind whatever I have said to you" (Jn 14:26)? Such a retreat lacks proper spiritual "color." We are not unmindful of the good will and the earnest efforts of most of our retreat masters, but, no doubt, here is a field which thus far has not been sufficiently explored. If, at times, retreat masters complain about the "sterility" of their retreats, here may be found a partial answer. One thing is certain, living with the Church, appreciating the transforming power of her seasons and feasts, will awaken a joy that becomes irresistible, a *joy* in the Lord, which will make our *moderation* be known to all men, because the Lord is *nigh* (cf. Phil 4:4–5).

V. GRATIAS AGAMUS!

We are thankful to our Lord, to His Holy Spirit, and to His Church for the majestic year of redemption and life, in the course of which we are made "partakers of His Divinity who has condescended to become a partaker of our humanity, Jesus Christ, Our Lord" (mingling prayer). There is no better way for growing deeper into the life of the divine Head and His Mystical Body than the liturgical year. Here is the way which Mother Church not only approves and recommends, it is *the* way on which, with maternal solicitude, she herself leads her sons and daughters toward that glorious Parousia, the completion and culmination of all redemption, toward the everlasting victory and glory of the beloved Shepherd and His loyal sheep. "The former things have passed away. And he who was sitting on the throne said: Behold, I make all things new" (Ap 21:4–5).

...15...

Rites and Blessings for Children

FRANCIS X. WEISER, S.J.

THIS short historical sketch is restricted (1) to rites and blessings performed outside the administration of sacraments and (2) to those religious practices which were widely used within liturgical functions and recorded in the sacramentaries (rituals) of the Middle Ages. Hence we exclude the whole field of popular religious folklore which concurrently developed in those centuries and found its expression in ceremonies, prayers, incantations performed by lay people, and sometimes even by the clergy, but without the official approval of the ecclesiastical authorities, and often against their outspoken condemnations.

THE UNBORN CHILD

For lack of better biological and medical knowledge, the "sufferings of pregnancy" were painted in darkest colors by medieval religious and medical writers, and frequently exaggerated beyond measure. "Every woman who has conceived," writes Vincent des Beauvais, "must endure sufferings and give birth in pain. . . . Her face turns pale; her body swells; her gait becomes feeble, the body tired; she suffers from weakness, sleeplessness, fear and fright. Thus she is constantly tortured by worry about herself and about the fruit of her body. She refuses nourishment, avoids those foods which might help her, and craves harmful things. . . . In sadness and pain does she give birth, nurses her child with solicitous labor, watches over it with anxiety and fear."[1]

---

[1] *Speculum Morale*, III, 11.

Protection

According to the traditions of civil law pregnant mothers were granted special protection in all Christian nations. The Church, too, extended loving concern to them and their unborn children. Pregnant women were generally dispensed from the rigid provisions of the Church law concerning fast and abstinence; husbands were warned of the serious obligation not to impose heavy burdens of work on them; striking and physical maltreating of expectant mothers were even punished by excommunication.

Liturgical Blessing

To mothers approaching the time of birth the Church offered spiritual assistance through a special liturgical benediction in which the priest prayed for the health of the mother, a successful and happy birth, protection against the wiles and attacks of the devil, and God's blessings upon the child to be born.

From the eighth to the tenth centuries the texts for this blessing of expectant mothers were simply taken from the ritual of marriage blessing, and thus phrased in general terms except for a short addition referring to the childbirth, like this formula of the tenth century:

> O God, who from the beginning made man and gave to him a helper like himself, that men might grow and multiply on earth, give mercy to this Your servant N., that she may prosper and give birth without grave pain. Have mercy on us, Lord.[2]

These short and simple prayers were gradually amplified by texts taken from liturgical blessings for the sick, and especially by those two prayers which the Roman Ritual still provides at the end of the rite of extreme unction.

---

[2] "Deus, qui ab initio fecisti hominem et dedisti ei adjutorem similem sibi, ut crescerent et multiplicarentur super terram, da misericordiam tuam huic famulae tuae N., ut prospere et sine gravi dolore parturiat. Miserere nobis, domine." *Codex Palatinus Vindobonensis*, p. 7. — The Latin texts are taken from the collection of medieval liturgical documents in A. Franz, *Die Kirchlichen Benediktionen im Mittelalter*, 2 vols., Freiburg, 1909. For easier reading, errors in the original Latin, or unusual spellings, have been corrected by the author of this article.

In the Greek Church the blessing of mothers before childbirth was conferred with a more solemn ritual: prayers outside the house, an incensing of the whole home, and finally the benediction at the bedside of the expectant mother.

The *Rituale Romanum* still contains a "benedictio mulieris pregnantis (in periculo partus)," with three prayers, Psalm 66, two liturgical blessings, and sprinkling with holy water (Tit. VIII, Cap. 5).

Other Rites

Pregnant mothers were generally exhorted in medieval times to prepare themselves for the difficult hour of childbirth by confession and Holy Communion, and by frequent attendance at Mass. Communion was usually brought to them at the onset of labor pains. After reception of the Holy Eucharist, it was usual for the mother to draw the name of one of the Apostles from a box held by the priest. This Apostle was to be her special helper in the sufferings and dangers of birth, and a heavenly patron for the healthy issuance of the child. Many parents imposed on their children in baptism the name of this particular Apostle, thus making him also the "baptismal saint."

When the day of birth was nearing, votive Masses were offered for the mother in her parish church. In the High Middle Ages it was mostly a Mass in honor of St. Margaret, the popular patron saint of parturient mothers. From the fourteenth century on, St. Ann shared in, and often superseded the veneration of St. Margaret in this particular patronage. Also Masses of the Blessed Virgin and of SS. Philip and James were taken as votive Masses *pro parturientibus*. The Collects, Secrets, and Postcommunions (*complenda*) of these votive Masses expressed the petitions for the expectant mother. The text of the Postcommunion in a missal from Passau (Germany), printed in 1522, may serve as an example:

> Postcommunion (*complenda*): Having received the sacrament of the body and blood of Your only-begotten Son, we humbly beseech You, Lord, that the merits of blessed Margaret, whose memory is

celebrated, may become for Your servant N. a means for avoiding the peril of childbirth and for seeing the fruit of her womb safe from all harm, through Your grace.[3]

Another spiritual means of devotion, consolation, and help was the invocation of saints and imposition of their relics on mothers facing the hour of birth. Many are the saints who were invoked in different sections of Europe. Mothers vowed candles, pilgrimages, works of mercy, and special prayers to these saints, if they themselves and their offspring should emerge from the ordeal in good health. An interesting illustration of this practice can be seen in the famous relics of St. Elizabeth — her cup, girdle, and spoon — which traveled constantly through fifteenth-century Germany, to be kept for a few days at one princely palace or another, wherever a new child was expected. Nor did the aristocratic ladies neglect to share this privilege with the common people; St. Elizabeth's cup was filled with wine many times over, and this wine was then distributed in small quantities to expectant mothers among the subjects of the prince.

A specially potent help to secure a happy and easy birth was the *Aqua Sancti Alberti*. This saint, a Carmelite monk, who died in Sicily in 1306, soon came to be venerated as a favorite patron by expectant mothers, especially against the dangers of child-bed fever. Water blessed in his honor was given such mothers to drink, or was sprinkled over them. The first formulas for the blessing of St. Albert's water date from the fourteenth century — soon after his death. Some of them expressly refer to pregnant and parturient mothers such as this text from the fifteenth century:

The Blessing of St. Albert's Water for Pregnant Women

. . . Show, we beseech You, Lord, Your tender affection and loving concern, and infuse Your holy blessing upon this creature water, that whoever, about to give birth, partakes devotedly of this water

---

[3] *"Complenda:* Sumptis, domine, corporis et sanguinis unigeniti tui mysteriis te supplices exoramus, ut beatae Margarethae merita, cuius commemorationis sunt votiva, fiant famulae tuae N. ad evadendum partus periculum et ad videndum salvum ventris sui fructum te donante proficua." Franz, II, 193.

may be saved from all dangers by the merits of Your most holy mother Mary and by the relics of Your devoted and holy confessor Albert. May Your wrath fall mercifully upon her in giving birth, and may her child be brought forth from her womb fully healthy and may he be sustained carefully in Your service.[4]

A blessing of water in honor of St. Albert may still be found in the Roman Ritual (Tit. IX, Cap. 11, 50); the present liturgical text, however, does not expressly mention expectant mothers but only the general classification "all those who suffer from fever."

BIRTH

In earlier centuries — up to about A.D. 1000 — priests often remained with a woman during the birth of the child, reciting prayers and blessing both mother and child. Formulas of such blessings *in partu* are preserved in ancient manuscripts; but they did not enjoy an official character, and the Church authorities generally opposed the practice. By the eleventh century it had completely disappeared, and priests were not present at the actual birth. Durandi recorded this in his *Rationale*: "For it is not proper for the priest to remain long with a woman in labor at the time of her delivery."[5]

Nevertheless, the invocation of divine help and an imparting of blessings seemed especially called for during the time of birth. Thus the custom developed that monks and clergymen would write prayer texts and instructions for sprinkling of holy water, imposition of relics, lighting of candles, etc., on pieces of parchment. These "letters" were then read — and the rubrics observed — by lay people, mostly women, who assisted at the birth. The following prayer of the twelfth century may serve as an example:

[4] *"Benedictio aquae de sancto Alberto pro mulieribus pregnantibus:* . . . Ostende, quaesumus, Domine, tuum pium affectum et effectum et huic elemento aquae tuam sanctam benedictionem infunde, ut quaecumque paritura hanc aquam potando pie susceperit, meritis sanctissimae genetricis tuae Mariae et reliquiis devoti et sancti confessoris Alberti ab omnibus periculis eripiatur et flagellum tuum in natum misericorditer suspendatur, proles eius cum omni prosperitate de utero educatur et in tuo famulatu iugiter conservetur." *Codex Rossianus,* VIII, 65; Franz, II, 196.

[5] "Nam inhonestum est, quod tempore partus presbyter diu cum ea (pariente) moretur." *Rationale divinorum officiorum,* Lib. VII, c. 7, n. 7.

Ann gave birth to Samuel, Elizabeth to John; Ann gave birth to Mary, Mary to Christ. Infant, whether masculine or feminine . . . I adjure you through the living God, the true God, the holy God, the God who was born of Mary the virgin, come forth. Your Savior calls you to the light. . . .[6]

An appealing practice was the fairly general custom of saying public prayers during Sunday Mass in the parish churches for all women approaching childbirth: "For all expectant mothers, that God may happily deliver them and let them joyfully behold the fruit of their bodies; and that the Lord may grant the children the holy sacrament of baptism."[7]

In many places a church bell was rung three times when a woman came into labor, to remind all parishioners to pray for her. While the mother gave birth, relatives and friends would gather in church, read the Prologue of St. John's Gospel and recite the seven penitential psalms. Frequently a parish priest officiated at such prayer services.

BLESSING AFTER BIRTH

This rite, not to be confused with the "churching," was imparted to mother and child soon after birth, and always in the home. In the Greek Church, it was given on the very day of delivery. The prayers invoked God's protection and mercy upon mother and child, implored forgiveness of sins and successful recovery for the mother, and also recommended to God the midwife and all other women who had assisted in the birth. For the first time the priest solemnly marked the baby with the sign of the cross. In later centuries, however, this liturgical signing with the cross was done on the eighth day after birth.

In the Latin Church, no benediction immediately after birth

---

[6] "Anna peperit Samuel, Elisabeth Johannem; Anna peperit Mariam, Maria Christum. Infans, sive masculus sive femina . . . adjuro te per deum vivum, per deum verum, per deum sanctum, per deum qui natus est ex Maria virgine, ut exeas. Te vocat salvator ad lucem. . . ." *Cod. Palat. Vindob.*, 850; Franz, II, 200.

[7] N. Surgant, *Manuale Curatorum*, Basle, 1520, p. 66.

was provided in early times. The first texts of such a *Benedictio post partum* appear in the eleventh century. They were subsequently approved and used in many dioceses, but never became universally accepted. St. Charles Borromeo forbade this blessing in his diocese because it was not listed in the Roman books.

Usually the *Benedictio post partum* was given on the eighth day after birth: "On the eighth day after the woman's delivery let the priest enter her room and say these prayers. . . ." The texts clearly follow the ritual of the blessing of the sick. Devils and demons, who are regularly mentioned in the prayers of the Greek Church as threatening mother and child, are passed over in silence in the Latin books. The child, although present and included in the blessing, is hardly mentioned in the prayer texts.

Churching

It is not within the scope of this article to treat the historical background of churching as far as it was considered a *purificatio* of the mother after birth. In the Western Church this aspect was never as pronounced as in the oriental Churches. The traditional title of the rite in the Latin liturgy was *Benedictio ad introducendam mulierem in ecclesiam.* The Ritual now calls it *Benedictio mulieris post partum;* both the text and the rubrics, however, make it clear that it is the *Introductio* rather than the ancient *Benedictio post partum* in the home.

In the Latin Church, the first formulas of this rite date from the eleventh century. Forty days after childbirth the mother was to come to the church to be solemnly introduced and blessed. Although this ceremony was prescribed by Church law in the East, it was never imposed as a strict duty in the West, but was always highly recommended. Some theologians in the fifteenth century considered it a fault deserving of ecclesiastical punishment for a woman to omit her churching; this opinion, though, was soon abandoned.

How highly esteemed this blessing was is clear from the fact that Pope Innocent III reserved it to pastors; the Roman Ritual has retained this provision up to now.

The prayers of the rite of churching have always stressed the character of thanksgiving and of petition for God's continued protection and blessing on mother and child. Here and there the Old Testament idea of a purification from moral stain is indicated in passing, as in the prayer *Aufer ab ea,* in the versicle *Cor mundum,* and in the recitation of the psalm *Miserere.* However, the more recent the texts are, the fewer become such hints at "purification." The present rite expresses nothing but happy gratitude and joyful confidence in the Lord's goodness and mercy; and, reading it, one gathers the definite impression that the Church wishes to honor the dignity of Christian motherhood by the deliberate choice of these beautiful prayer texts.

In medieval times a mother who had suffered a miscarriage was also blessed with the usual rite of churching. Many liturgical books, however, have the notation that in this case the mother should not carry a burning candle, but an unlit one.

Churching and Child

Mothers were at no time required to bring their children along for the churching. However, it became a widespread custom to do so in the eleventh century, especially in Germany, Austria, Switzerland, and France.

After the liturgical rite was completed, the mother would hand a gift of gratitude to the priest. These donations consisted of the candle which she had brought along, and of money or other things, like altar linen sewn by herself during the days of confinement. St. Elizabeth, Duchess of Thuringia, is reported to have offered a lamb besides the candle.

The child, too, was "offered" to God in a symbolic ceremony; the priest would carry it to the altar, present it to the Lord in a short prayer, then hand it back to the mother with the words of the antiphon, *Cum inducerent puerum Jesum . . .*

In France, Italy, and England the churching used to be followed by the votive Mass, *Salve, sancta parens,* after which the priest read the Gospel *In principio* over the woman and gave her a small loaf of blessed bread.

Additional Rites

An interesting custom was the *Sumptio ablutionis* which took place in many dioceses after the ceremony of churching. The child was brought to the altar and the priest moistened its lips with a few drops of the wine that he had kept from the ablution after his own Communion. He did it in the form of a cross over the mouth of the child, saying, *"Ablutio domini nostri Jesu Christi custodiat te in vitam aeternam"* or a similar phrase.

This ceremony was a substitute for the ancient practice of giving children Holy Communion under the species of wine immediately after baptism. Although the ecclesiastical authorities did not invest the *Sumptio ablutionis* with official standing, it was approved and encouraged by the bishops through many centuries. As late as 1823 a diocesan directive in Switzerland warned pastors not to refuse this pious and ancient rite to those who asked for it.

Among the common people a belief became widespread in the thirteenth century that the giving of the ablution made the little ones bright and intelligent. This superstition accounted for the popular term of the rite in German-speaking countries (*witzen:* "to make smart") and found its way even into liturgical handbooks (*dare sapientiam*).

During the earlier centuries, a special Mass for the first anniversary of birth was recorded in the *Gelasianum* and other liturgical books (*in natale genuinum*). The prayers of this votive Mass implore God's continued protection and blessing over the child; no mention is made of the mother.

SCHOOLCHILDREN

The oriental Churches had special prayers of impetration and blessing to be said by a priest over children who started going to school. This practice seems to have come to Europe during the time of the Crusades. We find the first prayer texts for this rite in manuscripts of the thirteenth and fourteenth centuries. They remained private devotions, though, and were never incorporated into the official rituals, although we find them occasionally placed there by individual writers of manuscripts. Many of these formulas abound in long prayer texts, cabalistic words, invocations of legendary angels, and in the use of magic signs. Their promoters claim that they secure for the child an easy memory, agility of tongue, and keen understanding, provided they are said exactly according to instructions on every first day of a month or on an empty stomach, or after having washed the head in running water, etc.

A book for priests, published in 1522 in Vienna, Austria, mentions St. Augustine and St. Thomas Aquinas as special patrons of students and provides prayers which allegedly were composed by these saints. It also prescribes that those using the devotion must keep themselves free from all sins of the flesh, receive the sacraments, and have three Masses offered in honor of the Holy Trinity. So far, so good. Then, however, the superstitious promise is added that students who perform these prayers faithfully, and fulfill the required conditions, will infallibly "learn more in one week than others in six years."

Fortunately, such aberrations disappeared from liturgical and quasi-liturgical books quite soon, and in their place the Benedictine Fathers introduced for their schools a short and dignified priestly prayer of blessing which may be found in many monastery rituals from the twelfth century on:

> O God, who founded all things in wisdom, that is, in Your eternal Son, give, we beseech You, a docile mind to Your servant, that he may make progress in his studies and merit to become capable of everlasting doctrine.[8]

The modern Ritual, in its *Benedictio pueri ad obtinendam super eum misericordiam Dei*, continues — and now within the official liturgy of the Church — the ancient practice of prayer and blessing for children, "that they may grow in virtue and wisdom among God and men . . ." (Tit. IX, Cap. 4).

---

[8] "Deus, qui in sapientia, hoc est coaeterno filio, omnia condidisti: da, quaesumus, famulo tuo docibilem mentem, ut et in exterioribus studiis proficiat et aeternae mereatur fieri capax doctrinae." *Rituale Sti Floriani*, 107, 26; Franz, II, 260.

THE CUTTING OF HAIR

In pre-Christian times an offering of human hair was generally made to the gods as a symbol of dedication. The hair of the head served as an external token of life itself. When animals were offered, the hair of their foreheads was cut away as a sign that they were "handed over" to the god as his possession. This practice subsequently developed into the ceremony of initiation into manhood among the Greeks and Romans, in which locks were cut from the heads of adolescents, put in a box of gold or silver, and placed as votive gifts in the temple of a favorite god. St. Gregory Nazianzen mentions this custom when, among the annual festive celebrations of a civic nature, he lists the *kourosia* (cutting of hair).[9]

After their conversion, the Christian nations both of the Orient and Occident retained this ceremony, using it now as a symbolic dedication of their children to God. In the Greek Church the cutting of hair (*trichokouria*) was performed immediately after baptism (and confirmation). The officiating priest, cutting in the form of the cross, severed some locks from the top of the head. The ceremony was accompanied by prayers which expressed the fact of dedication. The hair was then put in a repository within the sanctuary, or taken by the godfather and affixed to a cross in the home.

The meaning of this rite is clearly stated by Symeon of Thessalonike: "As the first-fruit and first offerings of the human body the baptized one dedicates some of his hair to Christ, because the hair is an incense-offering given by the body."[10]

In the Latin Church there was no such cutting of hair at baptism. About the eleventh century, however, it appears in the liturgical books as a rite to be performed on children — and always in church. The usual titles are: *Ad capillaturam incidendam* or *Ad tondendum parvulos*. The prayers contain petitions for God's

---

[9] *Eis to hagion Baptisma; PG,* 36, 360.
[10] *De sacramentis,* c. 67; *PG,* 155, 322.

blessing upon body and soul, for holiness and long life. Here is the text of a much used formula, from the twelfth century:

> Almighty Christ . . . who, imposing Your hands on the little ones brought to You, said that of such is the kingdom of heaven, bless this servant of Yours, N., whose superfluous hair we cut in Your name. Give him intelligence with increase in age, that he may fear You, know You, and guard Your commands and, with Your help, attain even to old age in the highest state of health.[11]

Despite the common basic significance, the tonsure of children has always remained distinguished, both in its purpose and liturgical text, from that of monks and clerics. It was intended for children without regard to their later calling in life. This holds true even in cases where the children's rite was listed together with the tonsure of clerics under the common heading, *Tonsura*: the prayers themselves show the difference.

During the fourteenth and fifteenth centuries the cutting of children's hair was gradually discontinued; the older texts are missing in later rituals, and in their place appeared a *Benedictio puerorum* which shows the same prayerful wishes for the spiritual and temporal welfare, and uses one or the other antiphon from the ancient texts.

The present *Benedictio puerorum* in the Roman Ritual (Tit. IX, Cap. 4, n. 5) marks the final stage in the development of the *tonsura infantium*. From a rite for individuals it has turned into a collective blessing of children. Its main prayer not only follows the tenor of the old formula of Gundecar, but even repeats verbatim some of its phrases. The addition to the title (*cum praesertim in ecclesia praesentantur*) also indicates the ancient practice according to which the *tonsura* was always held in church.

---

[11] "Omnipotens Christe . . . qui venientibus ad te parvulis manus tuae benedictionis imponens talium dixisti esse regnum caelorum: benedic hunc famulum tuum N., cuius in tuo nomine superflua incidimus capillorum; da ei intellectum cum aetatis augmento, ut te timeat, te intelligat, et tua mandata custodiat et te auxiliante usque ad senectutem cum summa sanitate perveniat." *Codex Gundecari*, 12b; Franz, II, 250.

SICK CHILDREN

There are no extra texts of blessings for sick children in the liturgical books of the Middle Ages. Children were blessed and provided with the same rites as grown-up patients. The rituals of the time abound in special blessings for all kinds of diseases — fever, epilepsy, hemorrhages, boils, rheumatism, arthritis, paralysis; diseases of the eyes, ears, blood, and skin; a number of nervous and mental disorders were also treated with exorcisms, since the common belief of the time ascribed them to the direct action of the devil.

The official liturgical prayers of blessings for the sick are generally couched in dignified religious terminology and abstain from any admixtures of popular superstitions. Besides these official texts, however, many people used private prayers, incantations, superstitious rites, and magic formulas. Even priests and nuns practiced them, until the repeated and emphatic ecclesiastical prohibitions effected a definite change and established a clear code of practice in the fourteenth century. In case of sickness only the following religious means of help were to be used: the sacrament of holy unction, devout private prayer, the sign of the cross, official liturgical blessings and sacramentals, and any other texts or actions which were publicly approved for use by the bishop of the diocese.

Among the popular practices which found ecclesiastical approval in medieval times and were often endowed with a liturgical character, the following ones deserve special mention.

Incubation

This was the first and most ancient custom in Christianity, dating from the fourth and fifth centuries. It was an external imitation of the ancient *incubatio* at pagan temples, but entirely different in purpose and execution. The faithful brought their sick, children and grown-ups, to the tomb of martyrs — and later also to the tombs or shrines of confessors and other saints — left them in the sacred place for the night, and meanwhile implored the help of the respective saint in fervent prayer. The lives of early saints abound with stories of miraculous cures obtained by means of this pious custom; many of the cured ones were children.

Use of Relics

The second, and more general, custom was (and still is) the veneration and imposition of saints' relics to obtain their special help in cases of sickness. Relics used to be imposed with prayers made for this occasion, or hung around the necks of sick children. The patients received water or wine which had been "blessed" by immersion of a saint's relic. Diseased parts of the body were touched with the relics or with objects that had been brought in contact with relics.

The above customs usually found the approval of the Church authorities. Many others, however, which contained superstitious beliefs or practices, had to be condemned, and repeatedly so. Such were the lists of specific effects that were claimed to follow the use of certain relics. The dust from the tomb of St. Martin of Tours, for instance, was said to be an infallible medicine for the "cleansing" of head, lungs, and stomach.

Weighing

This interesting practice was extensively used, and especially for sick children. In the presence of a saint's relic, or in front of a shrine, the sick person was put on a scale and weighed, with the promise of donating an equal weight of votive gifts (wax, candles, grain, bread, fruits, silver, gold) in honor of the saint, if his intercession would obtain a cure. This custom was widespread in Italy, France, and Germany. In some places it lingered as late as the seventeenth century.

Liturgical rites for the weighing of sick persons (*Ad ponderandum hominem*) are found in Italian rituals of the high and late Middle Ages. Here is the main prayer of such an *ordo*, taken from the list of liturgical blessings in the appendix of a Franciscan breviary (written in Italy), from the end of the fourteenth century:

Almighty, eternal God, Creator and provident Lord of the universe, who has made all things in measure, number, and weight through Your co-eternal Son, be quick to hear our humble prayers, that You may bless with a heavenly blessing, fortify with Your help, and keep from all adversity, Your servant N., who comes to this church of blessed Mary for the sake of weighing himself, insofar as he may merit, through the intercession of blessed Mary, to present himself as safe and sound to Your Church.[12]

For all these ancient blessings and practices the Church has substituted the appealing and dignified rite of the *Benedictio puerorum aegrotantium* (Tit. IX, Cap. 4, n. 6). Most of the old books had prescribed the reading of the Prologue of St. John's Gospel over the sick person. This practice has been retained in the modern blessing of sick children.

PRESENT BLESSINGS OF CHILDREN

The preceding short sketch might serve to clarify the historical background of the five blessings for children which the Church provides at present in the Roman Ritual. The genuine spiritual and temporal concerns which have inspired the ancient blessings are faithfully preserved in the modern rite. What has been dropped is but the framework of nonessential formulations, symbolisms, and practices of past centuries.

In the current liturgy of children's blessings every prayer and action manifests the pure and wholesome spirit of liturgical piety, without the slightest admixture of sentimental, erroneous, or dubious folklore elements.

For all this we cannot but feel deep satisfaction and gratitude. A good way of expressing this gratitude might be the sincere endeavor, on the part of all who love the holy liturgy, to make the Children's Blessings known, to inspire both clergy and parents with the desire and willingness to use more of these admirable treasures of the Church for the benefit of today's children.

---

[12] "Omnipotens sempiterne Deus, creator et dispensator universitatis, qui per coaeternum tibi filium omnia in mensura, numero ac pondere fecisti, adesto propitius humilibus precibus nostris, ut famulum N., qui ad eccelesiam hanc sanctae Mariae se ponderandi causa advenit, celesti benedictione benedicas et auxilio tuo munias et ab omni adversitate defendas, quatenus intercedente beata Maria salvus atque incolumis ecclesiae tuae se representari mereatur." Rosenthal library, Munich, Ms.; Franz, II, 464.

...16...

The Pyrrhic Victory of Florus of Lyons

H. A. REINHOLD

THE liturgical historian Adolph Franz published in 1902 a thorough and massive study of the Mass in the Middle Ages in Germany. This is still the best study, although the late Father Peter Browe and others brought up to date a few nonessentials, e.g., Franz's two Amalars, one of Trier and one of Metz, are now recognized as one bishop. Father John M. Hanssens, S.J., made a magnificent publication of all of Amalar's works in three large volumes. Amalar was indeed a formidable scholar for his period, the Dark Ages, that followed the Carolingian Renaissance. Amalar was not only a learned man but also a great traveler and a bishop of great pastoral concern. Apart from his controversy with John Scotus Erigena, he worked mostly in the field of liturgy. He published texts which now are a mine of information for liturgiologists. He still is a reliable source the world over. He had ample information even about the Eastern rites, since he was sent to Constantinople by his monarch on some Church and political business and he went there with his eyes wide open for differences in tradition. But he was also a reformer of liturgy. This made him enemies.

For a few years he administered the diocese of Lyons, whose bishop was absent for some mysterious reason which has eluded the Church historians. He tried to introduce a few changes into the Lyonese rite, probably what he considered to be Roman usage and therefore most authoritative. He obviously could not foresee that to this day Lyons would have its own local rite, Amalar or no

Amalar. He returned to Metz as its bishop, and there he probably died in or around 850. With the political pacification of the heritage of Charlemagne, Archbishop Agobard was allowed to return to his See in Lyons. It is obvious that the times were troubled. And it also appears that the gentle Amalar ran into more trouble when his teaching on the "Corpus Tripartitum" (the threefold Body of Christ) in the *Fractio Panis* of the Mass, together with arbitrary allegorism, was condemned by the Synod of Quierzy (838). The man who led the attack against him was a well-read, sober-minded and passionate fighter who led the grumblers in Lyons, a deacon by the name of Florus.

The two counts on which Amalar was taken to task were really born of the same mother: Amalar's indomitable inclination to allegorize. Allegorism is, of course, older than Amalar, as is proved by the allegorical explanations of Scripture by Philo of Alexandria and his followers. But Amalar went to Quierzy thinking it to be his own brand-new escape from a dilemma. He did not know that he had a long line of predecessors, from Pseudo-Denis, through Sophronius of Jerusalem (d. 638), Maximus Confessor (d. 662), to Isidor of Seville, to name only the more prominent liturgical allegorists. Biblical allegorism is even more prominent, owing to such names as St. Augustine, Ambrose, and Gregory the Great down to Bede the Venerable. The example best known to the clergy is St. Augustine's allegorical explanation of the thirty-eight-year-old paralytic at the pool of Bethesda — familiar to all who use the breviary, where it is read in Lent. The figure thirty-eight is arrived at by subtracting two divine virtues from the sacred figure forty to show the imperfection of the paralytic who lacked faith and hope. This is a sublime form of *léger de main* in which we have lost faith. The same is true about the explanation of the liturgy via allegory. Its classical miscarriage we all remember from grade school days where we were expected to believe that in washing his hands after the Offertory the celebrant "symbolized," of all people, Pilate. This strange explanation demands of us that we see in the celebrant, not the figure of Christ, but the cowardly opportunist who let himself be pressured by a screaming mob and its leaders into a sort of lynch justice. It obviously demands too much of the victim of this technique and renders all explanation unserious. Another example of the arbitrary way of allegoric explanation is Isidor of Seville's forcing numbers on the liturgy, as he does with the figure seven on the Canon of the Mass (Franz, p. 339). Adolph Franz locates in the ninth century the change from realistic and sober exegesis of the liturgy to abstruse allegorism. Each of its explanations receives now a "memorative" exegesis; each rite represents facts from the past and symbolizes a definite hope in the future. In everything that happens during Mass Amalar sees mysterious relations to the life and death of Christ (Franz, p. 351). As time went on there arose two allegorical traditions. One follows Amalar by forcing into the whole length of the Mass the different historical phases of the passion. It sees the Mass thus as an allegorical representation of all these phases in every liturgical action performed at the altar; in other words, a weird and strange *mysterium-repraesentatio*, not troubled by the *symbolical* character of the sacramental mystery. Naturally, this opens the door wide to the most arbitrary mystagogy. No wonder then that we find this method enlarged and expanded to a second, a super-allegory which not only sees in the Mass an allegorical synopsis of the whole passion and resurrection, but goes much further. The whole economy of salvation is allegorized with such choice "explanations" as Communion as the burial of Jesus' body (in the mouth of the faithful) and the last blessing as the parousia and last judgment in allegory.

As the Greek liturgy in its Proscomidy performs an allegorical sacrifice before the beginning of the liturgy, so there arises in the eighth century and thereafter an allegorical "development" of the Franco-Roman offertory. Even more astonishing is an intrusion which is still with us; the nonbiblical breaking of the Bread after the Lord's Prayer. This rite allegorizes the resurrection of Christ by reuniting the hitherto separated species in order to reassure the Christians gathered that they do not receive a "corpse" (to put it with medieval bluntness). This was, of course, not the only reason for the intrusion of the rite, but it is certainly its most startling allegorical explanation. That it is not the *Fractio Panis* proper, but a free development can easily be seen. The sacramental *Fractio* took place during the Agnus Dei and after the Kiss of Peace (*Bringing the Mass to the People,* H. A. Reinhold, Baltimore, 1961, p. 75). There is no sharing of the bread after this ceremonial breaking of the Holy Species. It has nothing to do with the communion of the sacred ministers and the people. It is something that would not have occurred after the thoughts of the classical scholastic teaching on the Eucharist, as in the *Adoro te devote,* became widespread in Christendom. Allegory lacks the simplicity, reverence, and reasonableness of symbolism, true and proper. While St. Augustine practiced biblical allegoresis its extension to the liturgy never occurred to him, nor to any other Father close to the liturgy — which, though symbolical, was clearly outlined and matter-of-fact. Bread had to be broken to distribute it, hands were washed in order to have them reverently clean, not because a hypocritical governor of Judea pleaded innocence in a lynching. All this was clearly seen by Florus, who seems to have felt that he had a mission against "pious drivel." What makes his fury a bit unreasonable is the following consideration. First, if anything is sure it is that Amalar, in his clumsy effort, wanted to preserve the fullness of Christ's redemptive action somehow contained in the Mass. He could serve as a witness for the *Mysterium* theory of the Maria Laach School and Anscar Vonier's *Repraesentatio*. Second, both antagonists missed the point, although this is easily understandable in the imperial period of the Church. The whole thing would probably never have come up if the Mass had been in the vernacular. What is obvious needs no allegoristic explanation. In time and space the controversy was close to the pioneer missionaries Cyril and Methodius, who translated the liturgy for raw nations, a liturgy far more complex than Rome's (and already invaded by allegorisms); therefore, they were at a disadvantage if we consider the early Roman form of the liturgy. The Gallican liturgy was full of rites of great and prolix splendor.

But I think I owe my readers a translation of Father Franz's sample Mass (p. 356), which goes like this:

The arrival of the bishop . . . arrival of Christ on earth

Gloria . . . reception of Christ by saints and angels after resurrection

The bishop sits down . . . Christ seated at the Father's right

Epistle . . . sermon preached by the Old Testament (sic)

Gradual . . . sermon of the New Testament (sic)

Gospel . . . sermon of Christ

Dominus Vobiscum (Offertory) . . . Christ greets the people of Jerusalem

Celebrant receives the gifts while choir sings . . . Christ accepts jubilation of the crowd

Celebrant offers the gifts . . . Christ enters the temple to sacrifice to the Father

Sanctus . . . the crowds cheer the Lord

First part of Canon . . . Christ suffers and disciples flee

After Consecration . . . Christ dies on the cross

Nobis quoque . . . the Roman captain confesses Christ to be the son of God

Celebrant moves the Host in cruciform gestures . . . Christ taken from the cross

Subdeacon takes the paten to the celebrant . . . women leave the tomb and return

Particle of Host dropped into chalice . . . Christ rises from the dead and reunites his body and soul (uniting bread and wine)

Agnus Dei and breaking of Host . . . disciples meet Christ on the way to Emmaus

Particles are three to symbolize tripartite Body of Christ (sic)

Last Blessing . . . Ascension after blessing the disciples (Franz, p. 356)

All this strange stuff is Amalar's interpretation of "Do this in memory of me" and First Corinthians 11:26. In his letter against Amalar the Lyonese deacon Florus cites further aberrations of Amalar: "The former Auxiliary Bishop of Lyons (PL, 119, 73 ff.) . . . carried to the synod such inept, absurd and fantastic writings, which he entitled 'Embolium,' that they should be laughed out of court. He teaches," Florus continues, "that Christ has three bodies; the one he assumed in Mary, the second the one we are in him, the Church, the third made up by those who

are dead and buried. And this is the basis for the threefold breaking of the host; the first is dropped into the chalice, the second
is on the paten, the third one for the deceased is on the altar.
He also teaches that the host is the body of Christ, while the
wine is the soul. This latter remains in our body until we are
buried, or is invisibly taken into heaven or if we cut a vein flows
away with the blood." One may blame this nonsense, pious as it
is, on the undeveloped teaching on the Eucharist in those primitive days. But this is an invalid excuse in the light of Amalar's
condemnation at the Synod of Quierzy and in view of the savage
attacks by the deacon of Lyons. The allegorical school lasted
through the heyday of scholasticism and was quite respectable,
minus the more wild speculations of our culprit.

As a second Florus, none other than the very master of St.
Thomas, Albert the Great, made a devastating attack on liturgical allegorism, if we can judge from the fact that Thomas is
more tolerant of nonsense and that other writers to our own day —
Gueranger — allegorized more or less. Albert also fought in vain.
In his *Opus de mysterio Missae* (Franz, p. 467) there is not a
description of the Mass rite, nor does this *Opus* intend to answer
the theological and liturgical problems of the Mass, but it pre-
sumes familiarity with rite and dogmatic foundation. It is a treatise
of ascetic theology. Its motto is the text from Isaiah (66:12):
"Behold, I shall descend on you as a river of peace and like an
overflowing torrent watering the glory of the nations which you
will drink" (Franz, p. 467). He divides the Mass correctly into
three parts. He concludes the entrance rite with the Collect.
This division was rediscovered by our present-day liturgiologists.
The second part ends with the Creed after the sermon; he calls
it the Instruction — also a modern achievement. This is true
about the rest.

Franz credits Albert the Great with a gift of total view of his
subject, a quality completely absent in Amalar and his imitators.
The only thing missing is an historical account — an understandable omission at this period. His strongest point is his reliance
on Scripture, where his good taste prevails. He has not a single

quotation from the authors after the great age of the Fathers. After Florus, Albert is the first writer to declare open war on allegorism. He permits no "explanation" doing violence to the text. His special targets for scorn are the many abstruse allegorical "explanations" of the signs of the cross during the Canon of the Mass. He speaks of *deliramenta hominum illiteratorum* (Franz, p. 472). It is his lack of knowledge of the historical development that causes him to retain the nonsense of the tripartite body of Christ; here his less erudite predecessor Florus follows his sounder instinct with the advantage of being closer to tradition. When Albert wrote, allegorism possessed the field; when Florus rejected it as so much theological nonsense it was a novelty easily spotted by an alert traditionalist. In the long run both the great prince of scholasticism and the little-known deacon of Lyons failed. Their battle was for the cause of sanity. They won it, but their cause lost the war in the long run. Any explanation after them "explained" the liturgy of the Mass in terms of allegorism and even in our day the method still has some champions, among them first-rate historians and theologians, probably swayed by the old argument that the long survival must indicate that a quasi-tradition has rubbed off on this method and endowed it with dignity.

The liturgy is symbolic, not allegoristic. How can the following allegorisms, quoted by Florus out of Amalar in his letter to the Synod of Quierzy, be of any significance? (*PL*, 119, 74.) "He calls the chalice of the Lord his sepulchre, the celebrant Joseph of Arimathea, the deacon Nicodemus, all three the buriers of our Lord. Another part of the mystical prayer (the canon) is meant to represent Christ praying at Mount Olivet, another section of the canon represents the Savior on the cross and after I don't know how many silly divisions he has him dying. When the celebrant bows it means that Christ bows his head and dies — 'et inclinato capite tradidit spiritum' (Jo. 19, 30). . . . When the gospel book is lifted from the altar, Amalar has the altar represent Jerusalem from which it is taken away. . . . When the Roman pontiff on the Saturday preceding Palm Sunday distributes alms, he represents Magdalene anointing the Lord. . . . He claims to

follow the example of the great St. Augustine." The list of Florus'
strictures against Amalar is too long to quote here, although our
examples are not even the worst reproaches dug up by Florus.
It is a sorry sight to see reasonable writers like Florus and St.
Albert the Great lose out against the complete misunderstanding
of sacramental symbolism and phantasts like Amalar and Duran-
dus of Mende.

I am not of a mind to unearth a forgotten and long-buried
curiosity by drawing attention to a second- or third-rate theologian
who lived at the time when the Carolingian Renaissance turned
into the Dark Ages. Florus is gifted with a curious and hitherto
underestimated clearsightedness which was a result of his own
perspicacity and the patristic tradition in all its honesty, sobriety,
and realism of faith, standing on the shoulders of Tertullian,
Hippolytus, and Jerome. Allegorism was a wild growth like morning glory which suffocated the trunk aand branches of a tree. At
this time the liturgy had become a sacred show to be watched
in awe and silence. The sober and translucid quality of the true
symbols in all their simplicity — bread, wine, water, oil, lighted
candles, incense — which spoke its language when accompanied
by the *Logos* (the sacramental word) to the simple as well as to
the complex mind and heart, had started to become enigmatic
with the loss of the people's tongue and the decay of the rites
into hollow and empty ceremonies. Let us return to our example
of breaking of the bread. This breaking (after the Pax and later
accompanied by the Agnus Dei), which was foreshadowed by the
very words of Consecration, vanished, and the secondary and
ceremonial breaking of the priest's own Host for the commixtion —
itself a novelty and a development of speculation — took its place
for the uninstructed faithful with half its content, the more
significant half at that, gone. No wonder then that the Mass rite
as a whole and in its parts was mute, and men like Amalar tried
desperately to make the mystery speak to the people. But this
à-tout-prix effort to give meaning to the mystery was, in a way,
worse than ignorance. It laid the foundation for misunderstanding
and introduced a naturalistic interpretation. We are still saddled

with such expressions as "drama" where there cannot be a drama, especially in the naturalistic sense of the word. What is dramatic in the solemn offering of bread and wine and the reality of the presence of Christ and His economy of salvation? Even the pomp and circumstance of a pontifical function could not be categorized as dramatic. The "pious exercise" (popular devotion) of Good Friday now becomes part of the liturgy; the sudden blaze of light after deep darkness during the Resurrection vigil might be called dramatic but the Eucharist is still and quiet with not the slightest resemblance to Calvary, Gethsemane, the trial and the Resurrection in gesture, declamation, or image. All the true "drama" is recondite in symbol, sacred objects, speech, and music. What is dramatic, like the Palm Procession, is added popular devotion, Gerald Vann's "histrionic liturgy" imported from Syria via the Gallican or Frankish liturgy and outside the framework of the Mass proper. How vain an effort the allegorists' to bring drama into the liturgy in an arbitrary and crude effort.

Yet Florus' victory at the Synod of Quierzy was a pyrrhic triumph. The brave and impatient man appeared out of due time and stands there alone for over 300 years, a witness to the true character of liturgy, his only ally Albert the Great. The change in attitude, the lack of comprehension by the world of the sacramental *mysterium* shaped the minds of those who reveled in allegorism and who took huge steps outside the road, *grandes passus extra viam*. There is hope for a better fate of Vonier's, Casel's, and de Lubac's discoveries — at least we hope so.

...17..

Liturgical Piety for American Catholics?

MARY PERKINS RYAN

IT WAS not so long ago that liturgy was confused with rubrics by the majority of American Catholics who thought they knew the meaning of either term. What has been taking place in the Church during the past sixty years has, we may hopefully believe, begun to change this condition. Particularly since the appearance of the *Instruction on Sacred Music and the Sacred Liturgy* of September, 1958, American Catholics have become increasingly aware of the fact that the liturgy is "the worship rendered by the Mystical Body of Christ in the entirety of its Head and members" and that "by its very nature the Mass requires that all who are present take part in it, each in the way proper to him."[1] Today American Catholics are translating the principles of this Instruction into practice. These and other promising signs encourage the hope that at last the faithful generally are beginning to find their way back to "the primary and indispensable source of the true Christian spirit — active participation in the sacred mysteries and the public solemn prayer of the Church."[2]

But the presence of forces still blocking and hindering this return is all too obvious. Many of these have been distinguished and analyzed, from trends in theology and piety during the past centuries to the psychological forces which make people resistant

---

[1] Encyclical *On the Sacred Liturgy* (America Press ed., n. 20) and *Instruction*, n. 22 (translation published in *Worship*, November, 1958).

[2] See Gerald Ellard, S.J., *The Mass in Transition* (Milwaukee: Bruce, 1956). The quotation is from the Motu Proprio of St. Pius X, *Tra le sollecitudini*, November, 1903.

to change, especially in the realm of religious practice.[3] But, among the forces operating against the liturgical renewal in this country, there is one which, it seems to me, has not yet been given the attention it deserves; and this is the idea, the vague picture, that comes to the minds of American priests and people alike when they hear or read such phrases as "living with the Church," "celebrating the Church's feasts and seasons," or "liturgical year." This notion, this picture, has connotations and implications that make the idea of centering Catholic life on the liturgy seem alien and alienating, romantic and completely unrealistic.

It may well be, then, that it is this current notion of what "liturgical piety" means and implies which — to a great extent at least — makes many zealous bishops, priests, lay leaders, and "ordinary Catholics" uneasy about, if not positively opposed to, the liturgical renewal and its aims, since these appear to be opposed to an effective apostolate in our society. And it is from what is presupposed by this same notion that flow several of the major difficulties explicitly raised and implicitly felt, even by those concerned in the liturgical renewal, as to the incompatibility between "living with the Church" and living in modern America, difficulties based on the uprooted, unnatural qualities of our civilization and the "antinuminous" character of our mentality.

But here is one obstacle that can be removed. The modern "return to the sources" in every field of sacred studies, together with the practical experience of Christians who have been trying to "live with the Church" in the modern world, make it possible to discern the defects in this current notion of liturgical piety and what it implies. The essential elements and the dynamic pattern of the Catholic Christian life as such are beginning to stand out, and, as they do so, it is becoming increasingly clear that truly traditional Catholic life is essentially "liturgical," that it is not dependent on any particular social pattern or civilization,

---

[3] See, e.g., Charles Davis, Liturgy and Doctrine (New York: Sheed & Ward, 1960); Godfrey Diekmann, O.S.B., Come, Let us Worship (Baltimore: Helicon Press, 1961), especially the first two chapters; and "A Layman Looks at Participation" by Dr. Thomas Caulfield, M.D., in Participation in the Mass (Washington, D. C.; The Liturgical Conference, 1960).

and that, far from being unrealistic or un-American, it is precisely true "liturgical piety" which appeals to everything that is best in our modern mentality, which appeals to those who are seeking God both inside and outside the visible Church, in our own country, and all over the world.[4]

There is urgent need, therefore, to distinguish between the current inadequate and misleading notion of what "living with the Church" means and implies and that true idea; to see how many difficulties disappear when this distinction is made. To indicate all this — if only to promote more, and more authoritative, discussion — is the purpose of the present essay.

Consider, for example, the picture that immediately comes to mind with the term "liturgical year." Isn't it that of a calendar (probably in some style of art considered to be particularly "liturgical" or "Christian") — a calendar with a special New Year of its own, and with every day characterized by some particular observance? And this calendar, presumably, is to replace the secular one in the mind of the truly liturgical Christian, so that, for instance, he would naturally refer to September 29 as "Michaelmas" rather than September 29.

Now the thought of living by such a calendar cannot help seem unrealistic, to say the least, unless Catholics are to live in isolated villages or ghettos and give up doing business with the rest of the world. And so, immediately, the idea of a life centered in the liturgy appears unrealistic to many apostolic-minded Catholics, because they see their vocation as one precisely of involvement in charity in the ordinary life of mankind.

Or think of the picture conjured up by the phrase "celebrating the feasts and seasons of the Church." Isn't it that of a congregation crowding out of a church, singing snatches of Gregorian chant (or a Gelineau psalm or some old French or German hymn tune), going home to say a special grace around "liturgically" decorated tables spread with "traditional" dishes, and looking forward to returning to church to take part in Vespers or some para-liturgical

[4] See, for example, *The Liturgy and Unity in Christ* (Washington, D. C.: The Liturgical Conference, 1961), esp. p. 106 ff.

service and to ending the day with a festivity including songs, games, and square dancing, followed by Compline?

Where does such a picture come from, and why has it come to be more or less accepted as the liturgical ideal? It would seem as though, in part at least, it projects the nostalgia of Catholics of various European origins for a way of life remembered from their own childhood or from the descriptions of parents or even grandparents — a way of life remembered as more integrally religious, more in touch with the realities of the faith, than is our chaotic, secular, materialistic American culture. And so this picture and what it connotes appeals also to other Catholics who feel, for one reason or another, the need for a way of life quite different from their own — especially, perhaps, parents and pastors who realize how much simpler their task would be if things could be ordered along some such lines. Many of us have, then, consciously or unconsciously promoted such a picture, or at least some of its elements, as being of the essence of "liturgical" living. And all this fits in far too well with the still widespread impression that liturgy is chiefly concerned with externals (and with the commercial instinct to promote anything involving objects that might be sold in the name of piety or written up and photographed in the name of publicity). And so it has come about that "liturgical customs," as well as "liturgical vestments" and "liturgical altars," have become an accepted part of the American Catholic vocabulary, all contributing to an almost completely misleading picture of what liturgical piety really means.

This is not, of course, to deny the value of any of the elements of the picture sketched out above. The point is that none of them is *essential* to a "liturgical" life, rightly understood, and, in the absence of any general realization of what *is* essential, they make up a picture of a way of life which could never be realized in America as we know it and which, in any case, would not be liturgically ideal.

To build up such a way of life is an unrealistic aim because it presupposes a community in which the social and religious interests of the majority of its members are not only interwoven but mainly limited to the community itself — a situation less and less true in our country today. Even if it were possible to work out a pattern of socio-religious life with elements taken from American rather than foreign cultures, people simply do not stay within parish or community limits consistently enough to allow such a pattern to take root and flourish as a native product.

But a pattern of this kind would not be liturgically ideal either. It implies a way of life in which nature, human customs, and supernature are harmoniously interwoven to constitute a complete context for individual, family, and social life — a context which presumably humanizes and Christianizes people almost by itself. But any pattern such as this is necessarily as much of a deterrent as an aid to mature Christian living — to "liturgical" living. Unforced, positive adherence to Christ and His life is of the essence of a life lived in awareness of the implications of Baptism, Confirmation, the Eucharist. Unforced, positive adherence to the Christian community as such and the readiness of that community to welcome anyone fully into its life is of the essence of a Christian life aware of the implications of the Eucharist. And such adherence is made more difficult, not less, by any inherited socio-religious pattern (including the racial-origins equivalent of the *"cuius regio, eius religio"* principle that still exists to some extent in the United States).

It may well be, therefore, that the physical and social mobility of American life will ultimately bring about a healthy kind of dispersion of racial and social groupings, helping to free each individual's personal commitment to the faith and to the whole community of the faithful from the limitations of racial and social bonds, and bringing out the possibility of, and the need for true Christian community. But, in any case, the liturgical renewal is in no way concerned with any program of trying to restore either the medieval village or the one-time American racial parish way of life in any form. It seeks to "restore all things in Christ" and therefore, necessarily, to foster in every way the possibility and the growth of each Christian in "that freedom wherewith Christ has made us free."

Even more deeply, perhaps, the present picture of a "liturgical customs" way of life presupposes, together with a more or less stable and static religio-social community, a more or less stable and static view of the cosmos and of human life. Such a view of the universe has taken many forms in the past, Christian and otherwise, all implying a sense of the unity of reality, a sense that nature, human nature, and whatever is above nature, all form one great and ordered whole.

And it is precisely this sense of the unity of reality which modern men are losing or have lost. God has vanished from their world picture. He can no longer be relied on, so to speak, to keep things going in their accustomed paths, in the cheerful Victorian sense that "God's in His heaven, all's right with the world." (In this light, the unconsciously blasphemous chumminess of such modern expressions as "the Man upstairs," "my copilot," and even "the Home Office," seem to be rather pathetic attempts to keep in touch with a God whose presence can no longer be taken for granted.) The universe no longer seems a familiar home for mankind; we feel it to be strange and hostile — as science-fiction abundantly indicates — even though we are preparing to explore it. And, while our lives may actually be far more strictly regulated by work patterns and social pressures than were our ancestors' by church and social customs, we feel that human life is essentially disordered. Increasingly aware of the strange depths and forces within ourselves and others, we hope against hope that somehow things must be "getting better and better," but suspect that instead the whole human race is being rushed pell-mell toward some unthinkable abyss. Nor is this state of mind limited to unbelievers; we are all affected by it to some extent.[5]

With such a sense of loneliness, alienation, disorder, and imminent disaster dominant in our times, the notion of trying to create or re-create a way of life which presupposes a sense of security in the ordered harmony of the universe seems not only

---

[5] See Hans Urs von Balthasar, *Science, Religion and Christianity* (Westminster, Md.: Newman, 1959).

unrealistic but almost frivolous, irrelevant to today's urgent needs and questionings. Many serious students of religion, in fact, are wondering how an essentially sacramental and liturgical religion can be made to seem in any way relevant to modern men. How can the Church flourish (or even survive) in a mentality increasingly cut off from mankind's deep roots in nature, from the harmonies between man and the various levels of being above and below him which have always nourished human cultures in the past, and which the Church counts on, so to speak, in conveying Christ's message in human words, in conveying His life through the sacramental signs?

Yet the fact is that the present sense of cosmic disunity and impending disaster is at least as close to the view of reality actually presented by Scripture and the liturgy as is the view it is replacing — which in the recent past of our particular civilization had degenerated into taking God for granted as part of a scheme of things designed automatically to give anyone who obeyed the rules "all this and heaven too."

The biblical and traditionally Christian view certainly sees all things as brought into being by God through His creative Word and life-giving Spirit, and so as essentially good, reflecting and praising His perfections in beautiful order and harmony. It sees God as present in all things, as indicated by all things. Yet it finds Him veiled in "inaccessible light," completely transcendent to His creation, the "Utterly Other," except as He freely reveals and gives Himself in His loving mercy to the creatures He has made to His image and likeness.

And this view sees the original order of creation as having been violated by a rebellion of created spirits that somehow involves material creation — spirits who seduced mankind, in the person of Adam, and so enslaved us to evil, pain, disunity, and death. Cosmic and human history is, then, a vast struggle between rebel spiritual powers and God's love, willing to re-create, to re-establish all things still more wonderfully than in the first creation. And the victory is to be won by love, for God not only respects but cherishes the free will and the dignity with which He has endowed His reasonable creatures.[6] And so He sent His own Son, His Word, to become one of us, "like us in all things save sin," to redeem mankind from within, as it were, by suffering, dying, and rising again as a Man, as the new Adam, in loving obedience to His Father's Will. God sent His Son to become our Brother, to win us over and enlist us in His work of redeeming mankind and the cosmos, to unite us in Himself as free human persons in a community of love, pouring out in our hearts the Spirit of love and unity. For His purpose is to re-create us and bring us to share His own life as the complete human persons He meant us to be, carried beyond the limitations of the human nature even at its integral best, so that we are to become "sons in the Son," sharing in Christ's own life with the Father.[7]

The biblical-liturgical view of reality, then, does indeed see human and cosmic history as ordered and ruled by God's Providence — but not to give us a cosy, comfortable, childishly secure life here on earth. Christ has conquered the powers of darkness, sin, and death. But God honors human freedom so greatly that He gives us the opportunity to accept or refuse His life and love, to take part in the redeeming and re-creating work of Christ or to remain enclosed in our own self-love, prisoners and instruments of the Enemy. He works in us "both the willing and the doing," if we will let Him do so, but in such a way that it is most intimately and personally our own.

Each Christian life really lived as a Christian life, then, is necessarily a struggle, a warfare, carried on in the strength of Christ against the Enemy of God and mankind. But not a lonely struggle — for it is carried on in and with the whole Church. And the life of the whole Church on earth is a struggle — but not an unending warfare, for it is oriented toward the day of the Lord's return

---

[6] Vincent Wilkin, S.J., *From Limbo to Heaven, An Essay on the Economy of the Redemption* (New York: Sheed & Ward, 1961) brings out many aspects of God's respect for the order of freedom and responsibility He has established. See, for example, p. 132 ff.

[7] See F. X. Durrwell, C.SS.R., *The Resurrection* (New York: Sheed & Ward, 1960).

in glory to make His victory complete in redeemed mankind as it is already complete in Himself, seated in glory at His Father's right hand. The whole history of mankind receives its meaning and purpose from this struggle, in and through which Christ's Mystical Body is being built up, and will reach its climax and conclusion at that unknown, always imminent, day of the Lord's return.[8]

The present view of reality, then, in its strange dynamism, may well be antipathetic to the static, "rationalistic" aspects of Christian truth and life which have been dominant in the catechisms, theological manuals, and works of apologetics of the past few centuries. It may well be simply indifferent to the "things I must believe and do" view of the Christian life. But it would seem to be open precisely to the dynamic aspects of Christianity which were underemphasized during the same centuries and are now being brought out once more by the "return to the sources" of recent times. (It should be stressed here, perhaps, that this "return to the sources" does not mean any attempt to return to the mentality of the first Christian centuries. It is rather the turning of the accredited "householders" of the Church to the treasury which is hers by divine endowment, to bring out "new things and old" — to make most fully available to men of the present age the truth and life that Christ continually communicates to His Church.)

Among these aspects might be mentioned: an awareness of the infinite "Otherness" of God which forbids us to take Him for granted and so enables us to welcome in overwhelming wonder the mystery of His love for us; of the actual state of fallen mankind and the cosmos as subject to the "rulers of this world of darkness"; of the tension between human self-centeredness and our deep need for union with one another and with God — a tension we cannot resolve by our own resources; of the responsibility of our stewardship with regard to material things; of the

---

[8] For a striking synthesis of the biblical-Christian view of reality, see Louis Bouyer, *Introduction to Spirituality* (New York: Desclée, 1961), particularly p. 143 ff.

crucial nature of human life and the dynamic character of time and history, not going round and round or toward something vaguely "better and better," but hastening on toward the final decisive event.

Above all, perhaps, the modern mentality is reaching out — through its experience of the loneliness of man, and of each man, in the universe, through its experience of the need for personal communion with other persons, for sharing experience and love with other persons — to the Christian reality of communion with other persons in the Body of Christ which is the Church, and, beyond all human dreams, of communion with the Father, as "sons in the Son," in the Spirit.[9]

It would, then, seem providential, in the deepest meaning of the term, that modern Catholic scholarship, pastoral work, spirituality and apostolic effort are now converging to bring out the profound, traditionally Christian meaning of what the catechism tells us is the purpose of our lives: "to know, love and serve God in this world and to be happy with Him forever in the next."

To "know God" does not merely mean to know truths *about* Him; it means to know Him with the mutual personal knowing that is at once knowledge, intimacy, likeness, union in love. This knowing is itself the true and everlasting life that Christ came to give us "abundantly": "I am come that they may have life, and have it in abundance. . . . This is true life, that they may know You, the one true God, and Jesus Christ whom You have sent."

To "love God" does not mean merely to "prefer Him to anything else" in the sense in which this is usually taken as meaning the avoidance of mortal sin. It means opening ourselves out to receive and communicate the very love of God Himself, poured out into our hearts by the Spirit — the infinitely generous, self-giving

---

[9] For the special challenge and opportunities presented to Christianity by the modern mentality, see particularly Hans Urs von Balthasar, *op. cit.*, and also his chapter "God Has Spoken in Human Language" in *The Liturgy and the Word of God* (Collegeville, Minn.: The Liturgical Press), and, in the same volume, the chapter by Charles Moeller, "Is It Possible, in the 20th Century, to Be a 'Man of the Bible'?"

love with which the Father and the Son love One Another, the love revealed and communicated to men in Christ, so that we can love God and one another with His own love.

To "serve God" does not simply mean a legalistic nontransgression of the Commandments of God and the Church. It means obeying the positive command to love God and our neighbor with Christ's own love, following His example, even to laying down our lives.

And "to be happy with Him forever in the next" means the fullness of this "knowing" — to "know even as we are known"; it means being fully "inspirited," body and soul, with the Spirit of vitality, power, love, sharing the glory of the Risen Christ. It means life in the city of God, the community of the redeemed, gathered in Christ into the very life of God "all in all."

But, equally, as Scripture and Christian tradition testify and as all the great movements in the Church today are once more bringing out, it is the celebration of the Eucharist in the "assembly," the community of the Church which is the focus of God's communication to men of this "knowledge" and "love" revealed and communicated to us in Christ. The whole sacramental life of the Church is ordered toward the celebration of the Eucharist. Her prayer-life radiates from it. Her life of practical activity is ordered toward gathering men here and now into the Eucharistic unity of the Church and toward the final purpose of the Eucharist Itself — the upbuilding of the Body of Christ to the final perfection willed for it by God, to the perfection of the life of the redeemed in the world to come, already, here and now, anticipated in the celebration of the Eucharist.

Therefore, when St. Pius X stated that active participation in the sacred mysteries is the primal and indispensable source of the true Christian spirit, he was simply stating the central fact of Catholic Christian life.[10]

---

[10] For a study of the biblical and Christian sense of the terms "knowledge of God" and "love of God" and their implications, see Louis Bouyer, op. cit. The same author gives a detailed study of these same terms in Volume I of the History of Christian Spirituality, by Fr. Bouyer and others. (The French work,

In the historical development of the liturgical renewal of our times, receiving Holy Communion, "knowing Christ in the breaking of Bread," was the aspect of this participation first to be restored to the faithful, by the decrees of St. Pius X on early and frequent Communion, followed by those of his successors making it increasingly available.[11]

Then came the restoration of active internal and external participation in Christ's sacrifice, in His great work of worshiping the Father "in Spirit and in truth," His great work of praise in which "the whole work of our redemption is renewed." And with this came a renewed emphasis on the social aspects of Christian worship and the correlative social responsibility of Christians to put themselves actively at the service of the Church and of their neighbor in order to carry out Christ's work of love in the world.[12]

But only quite recently, perhaps, has it become clear that active participation in the Mass is complete only when it includes actively hearing the Word of God in faith, and only so can we come to know Christ, and through Him the Father, in the full human-divine way He intends. God wishes to deal with us in the Church as the human persons we are, made and remade to His image and likeness; and so He wishes to communicate with us through His word *in human words* at the same time as He gives us His life through that creative Word and His life-giving Spirit, enabling us to respond to His love through and with His Incarnate Word.

And so, in the Church, the inspired Word and the sacramental Word have always been associated — the Word spoken to us and the Word acting on us and in us. The whole liturgy not only contains the inspired Word, but is woven of it throughout its whole texture. In all the sacramental rites, the sign and what it effects involve each other; the rites built up by the Church around the

Histoire de la Spiritualité Chrétienne, is published by Aubier, Paris, 3 vols. An English translation is to be published by Desclée, New York).
[11] See G. Ellard, op. cit., particularly p. 256 ff.
[12] Ibid., especially pp. 68 ff. and 166 ff. A beautiful summary of participation in this whole sense was given by Cardinal Lercaro in his talk at the Liturgical Week of 1959 (Participation in the Mass, p. 31 ff.).

essential sign are essentially biblical, and their purpose is further to open out, to communicate its meaning. Here, as in human communication, gestures and the use of things are an integral part of "speech" as a whole. But it is the spoken word which is the normal means of communication, itself enabling us to go beyond words in our intercourse with one another. So too in our intercourse with Christ in the Church. Here, again, as in human communication, speaking together cannot be neatly distinguished from the total effect of persons on one another. Christ communicates His life to us through the sacraments at a level beyond the reach of our ordinary consciousness, but He does so through the sacramental signs that signify what they effect, so that we may come to know Him with our whole human selves, with all our powers of mind and heart.[13]

Once we begin to realize this essential place of the inspired Word in the sacramental life of the Church, then we realize also that each sacrament is intended to be a fully human, personal act of communication with Christ — although it goes so far beyond the human. In the Mass, above all, we hear Him speak to us — to each of us personally in the holy community of the Church, revealing Himself and the Father, telling us about one or another aspect of His redeeming work, inviting us to share in it, opening out to us what God promises to those who accept His Word and His love; and we welcome this Word with the response of faith which He Himself enables us to give. So we are prepared to take part in Christ's work, to respond to the Father's love by taking part in Christ's own Eucharist. And, by taking part in the sacrifice, by joining our self-offering with His, we come to know Him in another way, as we come to know another human person well

---

[13] The Congress of the *Centre de Pastorale Liturgique* held at Strassbourg in 1958 might be said to have marked the confluence of the liturgical and scriptural aspects of today's renewal. The papers given at this Congress, published by the Liturgical Press in *The Liturgy and the Word of God* are invaluable for awakening and clarifying our sense of the place of the Word of God in the liturgy and in Christian life. Also especially worthy of attention in this connection are the first four chapters in Louis Bouyer's *Introduction to Spirituality*, and the section on "Liturgy" in Hans Urs von Balthasar's *Prayer* (New York: Sheed & Ward, 1961), p. 88 ff.

by sharing in his work, becoming one with him in act and purpose. Then, finally, we are united with Him in sacramental Communion, sharing His very life.

Once we begin to gain this realization that God really wants to speak with us, to "get in touch" with us as human persons, through His Word, then everything in the Christian life begins to take on its true sense and proportion. We see the reason for the various feasts and seasons of the Church — so that Christ can communicate God's message, His plan, His demands, His promises to us in a way that our human minds and hearts can assimilate; so that we can respond to the various aspects of the one great work of Christ, thus presented to us as it were separately, with the one thanksgiving of Christ's Eucharist.

We see also that this Word spoken to us at Mass — where it is proclaimed by the Church in whom Christ is present and active and received in the assembly of the Church vivified by the Spirit — cannot be fully received and assimilated only *at* Mass. We need to hear it, be fed by it, and formed by it every day. And so we see the necessity for a daily prayer which is organically connected with the Mass, a prayer in which we listen to Christ speaking to us through His scriptural word, and respond to Him with a response formed by that same word, offering ourselves with Him to the Father in the Spirit.

Again, we see that our moral life, our obedience to God's Law, is not meant to be so much the following out of a code of things to do or not to do, as our response, by His grace, to what He asks of us by way of cooperation with His plan — what He asks of us in each Mass and in our prayer, through the inspired words of Scripture which His grace opens out to us and enables us to receive in "good and noble hearts." And we see that this necessarily involves the effort to "die daily" to our sinful and selfish selves, in cooperation with the grace of Baptism and Penance, in order to be free to live His life, to serve one another after His example, to take our part in His work.

Thus we realize that our lives are not meant to be a disconnected assortment of "prayers, works, and sufferings," but integrated, increasingly "spiritual" lives; that is, lives vivified by the Spirit; lives of coming to know Christ, and one another in Christ; lives of loving service of Him and of one another, in the joy of union with Him and one another. We see that our lives are meant to be "eucharistic" in the most profound sense, as sharing in the Eucharist of Christ, as sharing in His intercourse with His Bride, the Church, drawing her and ourselves as her members, into His own response to the Father in the Spirit.

"Active participation in the sacred mysteries" is thus seen as being the most direct and effective — because the God-designed, the truly traditional way — of coming to "know Christ" in this full sense. Hence it is also clear that such "liturgical piety" is what will enable us most effectively to carry out our task of sharing in His redeeming work in our world. Because we are coming to know Christ and His love, we can witness to what He means to us — or, rather, He witnesses through us to what He wills to do in and through the most ordinary of human lives. Because we are coming to know all the dimensions of His plan for mankind, we realize that He came — He comes — to redeem and transfigure real human nature, so that with His grace all true human progress, all development of human potentialities, everything that enables men to be more fully human, contributes to the final perfection of the City of God. Because we are trying to take part in His redemptive sacrifice in the Mass, we see the need to make our daily work a sacrifice of thanksgiving and of loving service of our neighbors' needs. Because we take part in the one Bread that makes us one Body in Christ, we do everything in our power to remove whatever interferes with the human unity of mankind, to remove all the constraints of fear, overwhelming need, insatiable wants, prejudice, compulsion from without or within, that prevent men from hearing God's message and responding to Him, from entering into the unity of redeemed mankind in Christ. All this is part of our Christian task today; all this is implied by active participation in the Mass.[14]

---

[14] Nor is this simply a theoretical deduction from the principles of participation. Anyone who has had the privilege of knowing and working with the

Living a "liturgical" life, then, means actively committing ourselves to — rather than being passively carried along by — the current of the Church's life of communication with the Incarnate Word, present and active in her, as she progresses through the years of human time toward the final consummation. It means actively committing ourselves to taking part according to our vocation in "redeeming the times," not in escaping from them.

For liturgical living is simply full Catholic living, carried out in our own times according to the primordial pattern of Catholic life, in the most direct communication possible with the source of that life: Christ communicating with His Church and with each of her members, giving Himself to us inseparably in the Bread of the inspired Word and the Bread of the Eucharistic Word; inviting us to respond to the Father's love with Him in the "spiritual sacrifice of daily life" to be offered by spending ourselves unstintingly for our neighbor in union with His Eucharistic Sacrifice; communicating to us the Spirit who enables us to hear and to respond, who works in us "both the willing and the doing."

And so such a life might be very simply defined as "hearing the Word of God and doing it" — receiving the Word and putting it into practice — the Christian life of which the holy Mother of God is the supreme exemplar.

In this light, the place and value of what are now called "liturgical customs" becomes quite clear — as reminders and extensions in our daily life of the Word we receive in the Church and of our eucharistic response to and with that Word to the Father in the Spirit. When any such practices are adopted or grow up in families or parishes from a real hearing and doing of the Word, then they do not seem superficial or alien, but "right and availing to salvation." But the pastor who recommends the use of Advent wreaths, for example, to his Ladies' Guild (or the parents who

pioneers and leaders of the liturgical renewal in this country realizes that their "witness" has been a primary factor in his own "conversion" to the liturgy and that this witness is the best proof of the value of what they have been inculcating. See Bishop Wright's summary of this opinion of the liturgical movement, its leaders and its effects, in *The Liturgy and Unity in Christ* (Washington, D. C.: The Liturgical Conference, 1961). In this same volume, see also "The True Christian Spirit at Work in Today's World" by Rev. Thomas Carroll.

try to incorporate this practice into their family life) without first and continually working at the essential — to proclaim and open out and do the Word given us by the Church during Advent — is only adding one more burden to lives already overcharged and overexternalized with "things to do." For, except in relation to this hearing and doing, such customs all too easily become simply another form of pious "gimmick."

In this light also, it is obvious that living with the Church cannot mean trying to live by a Church calendar as opposed to the secular one. The fact is that the Church never had any intention of setting up a "liturgical year" in this sense.[15] It is quite true, however, that it used to seem so. In the past centuries, the true flow of the Church's sacramental life had become overlaid with various growths that obscured the real bearing of her "seasons." But the legislation of recent decades, from the reforms initiated by St. Pius X to the latest decree on the simplification of the rubrics — with the promise of much more to come along the same lines — is once again bringing out the real nature of the Church's seasons and celebrations.

These are in no sense meant simply to mark the passing of time, or to differentiate one day from another as a separate static entity. Instead, they constitute the dynamic current of the Church's existential inner life, in which she communicates with her Lord, with Him worships the Father in Spirit and in truth, builds herself up, and sanctifies her children. It is this current of the Church's life, centered in the Eucharistic Sacrifice, which makes each year of human history since the Resurrection a "year of the Lord." And so we help to make each year a "year of grace" for ourselves and others by uniting the current of our lives as intimately as possible with this current of Christ's life in the Church and hers in Him.

---

[15] It is interesting to note that Dom Guéranger's great pioneer work was called *The Liturgical Year*, while Dr. Pius Parsch's later one is entitled *The Church's Year of Grace*. And the latter, in the English translation published by the Liturgical Press in 1957, contains a second introduction: "The Liturgical Year, a New Evaluation," bringing out this fact that there actually is no such thing as a "Church year," but rather liturgical or festal seasons unfolding within the context of the civil year.

Moreover, as Pius Parsch says so succinctly,[16] the rhythm of this current of the Church's life is that of grace, not nature. In the seasons dependent on Easter, the Church celebrates Christ's going from this world to the Father: His Exodus from the life of the "flesh" — that is, of human nature as it has been made by sin — "to the life of the Spirit": the power, the vitality, the creative love of God charging the whole of human nature with His glory — and our going with Him and in Him. In Advent and Christmas time, she celebrates Christ's coming from the Father to undertake and carry out and complete this work, of making us "sons in the Son." In the weeks "after Pentecost" and "after Epiphany," the Church simply lives the life Christ gives her, the life He gives us in her, so that we may praise God for it and live it more fully.

The feasts of the saints are not meant to interrupt or distract us from this basic rhythm of the Church's life. They are to celebrate Christ's victory in His members — above all, in her who supremely "heard the Word of God and kept it" — to unite us with our brothers and sisters of every century, to give us the hope and encouragement of their example and the benefit of their intercession, as we go on our pilgrim way in the pilgrim Church, still *in via.*

True "living with the Church" according to her feasts and seasons, then, means hearing, and responding with, the Word as she gives it to us, above all in the Masses of the "Proper of the Time" and in the reading of Scripture appropriate to each season[17] and trying to carry out in our daily lives what is suggested to us by that Word. And this cannot distract us from our particular involvement in ordinary human life; rather it enables us to live as true witnesses to Christ and servants of our neighbor.

Once we see the Christian life as essentially that of "hearing the Word of God and doing it," it becomes clear that many of the difficulties raised as to the incompatibility between the life Christ gives us in the Church and the modern mentality flow

---

[16] *Op. cit.*
[17] See L. Bouyer, *Introduction to Spirituality,* pp. 48–49.

from a mistaken notion of the essentials of the Christian life.

In order fully to "live with the Church," we do not need, for example, to be living a life closely bound up with nature's seasons. The primordial Christian celebration of Sunday as "the day of the Lord" has no analogue in nature. It flows entirely from the Word of God and His saving intervention in human history. The great Paschal celebration — toward which flow the pre-Lenten and Lenten seasons, and from which flows the Easter season — may have had its far-off anticipations in Canaanite spring rites. But God's intervention in the Exodus — revealing Himself to His people, redeeming them from slavery, making them His own by covenant — transformed, many centuries before Christ, whatever spring festival the Israelites may have held into a celebration of God's great redemptive work for His people. And it was this celebration — praising God for His great works of the past, renewed in the blessings of the present, anticipating and calling for those of the messianic future — which Christ took up and fulfilled in His Eucharist at the Last Supper.[18]

In this Eucharist, He celebrated the Sacrifice of the New Covenant, His Exodus to the Father through His passion and death. And it is this Exodus — with all its preparations and foreshadowings in the Old Testament, its re-presentation here and now in the sacramental life of the Church, its final consummation when the whole Church finally shares in the glory of her risen Head — this is what the Church celebrates in every Eucharist, on every Sunday, and in the Paschal feasts.

It is true that the feasts of Epiphany and Christmas seem to have been placed where they are in connection with the winter solstice in the Northern hemisphere: the pagan rejoicing at the "rebirth of the unconquered light" suggesting to the Christians the appropriateness of a celebration of the Coming of the True Light.[19]

---

[18] See F. X. Durrwell, The Resurrection (New York: Sheed & Ward, 1961), esp. pp. 17 ff., 48 ff., 319 ff.

[19] See J. Jungmann, S.J., The Early Liturgy (University of Notre Dame Press, 1959), p. 147 ff. The winter solstice is also the reason for New Year's being where it is in the Roman calendar on which our present calendar is based. Christmas and New Year's, therefore, would seem to be closely associated as

But it is not any annual natural phenomenon which the Church celebrates in Advent and the Christmas-Epiphany season; it is the unique Coming of the Son of God to make us "sons in the Son" — His whole Coming to mankind, initiated by the Incarnation, continued here and now through the Church, completed by His visible manifestation in glory at the Last Day.

Now, it was certainly not by accident that Christ "by dying destroyed our death and by rising again restored our life" at the time of year when nature is as it were re-created: there is an analogy between the Paschal renewal of the grace of our Baptism and the renewal of nature in the springtime; and nature's spring each year can be seen as a kind of natural picture of the final making-new of all things in Christ. There is certainly also a connection between the significance which the pagans of the first centuries attached to the winter solstice — the victory of good over evil, hope over despair — and the Coming of Christ that fulfills all hopes.

But none of these concordances can be carried too far (how is Advent, for instance, comparable to the onset of winter?) — above all, because nature's seasons are repeated year after year. But Christ became incarnate, died, and rose again once for all, some two thousand years ago. And each year of human time since then is, not a repetition of the same yearly cycle, but *another* "year of the Lord," through which the Church, within human history, is growing, progressing toward the final consummation. (And if the Church's seasons were in any essential way dependent on nature's,

---

to origin; and it is actually on Christmas Day that ambassadors to the Holy See present their New Year's greetings to the Holy Father. When the liturgical books first came to be put together in their present form, it was natural to begin with the season of preparation for Christmas, as associated with the civil beginning of a new year. (See Bouman and Ryan, *Key to the Missal*, Fides, 1960, pp. 27–28.) The First Sunday of Advent, then, was never meant to be the "New Year's Day of the Church" or the beginning of the liturgical year; it cannot have a beginning in this sense, although, certainly, a new beginning in our yearly effort to live Christ's life is indicated at Septuagesima. It is interesting, in this connection, to note that in the recent decree on the simplification of the rubrics, the first of January, while still a feast of the "first class," is now the "Octave Day of Christmas" rather than the "Feast of the Circumcision," indicating that it is a holy day in order to sanctify the beginning of a new year of human time as our civilization reckons it.

then the dates of Easter and Christmas would have to vary with degrees of latitude and particular climates, and be held at the opposite pole of the year in Australia and New Zealand — something which not even the most ardent proponent of adapting the liturgy to the needs of different peoples and cultures has seriously suggested.)

The fact that our present culture is not intimately attuned to the yearly cycle of nature is, therefore, no real obstacle to our participating in the Church's seasons. No more is modern man's apparent lack of a sense of the symbolism of natural things a real obstacle to our living the sacramental Christian life.

Actually, there are three different questions involved here, and they need to be distinguished rather carefully. The first is the fact that some of the particular things used and referred to in the liturgy do not have the immediate human connotations in our culture which they had (and still have to a great extent) in the culture of the countries around the Mediterranean Sea, and which more of these things had in our own culture prior to modern times. Bread, for example, does not mean "food"; wine does not mean "drink"; olive oil does not have the connotations which we associate with butter, poly-nonsaturated fats, salves, ointments, perfumes, etc.

But this is not a peculiarly *modern* difficulty: the Chinese, South Sea Islanders, Eskimos always have had the same problem as modern Americans in this regard. And this difficulty is a necessary result of the very fact of the Incarnation and of all sacred history as God has planned it. In becoming man, the eternal Word had to become a particular man, born in a particular culture, at a particular time in history. In accepting God's self-revelation and self-giving, we have to accept the various effects of this "particularity." And, precisely by adverting to it, Christians learn to enter into the essentially historical character of God's dealings with mankind, with us: how it was precisely His plan to take one small people in one small corner of the world as His own in order to save and gather all mankind into His life. This difficulty, then, when it is accepted for what it is, can be made into a positive means of helping ourselves and others to understand and enter into God's plan.[20]

The second difficulty raised in this same connection is that modern men are no longer aware of, or responsive to, the natural symbolism of things: water does not connote either destruction or purity and new life; food does not mean re-creation; light does not mean emerging from the shadow of death. All these things come too easily and mechanically to civilized man for him to respond to them as, it is said, a human being should. He turns a tap instead of carrying water from a well or stream; drives to the supermarket instead of cultivating the earth in the sweat of his brow; pushes a switch and the lights come on. And so he has lost the sense of wonder and awe in the face of nature, and with it the possibility of responding to the sacramental signs.

Now it well may be true that our present primarily utilitarian view of material things and forces may inhibit some of the possible resonances of the sacramental signs in some of the levels of our psychophysical makeup. But the essential purpose of these signs is not somehow impersonally to affect our subconscious. They are Christ's instruments through which He communicates with us, Person-to-person, giving us His own life on that level of our being which is above ordinary consciousness and enabling us to "know" Him with our human minds and hearts (in the biblical sense of the latter term, as being the deepest center of our whole intellectual-volitional life). Modern men may not fear nature or wonder at it as did primitive man. But we still use and enjoy or endure it. We drink water, wash in it, swim in it, and sometimes drown in it, benefit from irrigation and suffer for the effects of floods. We still eat and drink, and center our family and community celebrations on some form of eating and drinking together. And it is such human use, endurance, enjoyment of created nature on which God has based His use of natural elements and forces in sacred history, in Scripture, and in the

---

[20] See A. Martimort, *Signs of the New Covenant* (Liturgical Press, 1962), particularly the first chapter; also L. Bouyer, *The Meaning of Sacred Scripture* (Notre Dame, 1958), p. 231 ff.

sacramental life of the Church. We do not, therefore, need to react to water with the wondering awe of "primitive man" in order to appreciate Baptism. We need to allow the Word of God to lead us from the known — our own direct or vicarious experiences with water — to the unknown: the realities of His life communicated to us, by means of what He tells us about God's use of water — from the primal waters over which hovered the life-giving Spirit, to the water of life that flows through the City of God. And the same thing is true of the other natural elements and things used and referred to in Scripture and the liturgy and, more deeply, of the experiences of God's people in the Old and New Testaments.

In connection with the previous difficulty, it is quite true that we have to become "spiritually Semites" as Pius XII said, in order to be truly and authentically Christian. But this means "in the Spirit," the Spirit who inspired Scripture, who animates the Church, who dwells in us to lead us into all truth — the truth which is Christ. And so the key to the Christian understanding of Scripture is to receive it and pray it primarily and focally in the liturgy, where we receive it most immediately from the Church in the context of her tradition, and where we receive it most immediately in the Church as an integral part of our total sacramental encounter with Christ. And, equally, the key to full participation in the liturgy is to realize it primarily as our most personal encounter with Christ in the living unity and community of the Church — the meaning of which He illuminates and opens out to us in all its dimensions through the sacramental signs and all Scripture.[21]

But the third key is needed if we are to come to know Christ in the liturgy and Scripture: we must be trying to "do the truth in love" in our lives. St. Gregory sums up these three essential elements of the Christian life and their interconnection in his commentary on St. Luke's account of the disciples at Emmaus

---

[21] See Cyprian Vagaggini, O.S.B., *Theological Dimensions of the Liturgy* (Liturgical Press, 1959), Vol. I, esp. p. 40 ff.; Louis Bouyer, *Introduction to Spirituality*, p. 25 ff.; Jean Daniélou, *The Bible and the Liturgy* (Notre Dame, 1956).

(Hom. 23 on the Gospel): ". . . and God, whom they had not known in the exposition of Holy Scripture, they knew in the breaking of bread. By hearing God's precepts they were not enlightened; by doing them they were enlightened. It is not those who hear the law who are just in God's sight, but those who do it. Therefore, he who wishes to understand what he hears should hasten to carry out in his deeds what he has already been able to hear. For the Lord was not recognized when He spoke, but deigned to be known when He was given food."

All Scripture, liturgy, and Christian tradition tell us the same thing from one or another aspect: we cannot truly know and love God unless we are truly trying to know and love our neighbor. But this vital fact tends to be overlooked in many discussions of how liturgy and Scripture can be made meaningful to modern men. They never can, by themselves. Their meaning must be opened up by the "doing" of those who have already heard the Word; their meaning must be opened up as necessarily leading from and to "doing the truth in love." And it is a fact that simple souls of every age, including our own, who are trying to serve the Lord in their neighbor (even though they may only know Christ in Scripture and not in the Eucharistic Sacrifice) do not find the Bible strange or incomprehensible. They recognize that its language is ultimately that of God's love, and they come to understand it by sharing in and communicating that love.[22]

---

[22] This does not mean in any way to say that we are excused from studying God's inspired Word and the liturgy from all the aspects and using all the means available in our given circumstances. Our degree of culture in this regard should at least equal that of our human culture. Nor does it mean that pastors, teachers, parents, "apologists" should not use every means at their disposal to "open out" Holy Scripture and the liturgy. Books and pamphlets are available in increasing numbers, putting the results of modern scholarship, in the context of the Church's tradition, within the reach of anyone willing to make the effort to obtain and use them. And, in the present stage of transition in the life of the Church, when this "opening out" is not as yet commonly done in the ordinary course of Christian life and instruction, and the sacramental rites are still awaiting the long-promised major reforms to make them once again clearly the "signs" they are meant to be — it is doubly necessary for the individual Catholic who is aware of his need to make use of these aids. But this fact of the basic availability of God's Word to people who are truly "seeking God" and seeking to serve Him in their neighbor shows how many of today's objections to the "strangeness" of

So the solution begins to appear to the third difficulty raised in connection with modern man's loss of a sense of symbolism. Our present alienation from our roots in nature, our secularism and scientism, have brought it about that neither things, nor gestures, nor particular persons and places seem "sacral," "numinous," "mysterious," to modern men. They have lost the sense of the possibility of getting in touch with the divine through rites and ceremonies, made up of all these elements. How, then, can the sacramental, "ritual" life of the Church become the focus of religious living in the modern world?

In a sense, this is rather like asking how a child who has had and lost faith in Santa Claus can grow up to celebrate Christmas. The modern Santa Claus is a commercialized perversion of the real St. Nicholas who was, in his special order of Christian sanctity, a "sign" of God's loving providence. And the primitive sense of what may be expected from carrying out ritual acts is a perversion of the primitive revelation of the Creator and His providential care for men through natural forces. But a child who has become disillusioned about Santa Claus cannot and need not go back to his childish "faith" in order to attain true faith in Christ and hope in His Coming. So with modern men. We cannot return to the lost sense of the "sacral." But we can go on. We can learn to see created nature, not as primitive man saw it, but as Christ sees it. We can learn to use it as He would have us use it, drawing it, by our appreciation and use into His praise of the Father and His redeeming work for mankind, looking forward to His final redemption of nature and total human nature from its present "servitude to corruption" into the glory of the freedom of God's sons.

It would seem as though the Church, in times of mass conversions of more or less primitive peoples, did draw on and come to rely on this ambiguous sense of the "sacral" in nature in order to attract them to the sacramental rites. But this happened to the

the Bible arise from an ignorance of the basic purpose of Holy Scripture — to communicate the "knowledge of Christ," the knowledge which leads to love, love then leading to further knowledge. See Hans Urs von Balthasar, *Prayer* (New York: Sheed & Ward, 1961), p. 178 ff.

degree to which the faithful ceased to take active part in the celebration of the Mass, the sacraments, while the sacramental rites ceased to be thought of as signs,[23] and the faithful generally had less and less direct access either to the Eucharistic Bread or the "Bread of the Word."

This is, of course, a vast oversimplification of a very complex historical process. Nevertheless, it is true of this sense of the "sacral" as of all the other approaches whereby men can come to know of God "through the things that are made." All these means may be used by the Church, but they are not essential. Moreover, they are ambiguous for fallen man and, even within the life of a Christian or a "Christian culture" may lead, not to the true knowledge, love, and service of the living God but to the service of idols. In fact many men have not come to recognize God through His creation, even though they could have done so, and therefore God has had mercy on them and sent His Son to bring us to know Him and share His life.

And so we do not need any sense of the "sacral" in nature in order to participate in the sacraments; we need faith in God's loving mercy, revealing and giving Himself to us through Christ in the Church. We do not need any sense of the "numinous"; we need faith in God's Word spoken to us and acting on us and in us through the sacraments. We do not need any sense of the "mysteriousness" of rites and ritual; we need faith in what St. Paul calls the "Mystery" of Christ. And, as he uses this term, it means precisely the revealing and communicating to men of the secret of God's wisdom, the work of our salvation. It means Christ Himself, revealing and giving Himself to us in the Church, with all that this implies in the past, the present, and the future. The sacramental life is sacred, awesome, beyond any human sensing of the "numinous" because here, above all in the celebration of the Eucharist, this "Mystery" is realized, actualized, made present in its whole reality in our midst, in us: "Christ in you, your hope

---

[23] See Godfrey Diekmann, O.S.B., *op. cit.*, "Two Approaches to Understanding the Sacraments," p. 23 ff.

of glory."²⁴ And this faith is God's gift, not the product of any human mentality or culture — offered to men of today as to men of any other age.²⁵

It would be a tragic mistake, then, to try to insist that any particular human mentality is a necessary prerequisite to "hearing the Word," to participating in the life Christ gives us in the Church. The task of the Christian apologist (in the widest sense of the word) — whether as pastor, parent, teacher, or as "witness," is, as was said earlier, to try to enter fully into Christ's view of reality and then find the preparations for the Gospel existing in *today's* mentality. He may have to cease to rely even on a sense of wonder, of beauty, or of the ultimate "reasonableness" and goodness of reality. But his message is essentially based on none of these, for it is a message transcending all human hopes: "Christ and Him crucified," Christ and His love, revealed and communicated in the Church and so through the lives of her members.

Both the renewal taking place in the Church today and today's mentality, then, seem to be urging us to return to the "primary and indispensable source" and, living from that source, to take the true Christian spirit into today's world. This is why we need to pray with the faith that moves mountains that the Second Vatican Council and its effects may remove the obstacles to this return now existing in the liturgical rites themselves and the way they

²⁴ See Louis Bouyer, *Introduction to Spirituality*, pp. 35 ff. and 107 ff. The same author devotes a chapter in his *Meaning of Sacred Scripture* to St. Paul's use of the term as having purely biblical and Jewish connotations, and discusses the history of its use in the Bible and the Fathers in Volume I of the *History of Spirituality*. See also R. E. Brown, "The Pre-Christian Semitic Concept of Mystery," *Catholic Biblical Quarterly*, 20 (October, 1958), 417–443; "The Semitic Background of the New Testament *Mysterion*," *Biblica*, 39 (1958), 426–448; 40 (1959), 70–87.

²⁵ The same Volume I of the *History of Christian Spirituality* presents the results of an enormous amount of modern scholarship completely disproving the still widespread assumption that the Christian view of reality or any of the essential elements of the Catholic Christian life were taken over from any source other than the Judaeo-Christian tradition itself. For our present purposes, this would seem to be supremely valuable in relieving us of the idea that modern men will somehow have to be made either "primitive" or "Greek" or anything else *before* they can become fully Christian.

are celebrated — obstacles that are the result of many centuries' accretions from one or another past culture or mode of thought.[26] It is certainly true that, as things are, the sacramental signs seem "mysterious" in the wrong sense to the vast majority of the faithful, and do not reveal and open out to them the true "Mystery of Christ." But the solution is not to look to the study of natural "religious psychology" to try to find out how to make the sacraments seem "sacral" in the primitive sense. It is to celebrate and participate in them as meaningfully as possible, even while the above-mentioned still exist. It is to open out the Mystery of Christ to the faithful, as He wishes to be known in the liturgy, in Scripture, and in our neighbors, with faith in His power to "draw all things to Himself" in the ways He has set out in His Church.

Clearly, the Church, like the world, is in a state of transition. But clearly also the Church, like the world, is in a state of crisis. Even here in our own country (which, statistics report, last year provided one half of the dwindling number of vocations to the priesthood throughout the entire world), any extensive contact with young Catholics, so many of whom are more or less completely indifferent to the Faith as they know it, raises the question whether the renewal in progress in the Church will reach the majority of the faithful in time to prevent a great mass defection in the next generation. However well the current modes of instruction and devotion may have served their forefathers, they are not serving the fathers — or even the mothers — of the future. Too many Catholics today seem spiritually underdeveloped, one might almost say "retarded," because spiritually undernourished. They need, they most urgently need to be brought into direct contact with Christ Himself, speaking with them, inviting them and enabling them to come to know Him and His love in the sacramental life of the Church, to find Him and serve Him in all

<hr>

[26] See H. A. Reinhold, *Bringing the Mass to the People,* for a summary and presentation of the reforms of the Mass rites already suggested and presented to the Holy See for consideration. (Appendix C gives an invaluable clarification of the question of the "mysteriousness" of the Mass.) For suggestions as to the other rites, see *Worship: the Life of the Missions* (Notre Dame, 1958) and *Liturgy and the Missions, The Nijmegen Papers* (New York: P. J. Kenedy & Sons, 1960), both edited by Johannes Hofinger, S.J.

their human brothers — with all that this implies in modern life. It is not "liturgical piety" that is unrealistic and unsuited to the modern world, but the unliturgical, unscriptural, "gimmick" piety still prevalent today.

This is why it seems so necessary to clarify what liturgical piety really is and implies, so that all those who are kept away from it by a false and misleading picture may be able to see it for what it is: authentic Catholic Christian piety, hearing and doing the Word received in the Church, lived in the Spirit, to the glory of the Father.

Bibliography of Gerald Ellard, S.J.

Works in print, with the exception of simple book reviews, are listed here.

1923 "And the Light Shineth in Darkness," *America*, 30 (1923), 225–226.

1924 "Ctesiphon's Confession," *Queen's Work*, 16.5 (1924), 122–123 ff.

"Lady Miriam's Christmas Story," *Catholic World*, 120 (1924), 355–360.

"In the Year of Our Lord," *America*, 32 (1924), 247–248.

1925 "Open up the Liturgy," *America*, 33 (April 25, 1925), 37.

1926 "America Discovers the Liturgy," *Caecilia* (Sept., 1926), 192–193.

"Christ-Dust," *Magnificat*.

"Everyday Life in the Liturgy," *Catholic World*, 123 (1926), 38–43.

"The Mass of the Congress," *Columbia* (June, 1926), 7–8.

"Mass for the Feast of Jesus Christ, King," *Catholic World*, 124 (Oct., 1926), 36–40.

"The Sodalist and Mass Liturgy," *Queen's Work*, 18 (1926), 321–323.

"The Sodalists' Bond – the Liturgy," *Queen's Work*, 18 (1926), 288–290.

"The Sodalist's Prayer – the Liturgy," *Queen's Work*, 18 (1926), 261–263.

1927 "St. Theresa in the Missal" (Effingham: Catholic Women's Union, 1927), 134–136.

"Sodalists and a Liturgical Section," *Queen's Work*, 19 (1927), 11–13.

1928 "The Guest of St. Benedict," *Catholic World*, 127 (1928), 218–221.

"Liturgical Week in Louvain," *America*, 40 (1928), 8–9.

"The People's Part in Chrysostom's Mass," *Orate Fratres*, 2 (1928), 246–251.

1929 "Languages of the Mass," *Orate Fratres*, 4 (1929), 61–67.

"Liturgische Bewegung in den Vereinigten Staaten," *Stimmen der Zeit*, 117 (1929), 201–209.

"Movimento liturgico na Holanda e na Belgiea," *Broteria,* 5 (1929), 214–224.

1930 "As Chartres was Meant to be Seen," *Orate Fratres,* 4 (1930), 538–544.

"Corpus Christi in St. Andrä," *Orate Fratres,* 4 (1930), 443–449.

"From a Pilgrim's Note-Book: St. André bei Bruges," *Orate Fratres,* 4 (1930), 301–305.

"Remnants of a Tenth Century Sacramentary from Fulda," *Ephemerides Liturgicae,* NS 4 (1930), 208–221.

"Tiptoe on a Misty Mountain Top," *Orate Fratres,* 4 (1930), 394–399.

1931 "Mass in the Catacombs," *Orate Fratres,* 5 (1931), 502–507.

"Montserrat, a Centuries-Old School of Church Music," *Orate Fratres,* 5 (1931), 108–114.

"Sane Notes on Medieval Mass-Books," *American Ecclesiastical Review,* 85 (1931), 344–362.

1932 "Holy Week in Rome," *Orate Fratres,* 6 (1932), 202–208.

"The Liturgical Movement: In and for America," *Thought,* 7 (1932), 474–492; *Catholic Mind,* 31 (1933), 61–77.

1933 *Christian Life and Worship* (Milwaukee: Bruce, 1933).

Ordination Anointings in the Western Church before 1000 A.D. (Cambridge: Medieval Academy, 1933), 6 pl., xii and 124 pp.

"Liturgical Formation: the End and the Means," *Orate Fratres,* 7 (1933), 253–260.

"Liturgical Formation vs. Information," *Orate Fratres,* 7 (1933), 101–104.

"The Liturgy Course in College," *Journal of Religious Instruction,* 3 (1933), 689–696, 783–791.

1934 *Homage to Jesus Christ King* (St. Louis: CBCV, 1934), 3, 18 pp.

"Catholic Cult and Catholic Culture," *Catholic Mind,* 32 (1934), 41–53.

"Denver Liturgical Congress," *American Ecclesiastical Review,* 40 (1934), 407–418.

"Liturgy and Catholic Life," *Liturgical Arts,* 3 (1934), 157–167.

"Obliged to Communicate Before Mass," *Orate Fratres,* 8 (1934), 348–352, 395–399.

"What to Emphasize in Teaching the Mass," *Journal of Religious Instruction,* 5 (1934), 11–16.

"When Christmas was not Christmas," *America,* 52 (1934), 246–248.

1935 *The Religious and the Church's Corporate Worship,* Outlines for the Religious Communities of the Diocese of Brooklyn (Brooklyn, 1935).
"Dangerous Doctrine: a Demurrer," *Homiletic and Pastoral Review,* 35 (1935), 921–934.
"Pius X and Christocracy," *Orate Fratres,* 10 (1935), 8–14.
"Select, Annotated Bibliography on Liturgy and Catholic Life," *Liturgical Arts,* 4 (1935), 66–69.

1936 "Pius XI and Corporate Worship," *Orate Fratres,* 10 (1936), 553–561.

1937 "Bring the Faithful Nearer the Altar," *America,* 58 (1937), 102–103.
"The 'New' Liturgy: Its Functions and Its Challenge," *Catholic Mind,* 35 (1937), 64–77.
"The Spanish Revolt Enters the Liturgy," *Orate Fratres,* 11 (1937), 103–106.

1938 *The Mystical Body and Social Action* (Indianapolis, 1938), 24 pp.
"Needed: A Heresy or Two?" *Commonweal,* 27 (1938), 433–434.

1939 *Christian Life and Worship,* 2nd ed.
The Mystical Body and the American Bishops (St. Louis: Queen's Work, 1939), 160 pp.
Teacher's Manual for *Christian Life and Worship* (Milwaukee: Bruce, 1939).
"Liturgy: an Old Word with a New Meaning," *Liturgical Arts,* 7 (1939), 47–49.
"Progress of the Dialog Mass in Chicago," *Orate Fratres,* 14 (1939), 19–25.

1940 *Men at Work at Worship* (New York: Longmans, 1940), 307 pp.
"Alcuin and Some Favored Votive Masses," *Theological Studies,* 1 (1940), 37–61.
"Apostles of Uselessness," *Mount Carmel,* 20 (1940), 9–11.
"Black or the Color of the Day," *Orate Fratres,* 14 (1940), 161–165, 246–252.
"Eucharistic Questionnaires Again," *Journal of Religious Instruction,* 11 (1940), 234–241.
"Liturgical Week is Held in Chicago," *America,* 64 (1940), 150–151.
"Nocturnal Adoration in Rural Kansas," *Orate Fratres,* 14 (1940), 563–567.

"Shall I Come to You at Evening Mass?" *Commonweal*, 32 (1940), 37–39.

1941 "All Built on an Empty Tomb," *Orate Fratres*, 15 (1941), 193–198.

"The Church in Kansas Confers," *Commonweal*, 35 (1941), 253–254.

"Introducing the Dialog Mass," *Journal of Religious Instruction*, 12 (1941), 13–15.

"Odyssey of a Familiar Prayer," *Theological Studies*, 2 (1941), 221–241.

"Red Easter," *Orate Fratres*, 15 (1941), 289–294.

"Sacrificial Worship," *National Liturgical Week, 1940* (Newark, 1941), 97–105.

"Teaching Mass in High School," *Proceedings of the National Catholic Educational Association*, 1941, 338–345; *Journal of Religious Instruction*, 11 (1941), 902–909.

"Why a Liturgical Revival was Inevitable," *Proceedings of [Priests'] Liturgical Day* (Atchison: St. Benedict's, 1941), 5–12.

1942 *The Dialog Mass* (New York: Longmans, 1942), 233 pp.

Feast of Jesus Christ the King, An Evening Service of Love and Consecration (St. Louis: Queen's Work, 1942), 8 pp.

"Dialog Mass and its Place in the Liturgical Movement," *Journal of Religious Instruction*, 11 (1942), 577–586, 679–694, 776–778, 871–881; 12 (1943), 16–28, 109–117.

"Gift-Exchanges in the Correspondence of St. Boniface," *Review for Religious*, 1 (1942), 271–280.

"Hints for Sacristans," *Review for Religious*, 1 (1942), 194–195.

"Liturgical Birthday at St. Meinrad's," *America*, 68 (1942), 318–319.

"A Liturgist Among the Authors," *Book of Catholic Authors: First Series* (Detroit: Romig, 1942), 72–78.

"Liturgy in the Pattern of Modern Praying," *Review for Religious*, 1 (1942), 51–62.

"Liturgy in the Sodality Summer Schools," *Orate Fratres*, 16 (1942), 434–438.

"The Meaning of Priesthood," *The National Liturgical Week, 1941* (Newark, 1942), 29–38.

1943 *Lest They Assist Passively* (St. Louis: Queen's Work, 1943), 76 pp.

The Story of the Mass (with A. J. Heeg) (St. Louis: The Queen's Work, 1943).

"Bread in the Form of a Penny," *Theological Studies,* 4 (1943), 319–346.

"Dialog Mass: A Halfway Work," *Jesuit Educational Quarterly,* 6 (1943), 83–87.

"Dialog Mass, the Wichita Way," *Orate Fratres,* 17 (1943), 347–352.

"Differing Currents in the Liturgy, Too," *Review for Religious,* 2 (1943), 243–251.

"Non-Catholic Liturgical Movements," *Thought,* 18 (1943), 451–468.

"Nuns and the Liturgical Movement," *Orate Fratres,* 17 (1943), 198–203.

"Sisters as Big Sisters to the Liturgical Movement," *Orate Fratres,* 17 (1943), 246–255.

"But Song and Dialog Mass Combine," *Catholic Choirmaster,* 29 (1943), 99–101, 153–155.

"Sunday Mass Becomes a Talkie," *Epistle,* 9 (1943), 27–32 (reprinted as "The Dialog Mass," *Catholic Mind* [July, 1943], 42–48).

"Ten Liturgical Commandments in Wartime," *Homiletic and Pastoral Review,* 44 (1943), 1–8.

1944   *Community Mass: Missa Recitata* (St. Louis: Queen's Work, 1944).

"The Big Book on the Altar," *America,* 71 (1944), 389–391.

"The Body of Christ Which is the Church," *America,* 70 (1944), 429–430.

"The Christian Sacrifice Prefigured," *National Liturgical Week,* 1943 (Ferdinand, 1944), 4–13.

"Christmas and the Priest," *Alter Christus,* 7 (1944), 49–52.

"The Liturgy and the World Tomorrow," *America,* 72 (1944), 249.

"St. Ignatius Loyola and Public Worship," *Thought,* 19 (1944), 649–670.

"Towards a Uniform Version of the Mass," *Orate Fratres,* 18 (1944), 133–136.

1945   "The Council of Trent, 1545–1945," *Orate Fratres,* 20, 1 (1945), 49–58.

"Interpolated Amens in the Canon of the Mass," *Theological Studies,* 6, 3 (1945), 380–391.

"At Mass with Ignatius Loyola," *Orate Fratres,* 19 (1945), 99–102.

"Microphones for Altars," *Orate Fratres*, 19, 12 (Nov., 1945), 544–547.

"Saintly Sisters in the Shadows," *Review for Religious*, 4 (1945), 155–162.

"Saint Mark's, Burlington," *Priest*, 1 (1945), 45–47.

"Should Priests Pray the Mass?" *American Ecclesiastical Review*, 112 (1945), 103–109.

"Uniform Text in Peace and War," *Orate Fratres*, 19, 8 (1945), 374–376.

1946 *Defense Against the Atom-Bomb, the Eucharist* (Brooklyn: C. P. Bloud, 1946), 64 pp., paper.

"Holy Mass, the Body of Christ United in Social Worship," *National Liturgical Week, 1945* (Peotone, 1946), 50–58.

Symposium, Life and Work of Pius X (Washington, D. C.: CCD), "The Eucharistic Banquet," 159–181.

"Denver's Mile-High Liturgical Week, 1946," *Orate Fratres*, 21, 1 (Dec., 1946), 28–30.

"The Mass of the Martyrs," *Missionary Catechist*, 22.4 (March), 4–5; 22.5 (April), 4, 5–14.

"A Report," *Liturgical Arts*, 15 (1946), 28.

1947 "Catholic Youth and a Youthful Mass," *Jesuit Bulletin*, 26 (1947), 3–6.

"Liturgy as Social Sanctification," *Family Life in Christ* (Highland Park: Liturgical Conference, 1947), 45–51.

"Mass," *Encyclopaedia Britannica*, 15, 24.

"The Preservation of Society through the Mass," *Messenger of the Sacred Heart*, 82.6 (1947), 11–14.

"Seventh National Liturgical Week," *The Benedictine Review*, 2.1 (Jan., 1947), 7–9.

1948 *The Mass of the Future* (Milwaukee: Bruce, 1948), 360 pp.

Mediator Dei, with introduction and notes (New York: America Press, 1948), 112 pp.

Power: the Supernatural Powers and Helps Conferred on Man, by G. Ellard and John R. Gleason (Chicago: Loyola University Press, 1948), 346 pp.

"De Katholieke Kerk in de Verenigde Staten," *Streven*, 5 (Feb., 1948), 473–479.

"The Great Sacrifice," *Christ's Sacrifice and Ours: National Liturgical Week, 1947* (Boston: Liturgical Conference, 1948), 32–39.

"How Fifth-Century Rome Administered Sacraments," *Theological Studies*, 9.1 (1948), 3–19.

"The Liturgical Movement in Catholic Circles," *Religion in Life*, 17.3 (1948), 370–381.

"The Mass is Our Hope," *Messenger of the Sacred Heart*, 83 (1948), 11–17.

"At Mass with my Encyclical," *Orate Fratres*, 22.6 (April 18, 1948), 241–246.

"Pope Pius XII on the Liturgy," *America*, 78, 14 (1948), 378–379; 15 (1948), 407–408.

"Restoration and Innovation: New Encyclical on the Liturgy," *Action Now*, 1, 10 (June, 1948), 9.

"They Found the Child with Mary," *Catholic Art Quarterly*, 12 (Dec., 1948), 10–12.

1949   *Loyalty*, Religion Essentials Series, Book Two (with W. Farrell).

"Drawing the Liturgical Color-line," *Orate Fratres*, 23.5 (1949), 289–296.

"A March Date on a Mandate," *Orate Fratres*, 23 (1949), 216–219.

"Mediator Dei and Catechism Revision," *American Ecclesiastical Review*, 120, 4 (Apr., 1949), 289–309.

"New Fatima Development," *Actio Mariana*, 11, 4 (Aug., 1949), 12–14.

"Recent Work in Liturgy," *Theological Studies*, 10, 2 (June, 1949), 251–292.

"Rediscovering the Roman Mass," *America*, 81.1 (April 9, 1949), 10–12.

"Report on St. Louis Liturgical Week," *Liturgical Arts*, 18.1 (Nov., 1949), 5, 6.

"St. Leo Writes our Christ-Mass Prayers," *Jesuit Bulletin*, 28.6 (1949), 12, 13.

1950   *Christian Life and Worship*, 3rd ed.

"Liturgy and Education," *Second Maritime Liturgical Week* (Canso, N. S., 1950), 1–9.

"The Church's Wondering Welcome to Christmas," *Queen's Work*, 43, 3 (Dec., 1950), 22–23.

"Devotion to the Holy Cross and a Dislocated Mass-Text," *Theological Studies*, 11, 3 (Sept., 1950), 333–355.

"How Near is Evening Mass?" *American Ecclesiastical Review*, 122.5 (May, 1950), 331–344.

"The Master of Ceremonies in Relation to Church Planning," *Liturgical Arts*, 18, 3 (1950), 59–62.

"*Missarum Sollemnia* Looks to the Future," 364–374, *Die Messe in der Glaubensverkündigung* (Freiburg: Herder, 1950), 392 pp.

"Papal Pronouncements on Sunday Observance," *Sanctification of Sunday* (Conception: Liturgical Conference, 1950), 76–80.

"The Week in Retrospect," *Second Maritime Liturgical Week*, 118–122.

1951 *Service: Essentials in Religion*, Book IV by Gerald Ellard and Sister Anne Burns, O.S.B. (Chicago: Loyola University Press, 1951), 373 pp.

"The American Scene, 1926–1951," *Orate Fratres*, 25, 11–12 (Oct.–Nov., 1951), 500–508.

"The Dialogue Mass, A Brief History of," *For Pastors and People: National Liturgical Week, 1950* (Conception: Liturgical Conference, 1951), 91–95.

"*Orate Fratres*' Silver Jubilee," *America*, 85, 20 (August 18, 1951), 477–478.

"The Ritual is an Unfinished Book," *Liturgical Arts*, 19.2 (1951), 44–45.

"Sunday Evening Service in *Mediator Dei*," *Orate Fratres*, 25, 9 (Aug., 1951), 415–420.

"Vernacular in Recent Rituals: Ten Years' Progress," *American Ecclesiastical Review*, 125 (Nov., 1951), 324–342.

1952 "The Extension of Mass into Daily Life," *The Priesthood of Christ* (Conception: Liturgical Conference, 1952), 99–105.

"Laymen's Retreat and the Liturgy," with G. Augustine Ellard, S.J., *Woodstock Letters*, 81, 1 (1952), 13–23.

"The Place of Liturgy in the College Course," contribution to *Proceedings, Jesuit Institute on College Religion* (Fairfield Univ., 1952).

1953 *Christian Life and Worship*, 4th ed.

Follow the Mass (St. Paul: Catechetical Guild, 1953), 64 pp.

"Easter Restored: Liturgical Event of the Century," *Queen's Work*, 45, 7 (1953), 6, 7.

"Liturgy, as Giving the Holy Ghost a Chance to Teach," *Lumen Vitae* (English ed.), 8, 1 (1953), 69–72.

"Mary's New Assumption Mass," *Jesuit Bulletin*, 32 (1953), 10, 11.

"The New Easter Light and its Growing Vision," *The Easter Vigil: National Liturgical Week, 1952* (Elsberry: Liturgical Conference, 1953), 9–19.

"Will the Mass go Vernacular?" *Queen's Work*, 45, 4 (Jan., 1953), 12, 13.

1954   *Evening Mass: Our Latest Gift* (Collegeville: Liturgical Press, 1954), 90 pp.

   On the Sacred Liturgy: Mediator Dei, Notes, Introduction (New York: America Press, 1954), rev., 108 pp.

1955   *The Christmas Missal* (St. Paul: Catechetical Guild, 1955), 32 pp.

   The Little Missal (St. Paul: Catechetical Guild Educational Society, 1955), 32 pp.

   "New Use of English in the Liturgy," *Queen's Work*, 48, 2 (Nov., 1955), 18, 19.

1956   *Christian Life and Worship*, 5th ed.

   The Mass in Transition (Milwaukee: Bruce, 1956), 387 pp.

   Master Alcuin, Liturgist, Jesuit Studies (Chicago: Loyola University Press, 1956), xiv + 266 pp.

   The Rubrics of the Revised Holy Week Liturgy in English, with F. Prucha, S.J. (New York: Jubilee, 1956), 24 pp.

   "A Report, *First International Congress on Pastoral Liturgy*," *Liturgical Arts*, (Nov., 1956), 19–20.

   "The Resurrection and the Life," *Catholic Digest*, 20, 6 (April), 8–11.

   "Second Jungmann Volume," *Homiletic and Pastoral Review*, 56, 10 (July, 1956), 886–888.

   "Year of the Lord" Series, *Treasure Chest*, 12, 6 (November 22, 1956), produced in collaboration with G. Augustine Ellard, S.J.

1957   *Teachers' Manual for Christian Life and Worship.*

   "Alkuin," *Lexikon für Theologie und Kirche*, 340–341.

   "Good Friday is a 'Better' Friday Now," *Liturgy*, 26, 3 (July), 1957, 64–68.

   "Recent Language Trends in the Liturgy," *Theology Digest* (Autumn, 1957), 164–172.

   "Recent Research on the Mass: Mohlberg's Leonine Sacramentary and Other Items," *Theological Studies*, 18.2 (1957), 249–253.

   "Rubrical Simplification," *The Catholic Educational Supplement II* (New York: Gilmary Society, 1957).

   "Survey of Holy Week, 1957," *Worship*, 31, 7 (Aug., 1957), 399–404.

1958   *"The Ancient Mass."* film-script, copyright by H. G. Whittington.

   The Rubrics of the Revised Holy Week Liturgy in English

tr. and ed. by G. Ellard, F. P. Prucha (Milwaukee: Bruce, 1958), 69 pp.

The Simple Rite of the Restored Holy Week, tr. and ed. by G. Ellard, F. P. Prucha (Milwaukee: Bruce, 1958), 95 pp.

rev. *Missale Francorum:* Vat. Reg. Lat 257, ed. K. Mohlberg-L. Eizenhofer-P. Siffrin (Rome: Herder, 1957). *Manuscripta,* 2, 1958, 106–107.

"Pius XII, Pope of Pastoral Liturgy," *Worship,* 32, 10 (Nov., 1958), 584–590.

"Priests for a Changing World," *The Jesuit Bulletin,* 37.3 (June), 1958, 3, 4, 18.

"Thanks for 'Liturgical' 1957," *Worship,* 32, 3 (June, 1958), 71–76.

1959 *Community Mass,* rev. ed. (St. Louis: The Queen's Work, 1959), 38 pp.

"Are We on the Right Track with the Layman's Missals?" *The Liturgical Year* (1959), 106–108.

The Story of the Mass, 2nd ed., with A. J. Heeg.

"Le Sacramentaire Gélasien: Vat. Reg. 316," by A. Chavasse (Tournai: Desclée, 1958), 816 pp.; *Theological Studies,* 20, 4 (Dec., 1959), 641–642.

"Liturgical Movement in the United States," *Het Liturgisch Woordenboek,* Nijmegen.

"What Priests and People Can Add at Mass Nowadays," paper, Charlotte Regional Liturgical Week, May, 1959; published, mimeograph. *Proceedings* pages not numbered: this is No. 3.

"Why not Longer Cycles of Biblical Readings?" *Liturgical Year* (1959), 193–196.

1960 *La S. Messa in Transformazione,* Pontificio Instituto Pastorale, Studi Pastorali, 1959, Edizioni Romane Mame, 1960, 360 pp.

"An Example of Alcuin's Influence on the Liturgy," *Manuscripta,* IV, 1 (Feb.), 23–28.

"The 1960 Liturgical Changes," *The Queen's Work,* 53, 3 (Dec., 1960), 14–15.

"People Need a Simpler Mass," *Worship,* 34, 3 (Feb., 1960), 131–137.

"Recent Publications in Liturgy," *Theological Studies,* 21, 3 (Sept., 1960), 454–459.

"Saluting the New Rubrics," *Theology Digest* (Autumn, 1960), 159–162.

"Sidelights of Recent Gelasian Research," *Theological Studies,* 21, June, 1960, 271–275.

1961   *Christian Life and Worship,* 7th ed.

    A Litany of Heroes and Saints, Notable Biographies and Lives of Saints for Students of Church History, compiled by Gerald Ellard, S.J. (Milwaukee: Bruce, 1961), 49 pp., paper.

    La liturgie en marche (Tours: Mame, 1961), 529 pp.

    "Surprising Vernacular Developments," *The Priest,* 17, 3 (Mar., 1961), 214–217.

1962   *Community Mass: Missa Recitata* (St. Louis: Queen's Work).

    "Manila Leads in the Liturgy," *Pastoral Life* (May–June, 1962), 5–12.

    "A New Mass 'For Ecclesiastical Vocations,'" *Sister Formation Bulletin,* 8, 4 (Summer, 1962), 29–31.